FACING EDEN

FACING EDEN
100 Years of Landscape Art in the Bay Area

Steven A. Nash

with contributions by

Bill Berkson, Nancy Boas, Michael R. Corbett, Patricia Junker,

Constance Lewallen, Ellen Manchester, and Marc Simpson

The Fine Arts Museums of San Francisco

University of California Press   Berkeley Los Angeles London

This book has been published in conjunction with the exhibition
Facing Eden: 100 Years of Landscape Art in the Bay Area.

The Fine Arts Museums of San Francisco
M. H. de Young Memorial Museum
25 June - 10 September 1995

The exhibition and catalogue are made possible by support from the
National Endowment for the Arts, a Federal agency, and the Ednah Root
Foundation. Additional funding is provided by USL Capital; Alex. Brown &
Sons Incorporated; LEF Foundation; McCutchen, Doyle, Brown & Enersen;
William A. Hewitt; Lorna F. Meyer; The Haley Trust; and Mr. and Mrs.
Melvin B. Lane. The catalogue is published with the assistance of The
Andrew W. Mellon Foundation Endowment for Publications.

Library of Congress Cataloging-in-Publication Data

Nash, Steven A., 1944 –
Facing Eden: 100 years of landscape art in the Bay Area / Steven A. Nash,
with contributions by Bill Berkson. . . [et al.].
       p.   cm.
"The Fine Arts Museums of San Francisco / University of California Press."
Catalog of an exhibition of the same name held at The Fine Arts Museums.
Includes index.
1. Landscape painting, American – California – San Francisco Bay Area –
Exhibitions. 2. Landscape painting – 19th century – California – San Fran-
cisco Bay Area – Exhibitions. 3. Landscape painting – 20th century – Cali-
fornia – San Francisco Bay Area – Exhibitions. 4. Art, American – Exhibi-
tions. 5. Art, Modern – 19th century – California – San Francisco Bay Area –
Exhibitions. 6. Art, Modern – 20th century – California – San Francisco Bay
Area – Exhibitions. 7. Landscape in art – Exhibitions. 8. San Francisco Bay
Area in art – Exhibitions. I. Berkson, Bill. II. Fine Arts Museums of San
Francisco. III. Title.
ND1351.5.N29 1995
704.9'4367946'07479761 – dc20   95-11934
                                                      CIP
ISBN 0-520-20362-3 (cloth)
      0-520-20363-1 (paper)

Printed and bound in Hong Kong

Contents

Foreword

There is no aspect of life in the Bay Area that affects one's identification with place more than the landscape. The natural and wild blended with the cultural and manufactured are visible throughout the region and provide a constant source of wonder, pride, and delight. Responding to this remarkable environment, artists and landscape architects over the past one hundred years have produced a rich body of work, revealing the many personal and collective meanings the landscape inspires. Their art is a reflection of society's constantly changing attitudes toward the land and its use. From William Keith, Bernard Maybeck, Childe Hassam, and Frederick Law Olmsted to Diego Rivera and Ansel Adams, then on to the more recent era of Richard Diebenkorn, Wayne Thiebaud, Christo, and Lawrence Halprin, the Bay Area tradition of creative interaction with the environment is one that few other regions of the country, if any, can match.

Facing Eden: 100 Years of Landscape Art in the Bay Area traces this distinguished tradition. It is particularly appropriate that the M.H. de Young Memorial Museum presents so ambitious a survey. The de Young Museum, now part of The Fine Arts Museums of San Francisco, was founded one hundred years ago in Golden Gate Park, one of the truly splendid elements of the region's landscape and an example of landscape design at its best. From the outset, the museum's collections featured American painting with a strong component of western landscapes, a strength gradually built on over subsequent years.

A great deal of new research has gone into the exhibition and this accompanying volume, celebrating both nature and art while also examining important issues that shape the environment around us, both current and future. Under the general guidance of Steven Nash, Associate Director and Chief Curator of The Fine Arts Museums of San Francisco, a team of seven other contributing curators delved into different aspects of landscape art, which they broadly defined to include not just painting, graphics, and photography, but also conceptual and site-specific art, video, landscape architecture, and even urban planning. We are greatly indebted to Bill Berkson, Nancy Boas, Michael Corbett, Patricia Junker, Constance Lewallen, Ellen Manchester, and Marc Simpson for the spirit of inquiry and the energetic research they brought to the subject. The chapters that each prepared for this book represent a lasting contribution to scholarship on Bay Area art. The objects they located and assembled make for an exhibition exciting in its visual experiences and juxtapositions. Never before has such a comprehensive, multidisciplinary examination been aimed at this key aspect of the region's art history.

To the many lenders to the exhibition, we extend a special expression of gratitude. Our project would not have been possible without their generous consent to part with treasured objects and share them with our museum audience.

Many other individuals also contributed importantly to the success of this complex undertaking. An accompanying list of acknowledgments gives credit to those whose help was most vital. A few members of the Museums' staff must be singled out, however, for special recognition. Kathe Hodgson, Exhibitions Coordinator, supervised many of the logistics of exhibition administration; Karen Kevorkian, Editor of the Museums' Publications Department, copyedited the catalogue and managed the myriad details of its production; Kelly Purcell, Exhibition Assistant, was indispensible to historical research, compilation of photographs, and manuscript preparation; Rob Krulak, 1994-95 NEA Intern, American Paintings, also assisted with research; Bill White, Exhibitions Designer, oversaw the exhibition installation; Therese Chen and Pam Pack of the Registration Department managed the assemblage of loans; Ron Rick, Chief Designer, provided the exhibition graphics; Vas Prahbu, Director of Education, and Jean Chaitin, Coordinator of Public Programs, organized the ambitious program of educational activities connected with the exhibition; Carl Grimm, Head Paintings Conservator, and others on the conservation staff, including Tricia O'Regan, Assistant, and Carrie Thomas, Getty Advanced Intern, worked skillfully to return many of the works in the exhibition to more presentable conditions; Elisabeth Cornu, Objects Conservator, and Robert Futernick and Debra Evans, Paper Conservators, helped with conservation and installation matters; Paula March, Manager, Corporate Relations, and Debbie Small, Development Associate, both worked on raising funds for the exhibition; Joseph McDonald, Photographer, provided much handsome new photography for the catalogue; Jane Glover, Secretary, American Art Department and the American Art Study Center, and Suzy Peterson, Secretary to the Chief Curator, in addition to assisting with the preparation of catalogue manuscripts helped in innumerable ways; Jack Stauffacher, well-known book designer, contributed his considerable talents; and Deborah Kirshman, Editor, University of California Press, worked with Ann Karlstrom, our Director of Publications and Graphic Design, to make the copublication of the book accompanying the exhibition a mutually rewarding venture. The highly professional standards of all these individuals were clearly apparent throughout the project.

Of course, the exhibition would not have been possible without the generous financial support of several sponsors. For their underwriting and the confidence they showed in our proposals, we are most grateful to the National Endowment for the Arts, a Federal agency, and the Ednah Root Foundation. Additional funding is provided by USL Capital; Alex. Brown & Sons Incorporated; LEF Foundation; McCutchen, Doyle, Brown & Enersen; William A. Hewitt; Lorna F. Meyer, The Haley Trust; and Mr. and Mrs. Melvin B. Lane. The catalogue was published with the assistance of The Andrew W. Mellon Foundation Endowment for Publications.

It is to the artists represented in the exhibition that we are most indebted. They help open our eyes to the landscape and reveal its many glories and mysteries.

Harry S. Parker III
Director of Museums
The Fine Arts Museums of San Francisco

Acknowledgments

Production of this exhibition and its catalogue has been truly a team effort. From the beginning, the contributing curators shared openly in a collaborative process and debate that broadened perspectives on the many issues involved in the exhibition, sharpening considerably our thinking about which objects would play the most expressive roles in this ambitious survey. Because of the breadth of the subject, research necessarily took many directions. The final realization of the project would not have been so successful without the generous sharing of information and ideas by other curators, collectors, historians, librarians and archivists, gallery owners and their staffs, and many involved in landscape architecture and criticism. The following is a list combined by the contributing curators of those individuals who helped at crucial points along the lengthy path of exhibition research and preparation. Given the complexity of the project, we are bound to overlook a few whose assistance was important, and to these individuals we apologize and offer thanks. We do not acknowledge here the many lenders to the show, who are listed elsewhere, nor do we list the artists who produced works included in the survey, certain of whom also freely shared information and perspectives on these works. It goes without saying that these are the ones who truly made the exhibition necessary and possible.

We wish to acknowledge the kind assistance of the following:

Louise Sloss Ackerman Fine Arts – Eugenie Candau; American Indian Contemporary Arts, San Francisco – Janeen Antoine; Gallery Paule Anglim, San Francisco – Paule Anglim, Edward Gilbert, and Jon Sorenson; Archives of American Art, Smithsonian Institution – Barbara Bishop, Caroline Jones, and Paul J. Karlstrom; Asian Art Museum of San Francisco – Terese Tse Bartholomew; The Atkins Family; Nicole Back; The Bancroft Library – Dr. Bonnie Hardwick, William M. Roberts, and staff; Beverly Bastian; Don Beatty; Kit and Peter Bedford; John Berggruen Gallery, San Francisco – John and Gretchen Berggruen and the staff; Don Birrer; Adelie Landis Bischoff; Ben Blackwell; Jane M. Oldfield Blatchly; Dorr Bothwell; Braunstein-Quay Gallery, San Francisco – Ruth Braunstein; Gray Brechin; Michael D. Brown; Ruth Vickery Brydon; Donald Cairns; Robert Cameron; Campbell-Thiebaud Gallery, San Francisco – Charles Campbell, Paul Thiebaud, Wendy Turner, and Diana Young; Paul Carey; Carlson Gallery, Carmel – Jeanne and David Carlson; Jehanne Bietry Salinger Carlson; Gary Carson; Center for Creative Photography, The University of Arizona, Tucson – Mark Williams; Mrs. Thomas Church; Church of the New Jerusalem – Dr. James F. Lawrence; Mrs. Joel E. Coffield; Harry

Cohn; College of Environmental Design, University of California, Berkeley – Cynthia Wardell; Gay Collins; Nancy Conner; Contemporary Realist Gallery, San Francisco – Michael R. Hackett; Frances Price Cook; Mr. and Mrs. Thomas Creighton; Susan Cummins Gallery, Mill Valley – Susan Cummins; Susan de Fremery; Delaney & Cochran – Topher Delaney and Andrea Cochran; Randolph Delehanty; Denenberg Fine Arts, Inc., San Francisco – Stuart and Beverly Denenberg; Phyllis Diebenkorn; Djerassi Foundation, Woodside – Carol Law; Sandy Donnell and Justin Faggioli; and Jennifer Dowley.

Also to be thanked are Susan Ehrens and Leland Rice; Filoli – Tom Rogers; 871 Fine Arts, San Francisco – Adrienne Fish; André Emmerich Gallery, New York – Louise Eliasof; The Exploratorium, San Francisco – Peter Richards; Fischbach Gallery, New York – Neil Winkel; Fraenkel Gallery, San Francisco – Frish Brandt and Amy Whiteside; Frumkin/Adams Gallery, New York – George Adams; Diana Fuller; Avesia Gallatin; Maxine Gardner; Garzoli Gallery, San Rafael – John Garzoli and Joel Garzoli; Kyle Gee; Gregory Ghent; Golden Gate Bridge District Office – Robert David; Golden Gate Park National Recreation Area – Stephen A. Haller; Marian Goodman Gallery, New York; Vice President Albert Gore; Colin Graham; Aaron Green and Associates – Aaron Green and Daniel Ruark; Paul Groth; Haines Gallery, San Francisco – Cheryl Haines and Todd Hosfelt; Mrs. John Haley; Grace Hall; Lawrence Halprin, Inc. – Lawrence Halprin and Dee Mullen; Monty Hampton; Wanda Hansen; Harcourts Gallery, San Francisco – Kim Eagles-Smith; Hargreaves Associates – Glenn Allen, George Hargreaves, and Jennifer Zell; Ann Hatch and William Farley; Dr. Phyllis Hattis; Headlands Center for the Arts – Donna Graves; Therese Heyman; Hirschl & Adler Galleries, Inc., New York – Joseph Goddu and Lane Talbot Sparkman; The Hirshhorn Museum and Sculpture Garden, Smithsonian Institution – Phyllis Rosenzweig and Judith Zilczer; Jan Holloway Fine Art, San Francisco – Jan Holloway; Edan M. Hughes; The Huntington Library and Art Gallery, San Marino – Jennifer Watts; and Mr. and Mrs. William Hyland.

Others who have helped are Mark Johnson; Mr. and Mrs. Roy Farrington Jones; David E. Junker; Helaine Kaplan-Prentice; William A. Karges Fine Art, Carmel and Santa Monica – Whitney Ganz; David Kelso; Diana Ketcham; Mary Julia Klimenko; KOCE-TV Foundation, Huntington Beach – Judith Schaefer; Anne Kohs & Associates, San Francisco – Anne Kohs; Koplin Gallery, Santa Monica – Marti Koplin and Eleana Del Rio; William Kostura; Clementina Kun; L.A. Louver, Inc.,

Venice – Kimberly Davis; Susan Land; Mitzi Landau; Susan Landauer; Julian Lange; Trudy and Oscar Lemer; Leah Levy; Li-lan; Susan Manilow; Claudia Marlowe; Maxwell Galleries, San Francisco – Mark Hoffman; Mr. and Mrs. Richard McDonough; Meridian Gallery, San Francisco – Anne Brodzky; Amalia Mesa-Bains; Amy Meyer; Lorna Meyer; Paul C. Mills; Mills College – Alice Erskine; Mills College Art Gallery – Dr. Katherine B. Crum; Marlborough Gallery, Inc., New York – Jack Mognaz; Montgomery Gallery, San Francisco – Peter Fairbanks and Elizabeth Peters; Achim Moeller Fine Art Limited, New York – Achim Moeller; Tobey C. Moss Gallery, Los Angeles – Tobey C. Moss; Gabriel Moulin Studios, San Francisco – Jean and Thomas Moulin; Mary Murchio; Geraldine Murphy; Museum of Fine Arts, Boston – Erica Hirshler; National Archives, Pacific Sierra Region – Waverly Lowell; Newport Harbor Art Museum – Betsy Severance; The North Point Gallery, San Francisco – Alfred C. Harrison and Barbara Janeff; The Oakland Museum of California – Janice Capecci, Drew Johnson, Harvey L. Jones, and the staff of Paul C. Mills Archives of California Art; Frederick Law Olmsted National Historic Site, Brookline, Massachusetts – Elizabeth Banks; Emmy Lou Packard; Recreation and Park Department, Golden Gate Park – Elaine Molinari; Pebble Beach Company Archives – Elmer and Elena Lagorio; The Art Museum, Princeton University – Peter Bunnell; John Roberts; Anne A. Robinson; Robyn Color; Runnymede Sculpture Farm, San Francisco – Mary Maggini; San Francisco Art Commission – Debra Lehane and Jill Manton; San Francisco Cinematheque –

Steve Anker; San Francisco Museum of Modern Art – Janet Bishop, Kara Kirk, Margaret J. Lee, Stephen Mann, Sandra Phillips, Tom Sempere, and library staff; San Francisco Museum of Modern Art Rental Gallery – Marian Parmenter; Norma Schlesinger; Kent Seavey; Sandra Shannonhouse; Johanna Raphael Sibbett; Mrs. Louis Sloss; Hassel Smith; Stanford University Libraries, Stanford University – Margaret J. Kimball and Linda J. Long; Francesca Stauffacher; Strybing Arboretum Society – Margot Sheffner; Roselyne Swig Artsource – Catherine Docter; Laura Sueoka; Sunset Publishing Company – Daniel Gregory; Terrain Gallery, San Francisco – Armando Rascon and Peter Wright; Pat Thomas; Trotter Galleries, Pacific Grove – Terry and Paula Trotter; University of California, Berkeley – Chancellor Chang-Lin Tien and Robert Jacobs; University Art Museum, University of California, Berkeley – Jacquelynn Baas and Lisa Calden; University of San Diego – Derrick Cartwright; Bruce Velick; The Vickery Family; Video Free America, San Francisco – Skip Sweeney and Sue Marcoux; Peter Walker William Johnson and Partners – Pamela Palmer and Peter Walker; Dee White; Caroline Wilson; Paul and Elizabeth Wilson; Stephen Wirtz Gallery, San Francisco – Stephen Wirtz; Philip and Mireille Piazzoni Wood; and the Yosemite Association – Steven P. Medley.

Steven A. Nash
Associate Director and Chief Curator
The Fine Arts Museums of San Francisco

Lenders to the Exhibition

Mr. Robert Aichele
Allan Stone Gallery, New York
American Craft Museum, New York
Anderson Gallery, Buffalo, New York
The Art Museum, Princeton University, Princeton, New Jersey
Jo Babcock
Ray Beldner
Robert Benson and Becky Evans
Gary Breitweiser
Ruth Vickery Brydon
Robert Buelteman, Jr.
Campbell-Thiebaud Gallery, San Francisco
Center for Creative Photography, The University of Arizona, Tucson
Zora and Les Charles
Christopher Grimes Gallery, Santa Monica, California
Gay Collins
Contemporary Realist Gallery, San Francisco
Liadain O'Donovan Cook
Lowell Darling
Robert Dawson
The Delman Collection, San Francisco
Denenberg Fine Arts, Inc., San Francisco
Department of Special Collections, Stanford University Library
Lewis deSoto
Stephen De Staebler
Phyllis Diebenkorn
Susan Ehrens and Leland Rice
Mrs. Pierre Etcheverry
The Fine Arts Museums of San Francisco
Fraenkel Gallery, San Francisco
The Friends of Photography/Ansel Adams
    Center for Photography, San Francisco
Frumkin/Adams Gallery, New York
Oliver Gagliani
Gallery Paule Anglim, San Francisco
William Garnett
Garzoli Gallery, San Rafael, California
Ms. Helen Gee
Judy and Sheldon Greene
Haines Gallery, San Francisco
The Harry W. and Mary Margaret Anderson Collection
Ann Hatch and William Farley
Terry and Eva Herndon
The Hirshhorn Museum and Sculpture Garden,
    Smithsonian Institution, Washington, D.C.
Douglas Hollis
Jan Holloway Fine Art, San Francisco
Pirkle Jones
Dr. Phyllis A. Kempner and Dr. David D. Stein
Martha Koplin, Los Angeles
Paul Kos
Mr. and Mrs. C. Richard Kramlich

Mr. and Mrs. Norman Lacayo
L.A. Louver Gallery, Venice, California
Robin Lasser
Dr. and Mrs. Oscar Lemer
Dennis Leon
Sukey Lilienthal
Ellen Manchester
Rose Mandel
Dr. and Mrs. Ian McGreal
The Metropolitan Museum of Art, New York
Mills College Art Gallery, Oakland, California
Douglas Muir
Alex and Eleanor Najjar
National Museum of American Art, Smithsonian
    Institution, Washington, D.C.
Newport Harbor Art Museum, Newport Beach, California
Museum of Art, Brigham Young University, Provo, Utah
The Oakland Museum of California
The Obata Family
Bill Owens
Mr. and Mrs. James R. Patton, Jr.
Mr. and Mrs. Thomas Peckenpaugh
Ron and Kathy Perisho
Private collections
Mrs. John Dowling Relfe
Peter Richards
Mary and David Robinson
John Roloff
Dr. A. D. Rosenberg
The Saint Louis Art Museum
The San Francisco Art Commission
The San Francisco Museum of Modern Art
Anne Schechter and Reid Buckley
Bonnie Sherk
Dr. and Mrs. Marvin Sinkoff
Stephen Wirtz Gallery, San Francisco
Roselyne and Richard Swig
Terrain Gallery, San Francisco
Paul LeBaron Thiebaud
Mark Thompson
Richard Titus
Triangle Gallery, San Francisco
University Art Museum, University of California, Berkeley
Valparaiso University Museum of Art, Valparaiso, Indiana
Vision Gallery, San Francisco
Mr. and Mrs. Mason Walsh, Jr.
Alex Weber
Thomas W. Weisel
Mr. and Mrs. Brayton Wilbur, Jr.
Williams College Museum of Art, Williamstown, Massachusetts
John Woodall
Richard York Gallery, New York

Selden Connor Gile, *Untitled (Cows and Pasture)*, ca. 1925
Oil on canvas, 12 x 16 in.
Robert Aichele, Menlo Park, *cat.no.58*

Introduction

Steven A. Nash

Wallace Stegner observed that "no place is a place until it has had a poet,"[1] although he might as aptly have stipulated "an artist." In this respect the San Francisco Bay Area has been fortunate. A great many talented artists have worked here during the past one hundred years, responding to a landscape renowned for its sensual pleasures by depicting in art their experiences of the environment or actually transforming physically some elements of the natural scene. Indeed, the Bay Area boasts one of the richest and most continuous traditions of landscape art of any region in the country, its diversity reflecting not just the glories of nature but also the exploration of what constitutes landscape in its largest, most complete sense.

At work in this book is a definition of landscape as a conjunction of geologic, historical, social, and economic forces. As a locus of cultural and philosophical values connected with issues of management and preservation, the landscape shapes our lives in ways both spiritual and practical. The landscape without constantly merges with the landscape within. Our exhibition aims at a deeper understanding of this phenomenon as place, symbol, and interaction of the natural and human.

That landscape has held such a strong grip on artistic consciousness in this region is not surprising. If one accepts the definition of a garden as the intersection of the best that is cultural and natural, then one can view the Bay Area as a garden of macro proportions. The geological processes that shaped the region – the patterns of uplift and depression of complex Franciscan formation rocks during the late Pliocene era approximately three million years ago, followed by river erosion and the raised sea levels at the end of the Ice Age that flooded the bay and defined the coastline – left a unique union of water and land, peaks and valleys. Combined with ever-changing atmospheric effects, this landscape provides a panoply of visual, physical, and emotional experiences challenging to artists and writers alike in their attempts to take its measure and to grasp some defining essence of its character (fig.1). In reality, of course, it is an environment combined of many microclimates, distinct topographies, and interwoven ecological systems. The lush valleys crouched low against the flanks of Mount Tamalpais, where ferns and redwoods hold dominion, contrast markedly with the arid domes of the Coast Range, which differ in turn from the fecund agricultural lands of the Napa and Sonoma valleys or the often fog-shrouded rocky coastlines. Any city dweller can attest to the wide swings in climate from one side of the San Francisco Peninsula to the other. Of course, some aspects of this environmental tapestry are less than congenial. Mark Twain, with typically acerbic directness, could find the region to be both a "paradise" and "a ghastly picture of fog, and damp, and frosty surf, and dreary solitude."[2] Floods, earthquakes, drought, and fires are accepted as part of the bargain of living here.

Generally speaking, however, a strong sense of nature's beneficence prevails and enters human awareness at levels both mundane and profound, from the premium placed on bay views in real-estate deals to philosophical and spiritual involvements reflected, for example, in ancient Native American religious beliefs centered on the land and in the birth of nationally influential preservationist movements. Even intrusions of the human into the landscape have often fared better than in other locales. The cubic whiteness of the city seen climbing high against the horizon and surrounding greenbelts, the sleek majesty of the bay bridges, or the miracle of urban planning as represented by Golden Gate Park all add importantly to this overall formulation of place. One factor contributing to the uniqueness of this marriage of the natural and cultural is the large number of artists from outside the region who have visited during the past one hundred years – George Inness, Childe Hassam, Diego Rivera, Charles Sheeler, Max Beckmann, Christo, and Richard Estes, to name a few – and worked in response to the landscape muse.

For the purposes of our survey, we have chosen a broadly inclusive view of landscape art. Not only are examples of painting, sculpture, graphic art, and photography included (fig.2), but also conceptual, performance, and site-specific work, documented in many cases by video and film. In addition, a key segment is devoted to the important tradition in the Bay Area of landscape design, city planning in relation to landscape, and architecture as it addresses the natural setting.

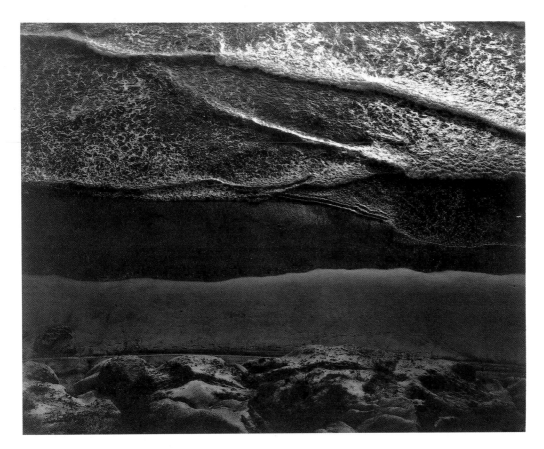

fig.1 Oliver Gagliani, *Untitled (Surf Sequence)*, 1965
Gelatin silver print, 9 x 11½ in. (one of four)
Courtesy the artist, collection of Ron and Kathy Perisho, *cat.no.53*

This book also surveys a diverse array of artists and designers and their myriad creative responses to the wealth of visual information encountered in the landscape on an everyday basis. Languages of expression vary, from different forms of realism that find their truths in replication of the visual world, to the synthesizing and generalizing paths of abstraction or the private realities of fantasy and symbolism. Especially in recent decades, evocative statements about nature have occurred in nontraditional forms, as in the idea-oriented realm of conceptual art or performance and "action" works. Direct manipulation of the landscape may also take many forms, from site-specific sculptures to major civic constructions and garden design.

Facing so vast an artistic terrain, choosing artists and works required difficult decisions; a fine line had to be negotiated between documentary representation and selective curatorial vision. The works gathered here very much reflect the personal perspectives of the team of contributing curators on historical importance, individuality of statement, and the expressive quality of a particular object. They attempted to avoid the merely picturesque, placing emphasis instead on fresh ways of looking at and thinking about the landscape, and on insights that juxtapositions in so large a survey can afford. Every object chosen emerged from a process of intense scrutiny, and while the latitude of choice means that a different team might have constructed a considerably different list, the results not only do justice to the subject but also provide much that is new and stimulating to consider. For greater thematic definition, we limited ourselves as rigorously as possible to the geographical region of the San Francisco Bay Area as defined roughly by the nine counties surrounding the bay and stretching from Napa and Sonoma in the north, eastward to Sacramento (which allows the expedient inclusion of important "Bay Area" artists who worked at the University of California, Davis), and south to Santa Clara. The landscape art of this region is rich and distinct enough to yield a study that can stand solidly on its own, without introducing the additional complexities of art depicting the Sierra Nevada and Monterey/Carmel regions, with their own important but idiosyncratic traditions.

At times this restriction proved difficult or even irrelevant to observe. For certain works it was hard to pinpoint an exact geographic location, and we undoubtedly strayed on occasion beyond our borders. The allegorical character of some objects enlarges particularities of site to broader statements about the Northern California landscape. Arthur Mathews's *California*, 1905, with its female personification of the state and view along an unspecific section of rugged coast, is such a work, as is Rinaldo Cuneo's beautifully painted folding screen, *California Landscape,* ca. 1928, which provides a generic ecologue of the fertility of Northern California plains and foothills. Especially with art of more recent vintage, metaphorical references commonly extend to generalized concepts on landscape and nature. Paintings by members of the so-called Bay Area figurative movement, for example, such as Richard Diebenkorn and Elmer Bischoff, often are not specific in terms of locale but, nevertheless, exhibit a geographical character deriving from the inspiration of immediate surroundings.

The arbitrary limitation of the survey to a one-hundred-year time span was imposed by the nature of the publication as part of The Fine Arts Museums of San Francisco's centennial celebration. It yields, nevertheless, a historical starting point with its own considerable logic. The early 1890s witnessed in the Bay Area the first stirrings of what can retrospectively be seen as a modernist spirit, which took landscape as its main expressive vehicle. Under the successive influence of certain national and international stylistic trends, most importantly the tonalist abstraction of James McNeill Whistler and George Inness and the liberated colorism of the impressionists, painters here began to break away from the main stylistic models of earlier decades. The age of romantic grandeur that had inspired so many bold western essays on the sublime, in painting and photography alike, was in its last throes, although it still beat strongly behind such works as Raymond Yelland's *Cities of the Golden Gate*, 1893, and Albert Bierstadt's vain efforts to inject transcendental drama into his *Golden Gate*, 1900.[3] Likewise, the more pastoral tradition of lush but somber naturalism deriving from the Barbizon School, so strong a motivation behind much late-nineteenth-century Bay Area landscape painting, had begun to run its course. More strictly topographical work, photographic in look and intent, was now especially old-fashioned.

For certain artists looking for new paths to explore, the soft light and smooth contours proffered by Whistler and Inness must have seemed particularly compelling as a visual language for key characteristics of the Bay Area landscape – the low, rolling silhouettes of surrounding hills, the filtration of light by fog and mist, and the muted colors associated with certain seasons and times of day. The nuanced, often daringly abstracted landscape views of Gottardo Piazzoni, Xavier Martinez, and Giuseppe Cadenasso, for example, give evidence of just how salutary a marriage of land and style resulted.

Slower to gain a following, but eventually dominating in influence, were the strong color, broken brushwork, and flattened pictorial spaces of the impressionists and postimpressionists. Gradual exposure to more work of this variety led artists such as Anne Bremer, Charlton Fortune, and members of the Society of Six such as Selden Connor Gile (page xii) to explore a new landscape art of vibrant color and light.

In photography, the golden age marked by the mammoth-plate images by Carleton Watkins and Eadweard Muybridge among others waned toward the end of the century, although it would continue to have influential reverberations in later work, for example, by Ansel Adams. Generally, the sharply focused grand perspective gave way to more intimate, luminous visions attuned to the tonalist style in painting that sometimes verged on pure abstraction.

The 1890s also brought powerful changes to the world of Bay Area landscape architecture, as projects such as Frederick Law Olmsted's design of the Stanford University campus, Phoebe Hearst's international competition for the design of the University of California's Berkeley campus, and the completion of Golden Gate Park ushered in a new era of professionalism in landscape design, setting precedents for landscape interventions on a major scale.

Although modernism had a later start in the West than in the East, and older currents long continued to flow through local practice, a strong spirit of change helped ignite the many developments documented in this exhibition and traced by our team of authors from the turn of the century to today. When surveying such a complex tradition, one is tempted to look for common features or salient connective strands that define a basic character or overall look or feel. Indeed, earlier writers have posited important common denominators generated very much by the nature of the environment itself. In a landmark study of California modernism, Henry Hopkins noted that the expressions of joyful response to geographical region in paintings by the Society of Six helped "set a pattern for Bay Area art which has continued to the present time." He elaborated further:

The Mathews, Piazzoni, the Society of Six, the Bay Area Figurative painters, the early and later Richard Diebenkorn, Wayne Thiebaud, the Photo Realists, William T. Wiley, William Allan, Joseph Raffael, Bill Martin and Gage Taylor, no matter what school title is devised to cover them all, each draws heavily upon the physical place of Northern California.... [T]his is the unbroken string that not only separates the look of the art of this region from most of that of the East Coast but that of Southern California as well.[4]

Others have spoken, for example, of a "deep alliance to the light and the land" in Northern California painting, and of "a certain quality that comes from the place."[5] Grace McCann Morley felt that even abstract art here came in part from "a space feeling, a spatial conception, the fact that this area, in the youth of [many of the abstract artists of midcentury] was still a countryside that wasn't extremely densely populated, that there were vast expanses, enormous distances and the scale of things was large."[6] For Wallace Stegner, space was a defining feature of western life, equatable with freedom.[7] For Morley, it was a prime generating force on Bay Area painting. Even abstract painters came under its sway in their search for a basic essence of landscape experience.

Such generalizations do indeed apply to a significant amount of Bay Area art. They describe a lyrical or Arcadian tradition rooted visually in enticing color, strong light, moderate climate, and deep, atmospheric space while also reflective of certain attitudes that extend beyond artistic into sociopolitical realms and important aspects of everyday life. From this perspective artists see nature in quasi spiritual terms as benevolent, enriching, even redemptive. Paintings by artists as diverse as William Keith, Selden Gile, and Arthur B. Davies, from the beginnings of our survey, to much later work by Richard Diebenkorn (fig.3) and Willard Dixon extol in such terms the beauties of Bay Area land and water. Even the urban landscape was subject to visions of purity and harmony as seen, for example, in Ansel Adams's *San Francisco from the San Bruno Mountains, California,* ca. 1952. The naturally given could also be creatively extended. A basic tenet of much landscape architecture developing out of the Bay Area was the mollification of harsher realities by the softening touches of nature applied as if by palette and brush. The urban and rural could join in the same Edenic continuum, aesthetically inspiring and rich in personal and social potential.

The Arcadian tradition, however, despite its strength in the Bay Area, cannot begin to account for the full diversity of expression in landscape art over the past one hundred years. The interpretation and uses of landscape are much too varied to fit comfortably within any one ideological or artistic mold. The early tonalists introduced notes of melancholy and even despair that deflated the symbolism of Edenic hope, and photographers who recorded so powerfully the grim landscapes of destruction following the 1906 earthquake struck an apocalyptic note that would recur in the work of later artists as well, a reminder of nature's dark forces. Again, by the time of the Great Depression, the mood in landscape art was far from sanguine. Many painters and illustrators around the turn of the century assisted the projection of a certain image of California that was useful to a national psychology of expansion and unlimited opportunity. By the late '20s the notion of California's bounty was severely strained, and landscapes and cityscapes by such artists as Maynard Dixon and John Langley Howard reveal how extreme the loss of belief had become. No more perceptive studies exist of the ironic relationships between beauty of place and oppressive social forces than the photographs of Dorothea Lange. Oppression of another sort is manifested in Chiura Obata's slightly later ink painting of the Bay Bridge from 1942, which seems so serenely unemotional until one learns that it was done from memory on the day of Obata's transfer out of Berkeley to a Japanese internment camp.

fig.2 Sonya Noskowiak, *Untitled (View of Ferry Building and Bay Bridge)*, 1940
Gelatin silver print, 8 x 10 in.
Collection of Ron and Kathy Perisho, *cat.no.118*

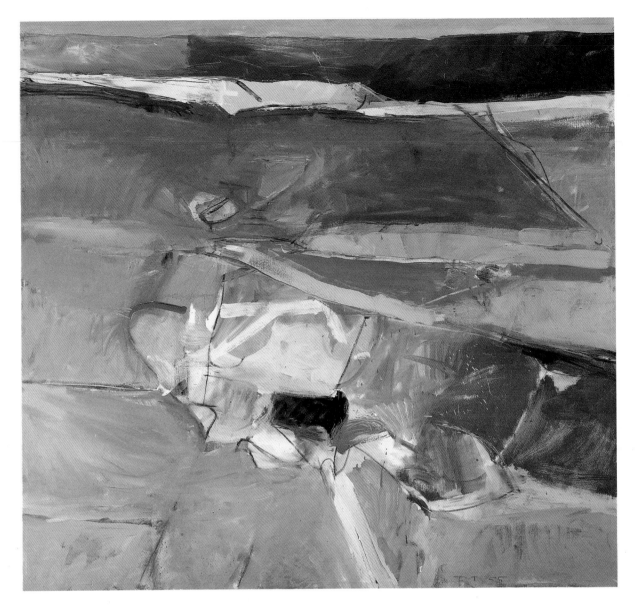

fig.3 Richard Diebenkorn, *Berkeley No.44*, 1955
Oil on canvas, 59 x 64 in.
Private collection, *cat.no.38*

The political and social consciousness that surfaces regularly in landscape images from the '20s and '30s is well represented by Diego Rivera's 1931 mural commissioned by Mrs. Sigmund Stern, the stylized realism of which is put to the service of both portraiture and a celebration of the fruits of agrarian labor. By midcentury, darker and far more personal symbolism had become common, often expressed abstractly, as in paintings seen here by Joan Brown, Jay DeFeo, and Sono Osato. Elmer Bischoff limned a particularly moving psychodrama of ambiguity and separation in his painting of two bathers at Land's End from 1957, and Christopher Brown similarly weighted his more recent sequential composition *The River, Evening*, 1984-85, with shadowy meaning, where nature becomes a cloak of imperfectly understandable forces.

At this same time, as awareness grew of the fragility of nature and of the growing pressures placed on it by development and pollution, works of art could both lament the situation and call for remedial action. Michael Gregory's *As if Twelve Princes Sat before a King* from 1988 presents a particularly Dantesque vision. Robert Colescott's *Christina's Day Off*, 1983, jocularly comments on the landscape of debris and refuse at a city dump, while Ray Beldner's *Lake Dolores* construction, 1994, highlights the problems of water mismanagement. Through photography Lewis Baltz and Robert Hartman cry out against despoiling the landscape, whether by careless neglect or massive building projects.

Numerous other themes and subthemes interweave through our topic. One important subtext is the variation of cultural or ethnographic perspectives that arise. Different population groups have identified with the landscape through their own distinct values and sensibilities. We have already noted Obata's moving invocation of the Bay Bridge as a symbol of lost freedom and homelife. José Moya del Piño's *Chinese Mother and Child*, 1933, a portrait set against the stunning backdrop of a view across the San Francisco Bay, stresses new identifications of home and place between a Chinese immigrant family and the natural setting of their adopted city. Brian Tripp's *In Memory of Mount Diablo:* TU-YOYSH-TAK (TY-YOY-SHIP) *Mountain to Mountain, When Straight Line Straightened out Circle*, 1992, and Frank Tuttle's *What Wild Indian?*, 1992, both comment from a Native American perspective on the loss of lands and traditions associated with European and American settlement of the area, while Lewis deSoto's video installation *Háypatak, Witness, Kansatsusha*, 1990/95, explores contrasting aesthetic and cultural reactions to the coastal landscape of Northern California by three different ethnic American groups – Asian, Native American, and Anglo. Works in the show by Carmen Lomas Garza and Robert Colescott provide snapshots of Latino and

African American experiences connected with the cityscape, while Peter Saul's *The Government of California*, 1969, is a bristling mixture of sardonic ethnic and political commentary.

For some artists, landscape provided a key to liberated imagination and fantasy. A strong surrealist strain in California art helped nourish the visionary paintings and drawings of Jess, Irving Norman, and William T. Wiley, and even surfaces in the less pliant sculptural forms directed toward natural imagery by Robert Arneson, Robert Hudson, and Richard Shaw. In these works, humor exists side by side with the bizarre and truly frightening. Joseph Goldyne's *Goya's Bull Coming in over Marin*, 1973, exhibits a similiar combination of fantasy and deadpan seriousness (fig.4).

For others, interpretations of place focused primarily on the constructed environment, whether on major technological and engineering projects such as bridges and highways, or the manufactured urban and suburban streetscape. In this way, interactions with, or the displacement of nature become primary themes, often with associated political or social meanings. The famous *Running Fence, Project for Sonoma and Marin Counties, California*, 1972-76 (fig.5), by Christo and Jeanne-Claude, is an example of one type of landscape intervention to which other site-specific works can be linked, even such technological projects as the surprisingly beautiful fields of wind generators atop Altamont Pass.

Artists from Ray Strong, Peter Stackpole, Charles Sheeler, and Erle Loran to Robert Buelteman, Jr., and Catherine Wagner have found images of power, beauty, and collective social will in the city's constructed topography. Wayne Thiebaud's dizzying visual essays on the spatial and geometric complexities of the San Francisco cityscape are renowned. Robert Bechtle frequently focuses on city side streets for their quiet, classic balance of hard-edged shapes carved by soft light, while Max Beckmann looked upon the city from a distant viewpoint and captured through his harsh outlinings an emblem of movement and strength. As guest curator Ellen Manchester points out in her essay, photographers have been especially drawn to the visual riches of the "right here" (the environments that exist at our urban and suburban doorsteps) rather than the "out there." (fig.6). The urban studies of Minor White, for example, reveal an array of small worlds easily overlooked by a less perceptive eye. John Gutmann's work shows how social commentary can be married to formal concerns, and Henry Wessel and Bill Owens have provided particularly wry comments on our everyday surroundings.

In a different mode, San Francisco's cityscape has been a fertile ground for conceptual and video or film works, as guest curator Constance Lewallen discusses in her essay. Mel Henderson's *Yellow Cabs* event of 1969, with its emphasis on political action and urban chaos

fig.4 Joseph Goldyne, *Goya's Bull Coming in over Marin* (version 2), 1973
Etching and monotype, 6 x 9 in.
Courtesy the artist and Richard York Gallery, New York, *cat.no.66*

fig.5 Christo [Christo Javacheff], *Running Fence, Project for Sonoma and
Marin Counties, California*, 1976
Charcoal, pastel, and pencil drawing, 42 x 96 in.;
topographical map, 15 x 96 in.; color photograph, 28 x 39¼ in.
San Francisco Museum of Modern Art, gift of the Modern Art Council, *cat. no.23*

fig.6 Douglas Muir, *Citicorp Atrium, San Francisco*, 1985
Ektacolor print, 12¾ x 18¾ in.
Douglas Muir, *cat.no.113*

fig.7 Mel Henderson, with Joe Hawley and Alf Young, *Yellow Cabs*, 1969
Documentation of performance on 19 November 1969, San Francisco

fig.8 Bob Walker, *Dougherty Valley*, ca.1986
Cibachrome print, 16 x 20 in.
The Oakland Museum of California,
Natural Sciences Division, *cat. no.162*

(fig.7), and Tom Marioni's *Studio 1979*, composed of filmed views using his studio window as a frame on modern life, are outstanding examples. Howard Fried's *Long John Servil vs. Long John Silver*, 1972, represents a photographic pilgrimage through time and urban space.

The theme of intervention in nature is, of course, most clearly manifested in San Francisco's important tradition of landscape architecture and design. In this arena, the paradigm of the "social landscape as garden" carries particular weight, and the action of social and political forces in shaping the landscape is especially evident. Architectural historian Michael Corbett has traced the development of this tradition, as it involves both the monumental level of urban planning and park and campus design and the intimate scale of domestic architecture and garden design vis-à-vis the natural setting. Historical accomplishments are many – one thinks immediately of the contributions of Frederick Law Olmsted, Bernard Maybeck, Thomas Church, Frank Lloyd Wright, Lawrence Halprin, George Hargreaves, and many others – and their influence nationally and internationally has been profound. A closely associated phenomenon is the preservationist movement that has been so strong a force in the Bay Area and its resulting social and environmental triumphs such as the creation of the Golden Gate National Recreation Area, Point Reyes National Park, and the Save the Bay campaign.

The power of local landscape to elicit the kind of awe and respect that have fueled the preservationist movement is a basic signifier of life here on the continent's edge. A central, related point emerging from our survey is the seemingly inexhaustible ability of the land to stimulate different personal meanings and metaphor. As Wallace Stegner recognized, a location takes its identity very much from the artistic interpretation and transformation it receives. From Arcadia to endangered species, from golden national dream to the depression's dystopian endgame, from extroverted joy to private melancholy, associations distilled from Bay Area landscape are myriad (fig.8). As the land and its uses continue to evolve, so will the interpretations they receive.

Notes

1. Wallace Stegner, *Where the Bluebird Sings to the Lemonade Springs: Living and Writing in the West* (New York: Penguin Books, 1993), 205.

2. From a letter to his mother and sister of 4 June 1863, and "Early Rising, As Regards Excursions to the Cliff House," 5 July 1864, reprinted in *Gold Miners and Guttersnipes: Tales of California by Mark Twain* (San Francisco: Chronicle Books, 1991), 5, 24.

3. Now located in the Thyssen-Bornemisza Collection, Madrid.

4. Henry Hopkins, *Painting and Sculpture in California: The Modern Era*, exh. cat. (San Francisco: San Francisco Museum of Modern Art, 1976-77), 25, 27.

5. Nancy Boas, *The Society of Six: California Colorists* (San Francisco: Bedford Arts, 1988), 10, and Grace McCann Morley in "Grace McCann Morley, Art, Artists, Museums and the San Francisco Museum of Art," interview by Suzanne B. Reiss, Northern California Oral History Project, The Bancroft Library, University of California, Berkeley, 1960, quoted in Boas, *Society of Six*, 187.

6. Morley, quoted in Boas, *Society of Six*, 187.

7. Wallace Stegner, *The American West as Living Space* (Ann Arbor: University of Michigan Press, 1987), 80-81.

100 Years of Landscape Art in the Bay Area

Kevin Roche John Dinkeloo and Associates,
The Oakland Museum of California, 1969

Rearranging the Environment:
The Making of a California Landscape 1870s to 1990s

Michael R. Corbett

Changes initiated by the Americans at the end of the Mexican war in 1847 were sudden and dramatic compared to those made to the landscape of the San Francisco Bay Area during thousands of years of American Indian occupation followed by seventy-five years under Spain and Mexico. Within a few years the framework for land division, ownership, and use that still exist today and have so decisively contributed to the look of the urban and rural landscapes were in place in the land survey grids of the cities and countryside. Within twenty years substantial progress had been made in re-creating the familiar look of the eastern United States by immigrants who considered California's landscape to be a strange and almost frightening place.

This brief history suggests the spectrum of activities over time that created a complex landscape that is the inheritance of every generation. It looks at mundane undertakings, whose effect is incidental to their purpose, and to activities such as park design, whose primary purpose is changing the look of the environment. As defined by J. B. Jackson, the landscape is the visible record of human beings living on the land, reflecting their needs, attitudes, and values.[1] If we know how to read it, all of it has meaning.

The hordes who came to California beginning in 1849 with the gold rush viewed the land pragmatically, seeing a great natural harbor with river access to interior mining areas and raw material such as trees and farmland to supply the needs of mining. Gradually another view of California arose, one that had a pervasive and long-lasting influence on the landscape, rooted in farming and gardening and expressed in romantic, aesthetic, and visionary ways.

In the early stages order was established on the land, as it was throughout nineteenth-century America, by means of grids meant to facilitate the recording of land transactions and ownership[2] that were laid down without respect to topography. In San Francisco, development was crowded in the flat, low areas by the port, leaving the hills largely barren. The countryside, in contrast, was almost empty, typically featuring a small cluster of farm buildings on parcels of one hundred acres or more.

As the population grew in San Francisco and the Bay Area, people began to consider more carefully the appearance of their surroundings and what improvements they might make. The discovery that almost anything would grow here led to the establishment of the first nursery in San Francisco, the Golden Gate Nursery, in 1849. By the end of the 1850s numerous nurseries and a vast selection of seeds and plants, from all parts of the world, were available.[3]

Given unlimited possibilities, most people chose to re-create what they knew. Since the new population was dominated by settlers from the United States and northern and western Europe, new inhabitants looked to gardens and landscapes they remembered from home and the prevailing fashions from England, especially for parks and private estates.

The first examples of landscape planning in the Bay Area were found in the of several blocks that were reserved for parks in the surveys of San Francisco made by engineers Jasper O'Farrell and William M. Eddy between 1847 and 1851 (fig.1). South Park, a private, green oval framed by Georgian-style houses, was built by George Gordon, an Englishman, in 1854 on the model of London real estate developments of the time (fig.2).[4]

About the same time that San Francisco set aside space for parks in 1847, it also reserved several sites for the military, including the large area of the Presidio.[5] Although not intended for public purposes, the withholding of this land from intensive development eventually led to important consequences for the park system. Another early contribution to the look of San Francisco occurred in 1854 after a great deal of work had been done leveling hills, cutting streets, filling the tidelands, and making new land by expanding the shoreline of the city (fig.3). Despite this early frenzy of earth moving, a commission advised that hills should remain to protect the beauty of the city.[6]

The look of the landscape and patterns of development were significantly affected by the construction of railroads in the 1860s, both the regional lines and the transcontinental railroad that arrived in Oakland in 1869. They spurred the development of agriculture and outlying towns, providing access to spas, resorts, and rural retreats; enabling the rich to build suburban estates, especially on the Peninsula; and quickly becoming

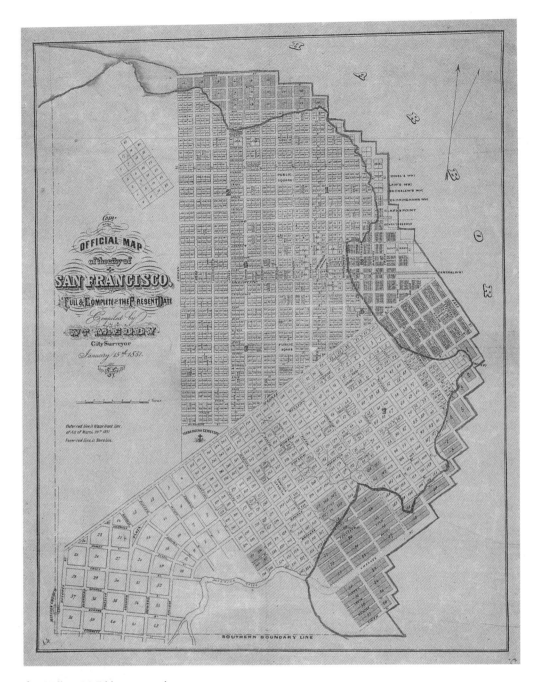

fig.1 William M. Eddy, cartographer
Britton and Rey, San Francisco, lithographers and publishers
Map of the City of San Francisco, 1851 (survey and publication)
Lithograph with applied color, varnish, mounted on linen, 23⅘ x 18⅘ in.
Courtesy of the California State Library, Sacramento

associated with the great wealth of the individuals and corporations manifested in the elaborate hotels and business buildings downtown and the conspicuously ostentatious mansions built on Nob Hill. Private gardens, established in San Francisco, Alameda, and Oakland, addressed the recreation needs of the new population, such as Robert B. Woodward's on Mission Street between Thirteenth and Fourteenth streets in San Francisco. Opened to the public in 1866, it embraced "a marine aquarium, museum, art galleries, conservatories, tropical houses, menagerie, whale pond, amphitheater and skating rink."[7]

Frederick Law Olmsted, the designer of the original Central Park in New York and the leading theorist and practitioner of landscape design in the United States, brought his views to California in the mid-1860s. He believed that, in addition to their aesthetic, recreational, and sanitary benefits, parks made better citizens of the urban populace, especially immigrants who were thought to lack the values most Americans were thought to acquire naturally by growing up on farms or in small towns.[8] Among his key projects were support for a park at Yosemite; the design of Mountain View Cemetery, now surrounded by Oakland, in the picturesque manner first made popular at Mount Auburn Cemetery outside Boston; a design for the new University of California campus and its surroundings in Berkeley; and his recommendation for a large urban park in San Francisco, equivalent to Central Park in New York.

The land set aside in 1868 for Golden Gate Park in San Francisco was mostly sand, including high dunes that moved with the wind and winter storms across an almost completely unpopulated area (fig.4). William Hammond Hall, the park's first superintendent, was an engineer whose grand vision for the transformation of nature through engineering was not only necessary for the challenging task of creating Golden Gate Park, but also represented a typically American view of California as a place infinitely alterable according to human needs and purposes (fig.5).

Outside the city, agricultural areas were dominated by wheat growing until the 1880s. As California's position in the world wheat market declined, however, many farmers in the Bay Area turned to other crops, especially fruit. The new agricultural landscape consisted commonly of vineyards and orchards interspersed with hay, grain, and grazing land on parcels of a quarter section and smaller, dependent on the availability of water from local artesian wells, springs, or streams. Efforts at rural landscaping on a public scale were made at county fairgrounds, as in Santa Clara County, where a boulevard of trees was planted in 1871 between Santa Clara and San Jose, with lines of shade and ornamental trees in four rows defining a roadway flanked by sidewalks.[9]

fig.2 George Robinson Fardon, *South Park*, from *San Francisco Album. Photographs of the Most Beautiful Views and Public Buildings of San Francisco*, 1856, albumen silver chloride print from wet-plate collodion glass negative. The Huntington Library, San Marino

fig.3 George Robinson Fardon, *Alcatras* [sic] *Island*, from *San Francisco Album. Photographs of the Most Beautiful Views and Public Buildings of San Francisco*, 1856, albumen silver chloride print from wet-plate collodion glass negative. This view additionally shows the tidelands with demarcations of water lots, conforming in shape to the city blocks, which would then be sold to individual purchasers and filled in with land. The Huntington Library, San Marino

5

fig.4 Isaiah West Taber,
Horse-drawn Carriage Rolling through Laveaga Dell,
Golden Gate Park, 1894
Courtesy Greg Gaar, San Francisco

fig.5 Golden Gate Park, viewed from the Pacific Ocean with the
San Francisco Bay and the East Bay in the distance, 1969
Courtesy Robert W. Cameron, Aerial Photographer, San Francisco

fig.6 Linden Towers, Menlo Park (home of James C. Flood), ca. 1890
Gardens designed by Rudolf Ulrich
Courtesy The Bancroft Library, Berkeley

fig.7 Carleton Watkins, *Malakoff Diggings Hydraulic Mine*, ca. 1880
Tons of debris from such operations washed into the San Francisco Bay
Courtesy The Bancroft Library, Berkeley

As retreats for city people, spas and resorts were built at scattered locations throughout the region. Most of these were associated with mineral springs and were promoted for their healthfulness. Many also advertised themselves as pleasure resorts, such as the Warm Springs Resort,[10] calling attention to vineyards, gardens, horse racing, and other sporting activities. The Rafael Hotel featured grounds designed by Rudolf Ulrich, a leading landscape designer of the period, noted for his invention of the "Arizona garden" and use of exotic plants.[11]

Between the cities and farms, a third type of landscape began to develop. By the 1870s many rich San Franciscans had built grand suburban estates, the largest such concentration in the West, in sunny areas accessible from the railroad lines in Marin County and on the Peninsula. Unlike their eastern and midwestern counterparts, owners of these fashionable homes could realize the ideal of growing diverse collections of exotic plants outdoors, instead of in greenhouses. Among the best-known gardens of the period were those designed by Ulrich at Thurlow Lodge and Linden Towers in Menlo Park (fig.6).[12]

Regionalism

In 1849 San Francisco was a small, isolated outpost and the Bay Area only scattered settlements and ranchos. Thirty years later a major industrial city existed, linked to the East by mail and telegraph, and described by the 1880 United States Census as "The Metropolis of the West." As a result of this growth the culture of the region changed dramatically. From being viewed by many as a temporary way station of opportunity, more settled generations sought to make the strange landscape familiar and to understand it for what it was.

The *Pacific Rural Handbook* of 1879 was a distillation of one of several farming and horticultural magazines published in the 1870s that reflected a widespread interest in practical and aesthetic issues associated with growing plants. Writing here, Charles H. Shinn expressed a widespread nineteenth-century view that the mix of climate, exotic plants, and diverse peoples was already producing a distinctive regional landscape in California.[13] Addressing practical issues of land management, Shinn couched them, like Olmsted before him, in the broader context of family life, aesthetics, and citizenship. Writing about windbreaks, for example, he presented a rich argument for a practice to enhance production, "add charm to the landscape," and improve life in general:
The judicious planting of tall and well foliaged trees has always been productive of good, and cannot be too strongly insisted upon. . . . We love wild places, . . ; we believe in bits of woodland, and belts of forest, and wind-breaks that wind along the horizon.[14]

fig. 8 Hillside above Sausalito showing windbreaks of eucalyptus
trees along roads and property lines, ca. 1910
Courtesy The Bancroft Library, Berkeley

fig. 9 Pre-1906 east view of inner campus quad with native plantings,
Stanford University, Palo Alto. Plan of campus by Frederick Law
Olmsted, buildings by Charles Coolidge of Shepley, Rutan and Coolidge
Department of Special Collections, Stanford University Library

Another major aspect of the development of the landscape in the Bay Area at this time and later was the public's role in relation to environmental issues. Public concerns were a factor in the decision to protect San Francisco's hills in 1854, and in the establishment of Yosemite as the first state park in 1864. Other major issues that emerged in the 1870s that would have long-term implications for the Bay Area were the antidebris and tree-planting movements. With the widespread adoption of hydraulic mining in the Gold Country in the 1860s, whole mountains were washed away by high pressure streams of water (fig.7). The runoff, with its huge amount of pulverized rock, called debris, silted up the channels of streams and rivers leading into the San Francisco Bay, ruining large amounts of farmland and aggravating flooding over a wide area. The antidebris movement, which began among landowners in the Sacramento Valley but spread to San Francisco, resulted in a court decision in 1884 ending hydraulic mining.[15] This victory established a powerful precedent for public action in environmental matters, which played a role in, among other things, the establishment of the Sierra Club in San Francisco in 1892.

Damage to the streams and rivers was reflected by the decimation of the redwood forests and oak groves that were such a notable feature of the landscape at the beginning of the American period, most of the lumber going into the construction of San Francisco. By the mid-1870s, laments were common concerning the loss of the trees, accompanied by proposals not only to replant lost forests but to plant trees widely over the bare landscape. Trees were seen as having both practical and aesthetic values: forests formed "a prominent and delightful feature in the landscape"; "the ocean, winds, and woods may be regarded as the several parts of a great distillatory apparatus" that also formed protective barriers.[16] Campaigns for tree plantings in various sections of the Bay Area were proposed in 1879[17] and an ambitious *Plan for the Cultivation of Trees Upon the Presidio Reservation* was proposed by Major W. A. Jones of the Army Corps of Engineers in 1883.[18]

By 1905 a state tax law encouraged private landowners to plant trees, with notable results: "More attention is being paid to planting ornamental and forest trees than ever before in the history of the state."[19] Various types of eucalyptus trees brought from Australia had been listed in catalogues as early as the 1850s and were the most common of many exotic trees planted beginning at that time (fig.8).

This view of the land as mere supplier to necessity only gradually yielded to awareness of a distinctive regional character to the California landscape in the 1870s, a quiet and largely unconscious development. The publication in 1884 of *Ramona*, a novel by Helen Hunt Jackson, is often cited as marking the beginning of a self-conscious sense of California as a special place, different from that of other parts of the United States, having its own landscape and history. Romantic views of the Mexican period in California's past popularized it as a time of easy outdoor living in comfortable adobe houses with beautiful gardens. The interest in *Ramona* spawned other novels and helped revive public interest in the severely deteriorated missions themselves.

Such interest in the spirit and character of California was an aspect of a much wider reaction to crowded industrial cities. It coincided with some of the main ideas of the arts-and-crafts movement, notably the emphasis in design on conveying the genius loci or spirit of the place, and on the garden as an outdoor room, ideas that shortly contributed to a new effort to express the distinctiveness of California in landscape design and architecture.[20] Among the first such efforts was the design for Stanford University, one of the first developments to attract the attention of critical observers outside California. Planning began for the Stanford campus in 1885 with a series of studies and plans by Olmsted. The buildings themselves were designed by Charles Coolidge of the Boston firm of Shepley, Rutan and Coolidge, with the regular involvement of the university's benefactors, Leland Stanford and his wife, Jane Lathrop Stanford.[21]

As built, the campus consisted of a formal grouping of buildings linked to the larger landscape by long controlled views. The buildings were constructed of sandstone with red-tiled roofs in quadrangles linked by round-arched arcades. Innovations included the landscaping of the quadrangles with concentrations of native and drought-resistant plants in otherwise empty courtyards (fig.9). The reference of the buildings and their landscaping was clearly to the missions.

Olmsted's overall plan linked the missionlike quadrangles to the domesticated landscape of the immediate surroundings and to the natural landscape beyond.[22] To outsiders and Californians, Stanford presented a powerful and, ironically, new image of what the state could look like. The style of the buildings was derived from a plausible, if manufactured, view of the area's history. The landscaping and relationship of the place to the larger landscape presented a model for planning and landscape design in the distinctive natural setting of the area.

Although few projects could match the grand scale and controlled environment of the Stanford campus, some of the same ideas that produced the new vision there began to affect the look of other places, both domestic and urban. Contemporary with the construction of the Stanford campus, new buildings in what was called the mission-revival style were built for two important temporary expositions, the World's Columbian Exposition in Chicago in 1893 and the

fig.10 Bernard Maybeck, pen and ink cover design of the
Hillside Club booklet, 1907
College of Environmental Design Documents Collection,
University of California, Berkeley

California Midwinter International Exposition in San
Francisco in 1894. These prominent events gave credence to the style as distinctive of the life and culture
of California. Various kinds of promoters soon adopted
it as part of a marketing strategy, including the Southern Pacific and Santa Fe railways. The Southern Pacific
operated railroads, ferries, and urban and interurban
electric lines in the Bay Area, and owned vast amounts
of land that it hoped to sell.[23] A string of mission-revival
railroad stations along its Peninsula line produced one
of the most conspicuous impressions of this imagined
inheritance of the Mexican era.

A different kind of landscape developed in Berkeley
from a related body of ideas, the collaboration of
Charles Keeler, a naturalist and writer interested in
William Morris, and the architect Bernard Maybeck.
Keeler and Maybeck were the leaders of the Hillside
Club, founded in 1898 to promote a set of principles
for design of the residential area north of the campus
of the University of California (fig.10). This was a middle-class area attractive to people associated with the
university and to others who wanted to live in a liberal
cultural atmosphere. In 1904 Keeler published a book
called *The Simple Home* in which he described his ideal
of the North Berkeley house on a hill as "landscape gardening around a few rooms for use in case of rain."[24]
The effort led to the remaking of a hilly grassland with
scattered oaks into a richly planted townscape that had
the effect of a single large public garden. Streets were
laid out with the topography, trying to avoid rock outcroppings and trees. The typical lot was developed with
a shingled or stucco house, colored to blend with the
landscape, oriented to a view of the bay and set in a private garden that merged with the planting of the hillside. Maybeck, who designed many houses in this area,
was as interested in the landscaping and the whole site
as he was in the buildings.[25] His designs reflected the
ideals of the arts-and-crafts movement for simplicity,
fine craftsmanship, the use of native materials and
plants, and an informal way of life integrated with the
natural setting. Although addressed to North Berkeley,
the informal house-and-garden idea was picked up in
scattered enclaves around the bay, which included the
area's first automobile subdivisions. After the earthquake of 1906 large new streetcar neighborhoods,
especially in the East Bay, were filled with bungalows
and small gardens, modest places with elements of
arts-and-crafts influence.

As San Francisco grew, the differences between city
and countryside became more pronounced and apparent. San Francisco was densely built up and widely
regarded as ugly, shabby, and architecturally unworthy
of the city's aspirations. The grid was almost devoid of
street trees. Houses were generally built near the building line, producing narrow, barren streetscapes with

fig.11 Carleton Watkins, *View of San Francisco from Telegraph Hill*, ca. 1865
Treeless hills with cheap wood houses constituted an unrefined and
uninviting cityscape. Courtesy The Bancroft Library, Berkeley

fig.12 San Francisco skyline from the 1920s
Courtesy Gabriel Moulin Studios, San Francisco

fig.13 Point San Pablo, Contra Costa County
This early aerial view shows a pattern of industrial shoreline development that began in the 1860s
Courtesy The Bancroft Library, Berkeley

fig.14 The Sunken Garden, Filoli, Woodside, 1927
Courtesy Gabriel Moulin Studios, San Francisco

shabby backyards hidden from view (fig.11).

The density, barrenness, and artificiality of the urban landscape was in sharp contrast to the countryside of the Bay Area as improved irrigation made expanded orchards, vineyards, and row crops possible in the 1880s and 1890s. If San Francisco was regarded as visually eccentric by sophisticated observers, the rural landscape was widely admired. Viewed from the undeveloped hills in rural areas all around the bay, the agricultural valleys below were mosaics of different crops with groups of fields in the same ownership often defined by tall windbreaks of eucalyptus trees. Each separate farm had a cluster of buildings; the main house was typically set in a garden of exotic plants and was approached by a tree-lined drive.[26] The beauty of this rural landscape was utilized in advertisements and articles promoting real estate in California, and rural scenes were commonly depicted on fruit and wine labels. With the explosive growth (and intermittent collapse) of the late-nineteenth-century real estate industry, the beauty of the distinctive rural landscape around San Francisco and beyond became a major element in the national projection of its identity.

Business, Industry, Professionalism, and Empire
It has been observed that the nineteenth-century mansions of the Big Four (Collis P. Huntington, Mark Hopkins, Leland Stanford, and Charles Crocker), the builders of the transcontinental railroad, stood out above San Francisco as conspicuous symbols of the power and wealth of a few individuals. About 1895 a new symbol of financial power emerged in the large buildings designed for a new type of organization, the modern corporation. When Michael de Young, William Randolph Hearst, and others constructed skyscrapers in the 1890s and 1900s, they also created prominent urban symbols for new ways of doing business. Collectively, by the time of the earthquake in 1906 they had helped to produce a new feature of the urban landscape – the skyline – that changed both the look and meaning of the city. By the end of the 1920s the new skyline was significantly expanded, visually suggesting an artificial hill among the natural ones and conveying a romantic sense of urban life (fig.12).[27]

The corporations that built the skyscrapers generated substantial wealth through industry. The Bay Area grew as an industrial center in the 1860s and boomed in the 1880s when the shore south of Market Street in San Francisco and along Contra Costa County were lined with smoking factories. Around the turn of the century, the transformation of the landscape accelerated as networks of industrial infrastructure developed. From about 1900 to the 1930s the construction of electrical, gas, water, road, and electric rail systems utilized huge amounts of capital and the skills of highly sophisticated engineers. These systems and their social implications were part of a chain reaction of growth and development across the landscape whose only precedents in scale were the railroad and telegraph.

The earlier establishment of water, sewer, electricity, and gas systems had a localized effect on San Francisco. For the Bay Area at large, important developments included the building of oil pipelines to new refineries, the first from Kern County to Richmond in 1901; a network of high-voltage power lines and steel towers for delivery of hydroelectric power from the Sierra Nevada, first in 1901 and at a large scale from the Pit River in 1921; and the aqueducts from Hetch Hetchy Reservoir in Yosemite and the Mokelumne River in 1923 and 1934. At Pacific Gas & Electric Company power plants and substations a consistent pattern of architectural and landscape design produced a unified landscape of electric power with a dominant Spanish-style reference.[28] Facilities of the Hetch Hetchy system created a similarly unified classical landscape.[29]

The road system was another important factor in this industrialization of the land. In the 1880s, even before the automobile, a Good Roads movement existed and a state highway department was established. State highway construction increased dramatically by the mid-1920s, with University of California landscape architect John Gregg serving as design consultant.[30] In the Bay Area highway construction concentrated on the Peninsula, with the Bayshore Highway opening in 1931.[31]

With the growth of the industrial economy came rapid population expansion. San Francisco's population had pushed westward aided by electric streetcar lines, and after the 1906 earthquake the East Bay boomed. The development of new electric interurban lines, part of the most extensive such system in the country, stimulated development in inland areas including eastern Contra Costa County, while the military expansion associated with World War II occurred primarily in Richmond, Oakland, and Alameda (fig.13).

In this rapidly and dramatically changing context a new profession emerged to address major landscape issues. The growing presence of professional landscape designers in the Bay Area had a counterpart in the rise of a wealthy class of clients and a new kind of garden. Where most nineteenth-century estates landscaped by skilled gardeners were either naturalistic like English parks or essentially collections of exotic plants, the new group of political and industrial leaders were generally interested in more formal designs and worldly symbolism. Mediterranean, French, English, and Japanese influences shaped private gardens of this era such as New Place, designed for banker William Crocker by Bruce Porter in 1905; Carolans, designed by Achille Duchêne in 1913 for Harriet Pullman Carolan;[32] and Filoli, designed by Bruce Porter in 1916 for William B.

Bourn II of the Spring Valley Water Company (fig.14).[33]

These grand tastes were reflected by the routine expression of imagery from imperial Rome and Renaissance Europe in architecture and landscape design for large public projects at the end of the nineteenth century, a tribute to the rising prominence of the United States in world affairs, called the City Beautiful movement. The World's Columbian Exposition in Chicago provided an inspiring example of a completely designed ensemble of architecture, landscaping, and sculpture in a single, unified plan. Believing that San Francisco should be the administrative and financial center not only of California but also of the Pacific,[34] leading San Franciscans supported a series of projects expressing their confidence and aspirations that established numerous enclaves and outposts of monumental classical design. These projects in San Francisco were led by a group of architects influenced by the teachings of the École des Beaux-Arts in Paris, the largest group of beaux-arts-trained professionals in America practicing outside of New York.[35]

The most ambitious of the City Beautiful movement projects was a plan for the entire city of San Francisco. Usually referred to as the Burnham Plan, it was primarily the work of Edward H. Bennett, an associate of Daniel H. Burnham (fig.15). As the chief planner of the World's Columbian Exposition and the McMillan Plan for Washington, D.C., Burnham was the leading figure of the City Beautiful movement in America.

The Burnham Plan proposed new diagonal boulevards across the existing grid of the city and a hierarchy of focal points, including sculpture, fountains, stairways, and a monumental civic center at the intersection of Van Ness Avenue and Market Street. The plan would create a new image for the city as did Baron Georges-Eugène Haussmann's design for Paris. Although completed just before the earthquake and fire of 1906, which seemed to clear the way for its implementation, the plan was rejected as impractical.[36]

Two other major City Beautiful projects in San Francisco were boosted by the earthquake. Public interest was revived in creating a civic center to convey the image of world prominence that San Francisco now claimed, and in 1912 a plan was adopted for a civic center complex with monumental classical buildings around a central plaza.[37] Burnham and others had thought that if appropriately grand public buildings were provided at civic centers and other nodes, private owners would be inspired to build in a like manner, replacing the fragile wooden buildings of the existing city and lining the boulevards with great structures equal to those of Paris.[38]

A second great City Beautiful project was entirely symbolic. To celebrate its recovery from the earthquake, unify its quarreling leadership, attract business

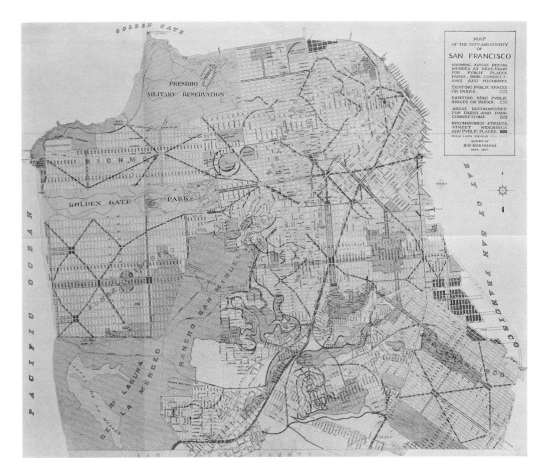

fig.15 Daniel H. Burnham, *Map of the City and County of San Francisco,*
from *Report of D.H. Burnham on the Improvement and Adornment of San Francisco,* September 1905
Collection of Albert R. Schreck

fig.16 Jules Guerin, *Bird's-eye View of the Panama Pacific International Exposition,* 1913
Ink and watercolor on paper, 49 x 97 in.
Collection of the Exploratorium, San Francisco

associated with the opening of the Panama Canal, and assert its preeminence in the West, San Francisco planned a great exposition. The Panama Pacific International Exposition (PPIE) of 1915 was organized and designed under the leadership of Edward H. Bennett and Willis Polk (fig.16). The core of the fair was a monumental sequence of three courtyards framed by colonnaded buildings decorated by different architects. The symmetry, axiality, and unity of the plan and the generally classical appearance of the buildings were in the beaux-arts tradition of other fairs since Chicago.

At the same time, this fair was a regional variation of the type. The scale of its courtyards, with high walls and narrow spaces, blocked the wind and fog. The colors of everything about the fair buildings, grounds, plants, banners, and uniforms of workers, were coordinated by Jules Guerin with a palette inspired by the natural landscape of California: the grassy hills in dry season, California poppies and other wild flowers, the blue bay, orange and gold. Landscape architects John McLaren and Donald McLaren worked with Guerin[39] to carry out the design principles with elaborate plantings and color mixtures. When it ended, the whole physical structure of the fair was torn down, except for Maybeck's Palace of Fine Arts and its lagoon,[40] which still stand in the San Francisco Marina district.

Projects with roots in the City Beautiful movement continued to be built through the 1930s in San Francisco and beyond. Major school building programs in Oakland and San Francisco in the 1910s and 1920s established landscaped outposts of monumental classicism and the Spanish colonial-revival style in neighborhoods throughout each city; veterans' memorial buildings were built in many cities and towns around the bay in the 1920s and 1930s; and Coit Tower, designed by Arthur Brown, Jr., for the top of Telegraph Hill, recalled an extravagant feature of the Burnham plan. The last major expression of the City Beautiful movement was the Golden Gate International Exposition (GGIE) on Treasure Island in San Francisco Bay in 1939-40.

Designed under the leadership of Arthur Brown, Jr., who had been a key figure in the planning of the civic center and the PPIE, its sheltered courtyards also provided protection from the fog and its color scheme too was completely controlled. The modernist style of buildings and statuary, however, contrasted with the classical themes of the earlier fair and spoke to the role of the Bay Area in a new and changing world.[41]

Among those who concerned themselves professionally with city planning in this period were many who called themselves architects, planners, landscape architects, landscape designers, and landscape engineers. From its establishment in 1913, the landscape architecture program at the University of California produced designers whose principal work in the area, in addition

to private gardens, was the designing of subdivisions (fig.17). As the increased use of the automobile made hilly areas more accessible and helped change attitudes toward life in the city, landscape architects participated in the first widespread layout of American streets to diverge from a rigid grid. Among the first such subdivisions in San Francisco were St. Francis Wood, designed by the Olmsted Brothers (Frederick Jr. and John C.) with John Galen Howard in 1912, and Seacliff and Forest Hills, designed in 1912 and 1915 by Mark Daniels.

In the countryside various technological improvements had a profound effect on both landscape and everyday life. The automobile and the developing road system ended the physical isolation of farms and gave farmers better access to markets. For the first time it became feasible to live on the farm and commute to work, and many farms were subdivided for new types of rural dwellers not dependent on farm income. Where the agricultural valleys of the Bay Area had previously been dominated by parcels of at least twenty acres, now narrow five- and ten-acre divisions lined the roads. Where the buildings on each parcel previously stood in isolation, they now were near neighbors, as in residential suburbs.

At least as important as the automobile was the arrival of electricity to farming areas. Rural electrification meant lights and other conveniences in the farmhouse and electric pumps for wells and irrigation systems in the fields.[42] In many cases, this meant that orchards, grapes, or vegetables could be planted for the first time, in place of dry-farm crops such as grains. With electricity and water, agricultural areas were transformed into the rich green landscape that exists today.

In addition to these technological changes, the state university began to provide standardized advice to farmers and others through the Agricultural Extension service, established in 1914. The landscape architecture faculty of the College of Agriculture of the University of California prepared plans and provided advice on the landscaping of schools, homes, parks, playgrounds, and highways.[43]

Rejections and New Directions
The collapse of the stock market in 1929 brought a concomitant decline in several main trends in land development, at least temporarily. Expansion of the main population concentrations in the Bay Area stopped, bringing to a halt the construction of new houses in central and western San Francisco, Oakland, and Peninsula suburbs. Expansion of industry, which was especially vigorous in the East Bay, slowed substantially. Developers stopped creating new subdivisions and wealthy individuals stopped commissioning gardens. All of these changes created a crisis among landscape architects, who had been extremely busy in the

1920s designing subdivisions, gardens, and parks. Most who stayed in the profession found work in government, where decision making and management often became more important than design.[44] By branching into new kinds of work, they established precedents that would ensure a professional role in public actions affecting the landscape in the future. In response to the economic crisis the public supported large bond issues and various levels of government responded with programs providing employment. In 1933 the Civilian Conservation Corps (CCC) established two-hundred-person camps around the state, each with a landscape architect, forester, and engineer among its leaders. In the Bay Area these camps made improvements to Aquatic Park in Berkeley and Mount Diablo State Park, built the Rose Gardens in Oakland and Berkeley and Aquatic Park in San Francisco.[45]

The most critical impact came with construction of new bridges across the bay (fig.18). Proposals had been made for a bridge across the Golden Gate as early as 1869 and for one from San Francisco to Alameda by 1871. Planning began for the Golden Gate in 1919 and for the Bay Bridge in 1921, but funding was not available for either until the 1930s, after the full economic impact of the crash had been felt.

Unlike the earlier bridge plans, the Golden Gate and the Bay Bridge were seen not just in practical and engineering terms but for what they represented to the Bay Area as symbol and sculpture. The appearance, both in outline and detail, was considered an essential aspect of each. The commission responsible for the Bay Bridge stated that not only would it be "the largest bridge in the world, but it must be the most beautiful,"[46] and that "the final design should be such that it will conform with the scenic beauty of the San Francisco Bay."[47] A team of architects consisting of Arthur Brown, Jr., Timothy Pflueger, and John J. Donovan, brought in after the design was far along, advised the bridge engineers under Charles H. Purcell on the western span, the suspension bridge between San Francisco and Yerba Buena Island. Under Pflueger's leadership a streamlined architectural expression was given to the bridge. The main San Francisco anchorage and the central pier were made to appear more massive and expressive, the towers of the bridge were made to appear higher, and the approach from San Francisco and the tunnel through Yerba Buena Island were detailed to enhance the experience of moving across the bridge.[48]

After earlier proposals for the Golden Gate Bridge were rejected because of their ungainliness in a setting that was already widely appreciated for its natural beauty and drama, Irving F. Morrow, an architect, was brought in to work with the team of engineers under Joseph B. Strauss. Morrow contributed to the choice of horizontal rather than diagonal braces on the towers with their subtle bracket supports, the telescoped shaping of the towers, and the streamlined detailing of bridge surfaces. Daniel Gregory has observed that Morrow "saw the bridge as a romantic expression of modern urbanism."[49]

The Bay Bridge opened in 1936 and the Golden Gate Bridge in 1937. Together they represented a triumph of modern engineering (and politics) against challenging environmental factors. Equally important, their sensitive designs made each a sculptural object of almost unprecedented scale that utilized its setting in a composition spectacularly incorporating the wider landscape.

The bridges began to make a physically unified metropolis out of a more loosely connected region.[50] The GGIE emerged as a celebration of the completion of the bridges and the creation of a single Bay Area metropolis (fig.19). Its location in the middle of the bay, where it was not a part of any one city, was significant; the whole Bay Area, visible across the water in every direction, became one of the fair's main exhibits.[51]

Another key development during the 1930s was the progress made on regional parks. A state bond issue had been passed for parks in 1927 and a State Parks Commission was established with Frederick Law Olmsted, Jr., as consultant. Olmsted's report called for an extensive series of parks in the East Bay hills as first recommended in the 1860s by Frederick Law Olmsted, Sr., for scenic highways, and protection of the coast.[52] Space became available in 1934 when the Mokelumne aqueduct was completed from the Sierra, and local watershed lands of the East Bay Municipal Utilities District were no longer needed. Public interest led to the initial acquisition of ten thousand acres of this land, including Tilden, Sibley, and Redwood Regional Parks, and establishment of the East Bay Regional Park District.[53]

This same period saw dramatic changes in the field of American landscape architecture comparable to the modernist revolution already underway in architecture. Much of the early development of these changes in attitude toward landscape design took place in the Bay Area, and it was notable that the first museum exhibition devoted to landscape architecture in the United States was held at the San Francisco Museum of Art in 1937.[54] Ironically, modernist trends in architecture were slower to evolve here and to a large extent developed in concert with landscape design.

Landscape architects who continued as designers were forced by the social and economic conditions of the 1930s to reappraise practices and the pool of potential clients. Designs based on historic models were expensive to construct and maintain and few could afford them. Newer approaches to landscape design stressed the practical, functional, and individualized. Design was based more on conditions of the site – topography, orientation, views, drainage, and existing

fig.17 A Study of Advanced Landscape Gardening,
San Pablo Park, Berkeley, 1915-16, from the *College of Agriculture Bulletin*,
University of California. Courtesy The Bancroft Library, Berkeley

fig.18 View of the Bay Bridge under construction at Yerba Buena Island
Photograph taken for the Yerba Buena Shoals Project, 6 March 1937,
official black and white photograph, 8 x 10 in., 88th Recon. Squadron,
Hamilton Field California, Air Corps – U.S. Army

fig.19 View of Golden Gate International Exposition,
Treasure Island, 1939-40
Courtesy Robert W. Cameron,
Aerial Photographer, San Francisco

fig.20 The front cover of *Sunset Magazine*
(*The Pacific Sunset Monthly*), February 1937,
featuring the "formistic" Griffin garden by
landscape architect Thomas Church
Courtesy *Sunset Magazine*

features such as trees or rocks – and on simplified palettes of color and plants. New technology and materials were introduced, and modern art, with its emphasis on freedom of form and space, was utilized as a key design source. New situations such as shopping centers and malls, freeways, urban renewal projects, farmworker housing, and urban housing became the concern of landscape designers. Even though modern landscape architects in the 1930s were mostly designing residential gardens for private clients, the ideas developed would have far-reaching impacts on the landscape after World War II.

An influential leader in this movement was Thomas D. Church, who had studied landscape architecture at the University of California and Harvard and opened his practice in San Francisco in 1929. The 1937 San Francisco Museum of Art show featured a number of Church designs for residential gardens, including one innovative example published in the catalogue with an asymmetrical layout, abstract forms, diagonal orientation, and the house linked to the garden through a plate-glass window. He collaborated in the design of the Potrero Hills and Sunnydale public housing projects in San Francisco in 1938-39 and designed two small gardens at the GGIE in 1939-40, introducing long curves into his compositions to create an illusion of increased space and movement in opposition to the typically rectangular boundaries of a site.[55] Many younger landscape architects whose work would become important worked for a while in Church's office, including Garrett Eckbo, Robert Royston, Lawrence Halprin, and Douglas Baylis, who later transformed *Sunset Magazine* in Menlo Park into an extremely influential source of information about garden design. In the years after World War II, largely as a result of the popularity of *Sunset* and other magazines, the modern garden replaced other models and was widely adopted by middle-class homeowners, not just in the Bay Area but throughout the United States (fig.20).[56] What came to be known as the California garden was an artistic, functional, and social composition.

While Church worked primarily on private gardens, Eckbo, Royston, and Halprin were at least as interested in applying new ideas about landscape design to the larger environment. Working for the Farm Securities Administration and the United States Housing Authority, Eckbo participated in the designs of farmworkers' housing in 1939-40 and housing for wartime workers in 1942-45. These experiences, plus his exposure at Harvard to Walter Gropius's progressive architectural ideas, gave impetus to the routine collaboration of landscape architects with architects, engineers, and others in the design of environments. These new ideas were expressed in what became the standard text of landscape architecture, Eckbo's *Landscape for Living* in 1950.[57]

Lawrence Halprin's impact on the public Bay Area landscape has been the greatest of those closely associated with the formation of modern landscape architecture. Working for Church in 1948 he participated in the design of a garden and pool in Sonoma County for Dewey Donnell, El Novillero, perhaps the most famous of the modern gardens of this period (fig.21). Some of his best-known projects in the Bay Area are Ghirardelli Square in 1968, with Wurster, Bernardi and Emmons (fig.22); the Embarcadero Plaza and Fountain in 1972, with Mario Ciampi, John Bolles & Associates, and the sculptor Armand Villaincourt; and the Market Street Beautification project in 1970, with John Carl Warnecke & Associates and Mario Ciampi.[58] These new types of public landscapes sought to make the urban environment welcoming through dynamic mixtures of people, architecture, and landscape; the replacement of formality with playfulness and intimacy; the emphasis on discovery rather than fully controlled movement; and the sensitive employment of a range of textures, colors, sounds, and even smells. Such principles, disseminated through the work of key Bay Area designers, became influential worldwide.

Contradictions: Environmental Crisis and the Best Regional Park System in America

World War II inaugurated an extended period of development and a transformation of the Bay Area landscape that was as revolutionary as changes in the 1930s, but far more extensive and long lasting. From World War II to the present a series of development booms (interspersed with recessions in the real estate industry) changed the Bay Area from a region characterized by a dominant large city, several smaller but important cities, and extensive agricultural land with small towns, to an area whose urbanized parts have nearly all grown together and whose agricultural elements have been greatly diminished. It was during this time that the military acquired much land for new bases.[59] Following the establishment of Moffett Field in Sunnyvale in 1931, with its enormous dirigible hangar visible from as far away as Richmond, many other new bases came into being around the bay after 1939 (fig.23). Large mudflats were filled to create a cluster of East Bay installations, again changing the bay's profile.

The war brought with it tremendous industrial expansion, particularly in shipbuilding. San Francisco Bay became the largest shipyard in the world, centered along the shore of the East Bay, from Alameda and Oakland to Richmond.[60] This expansion of military bases and industry brought huge numbers of people to the Bay Area and created a serious housing shortage.

Military expansion continued in association with the Cold War,[61] and the military remained a major presence in the Bay Area until after the fall of the Berlin Wall in

fig.21 Thomas Church, Landscape Architect; George Rockrise, Associate (for architecture); Lawrence Halprin, Associate; Adaline Kent, Sculptor. The Donnell House and Garden (El Novillero), Sonoma, 1948-50

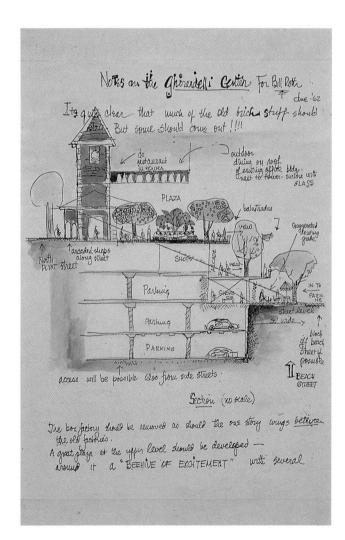

fig.22 Lawrence Halprin, Sketch for Ghirardelli Square, San Francisco, 1971

fig.23 Moffett Field, National Aeronautics and Space Administration,
Ames Research Center, Mountain View

fig. 24 The Marin Headlands with the Golden Gate Bridge leading
toward the Presidio in the background, 1969
Courtesy Robert W. Cameron, Aerial Photographer, San Francisco

1989. Since then the closing of several bases has produced prime new parklands, some development opportunities, and uncertainty about the future of key segments of Bay Area geography. Adaptation of the Presidio of San Francisco for a national park is one result of these changes (fig.24).

When World War II ended, the combination of a housing shortage, returning veterans, and federal loan programs resulted in a huge building boom. Demand for housing was satisfied by new, sprawling suburbs of single-family houses built over farmlands and new bay fill, along with schools, shopping centers, office buildings, and other developments. By the 1980s several new business centers had emerged outside the traditional downtown areas of San Francisco, Oakland, and San Jose, including Emeryville, Walnut Creek, Concord, Pleasanton, Foster City, and San Mateo.

Just as housing dispersed to the suburbs, so did industry. The closing of the shipyards after World War II marked the end of a long period of heavy industry in the Bay Area and initiated a new era of industrial development. It also changed the principal locus of industry from the Alameda and Contra Costa County shorelines to the Santa Clara Valley. Partnerships between business and the military established during the war for research and development provided the seeds for vast new electronics, computer, and biotechnology industries after the war. In addition to Silicon Valley in Santa Clara and San Mateo counties, major research industries developed in association with Stanford University, the University of California in Berkeley, and the University of California Medical Center in San Francisco. Among these, the Lawrence Berkeley Laboratory, with its carefully proportioned, domed cyclotron on the hill above the campus, and the corrugated metal, mile-long Stanford Linear Accelerator that runs under the freeway, characterize opposing approaches to design that each make monumental alterations to the landscape (fig.25).

All of these changes have a reciprocally supportive relationship with the automobile and the development of roads and freeways. While new freeways generally have been publicly supported, their design often created problems. Urban neighborhoods were cut in half, the poor and minorities were walled off, and the physical presence of these seemingly endless structures of unprecedented scale overwhelmed everything else around them. With restructuring of the physical environment to accommodate automobiles, the railroads scaled back; the interurban rail network, centered in Oakland and with connections to San Francisco and as far away as Marysville, died completely. The ports were reorganized to accommodate container shipping, resulting in the virtual demise of the Port of San Francisco and the growth of the Port of Oakland.[62]

fig.25 The Stanford Linear Accelerator Center, Stanford University, Palo Alto
Courtesy the Stanford Linear Accelerator Center and the U.S. Department of Energy

Changes were pervasive, from urban flight and the replacement of old houses in old city neighborhoods by multiunit apartments, to the visual disruption of the skies. While the first regular flights for carrying mail began about 1920 and the first airports opened in San Francisco and Oakland in 1927, it was during World War II that planes over the bay became ubiquitous. Since that time an invisible ingredient has been added to the air – "a dense 'soup' of electromagnetic radiation . . . with modified signals that permeate each other as well as all organic and inorganic matter," associated with telephone, television, computer, and radio transmissions.[63] The towers that support the equipment that sends and receives this radiation and the hierarchy of utility poles and towers that carry wires transmitting electricity, telephone, and cable television have spread far beyond their numbers before the war. The power used in all this apparatus was supplied by a proliferation of power sources, including the spectacular, sculptural array of wind-generating machines in Altamont Pass.

In the agricultural fields that remained, chemicals for fertilizer and pest control poisoned crops, animals, water, and soil. The flow of water through the Sacramento River became inadequate to maintain healthy conditions for wildlife in the bay. Agricultural, industrial, and residential runoff polluted the bay, rendering most of its food sources inedible. Industries and automobiles polluted the air. By the 1960s a major environmental crisis was perceived, encompassing the pollution of natural resources and the visual character of cities and countryside.[64]

The response to this accelerated, wholesale remaking of the landscape occurred on many levels. Of major importance was a new acceptance of the role of landscape professionals. The establishment of the Department of City Planning at the University of California in Berkeley in 1948, the Department of Landscape Architecture in 1949, and the College of Environmental Design in 1959, including architecture, landscape architecture, and city planning, reflected the institutionalization of the landscape professions and the collaborative structure necessary to address complex problems in a changing world. Both publicly and privately funded projects routinely incorporated landscape architecture in planning and design, including projects that had not traditionally included landscape design, such as office buildings, transit systems, and freeways, and new types of projects such as industrial parks, shopping centers, and the roofs of parking garages.

The boom in landscape architectural work was associated with the development of the local profession. Whereas before the 1930s leading landscape architects were commonly brought to the Bay Area from the East and Europe for major projects, after World War II Bay Area landscape architects were among the leaders of the profession internationally, producing not only most major designs in the Bay Area, but also much work across the United States and beyond. EDAW and Sasaki, Walker Associates (SWA), two locally based firms, were among the largest in the world, SWA, for example, preparing the massive master plan for the Golden Gate National Recreation Area in 1980. In the number of projects, quality of design, and influence, landscape architects created so many notable designs in the Bay Area alone that only a few of the most prominent and influential projects and project types can be mentioned here.

Among the individual public buildings produced were the Marin County Civic Center by Frank Lloyd Wright; The Oakland Museum, designed by Roche and Dinkeloo, architects, and Dan Kiley, landscape architect; and Foothill College, designed by Ernest J. Kump and Masten & Hurd, architects, and SWA, landscape architects. All attempted to establish a model relationship between a building and its landscape, for example, by placing Marin County Civic Center and Foothill College in suburban settings in which the surrounding landscapes were part of the designs. New construction, however, has so encroached upon Wright's design of arcaded linear forms linking hills across a valley that it has diminished much of the building's original relationship with nature. Wright's building has become a powerful illustration of the domination by economic and other ordinary forces over the best efforts of landscape designers (fig.26). Foothill College is a hilltop acropolis of classroom buildings clustered around courtyards, created within a landscape of gently graded mounds and lush plantings, and featuring a separation of pedestrian and vehicular domains (fig.27).[65] In contrast, The Oakland Museum treats an urban building as a park by landscaping its terraced roof with green lawns so that each level of the museum is a garden (page 2). Each of these projects incorporates landscape as artistic theme rather than simply as natural background.

The application of landscape design to freeways, a practice that has had a profound effect on one of the most common public places in the United States, was pioneered by Lawrence Halprin.[66] Landscape architects also were involved throughout the extensive Bay Area Rapid Transit (BART) system. The Stanford Industrial Park of 1959 with Thomas Church and the Cabot, Cabot & Forbes Industrial Park of 1965 with SWA set standards for this kind of development that were emulated across the country. Office buildings in downtown and suburban locations were routinely set in landscaped settings, many of them designed primarily to satisfy planning requirements or create an image. A few, like Crown Zellerbach, were aesthetically successful or encouraged pedestrian use. The landscape design of Levi Plaza, by Lawrence Halprin, succeeded in establishing a new

fig.26 Frank Lloyd Wright and Aaron G. Green, Associate,
Marin County Civic Center, San Rafael, 1957-62

fig.27 Peter Walker of Sasaki, Walker Associates
Foothill College, Los Altos Hills, 1957-60

model for an office building in balance with a usable public landscape (fig.28).

Federal redevelopment laws resulted in massive changes to urban areas in San Francisco, Oakland, and San Jose. Outside the framework of redevelopment, the urban landscape has been affected by a variety of planning tools generally encouraging conservation, such as the establishment of landmarks and historic districts, master plans, and zoning. San Francisco's Urban Design Plan, and more recently the residential design guidelines developed by architect Dan Solomon, have aimed at preserving the historic qualities of the city, if not its actual fabric. Outside the cities, some suburbs have attempted to create urban centers where none existed. San Ramon, Mountain View, and Walnut Creek have all built civic complexes in recent years with this goal.

Until the 1980s local landscape architecture continued to be dominated by the pioneering modernist generation of Church, Eckbo, Halprin, and followers like Peter Walker. From this point on, however, a new generation emerged whose work questioned some of the underlying principles of modernist landscape design. While building upon the freedom of form and space that modernism released, these landscape architects rejected the abstraction and artfulness of that tradition in favor of physical and psychological linkages between culture and nature that were more rooted in the historical setting, more accepting of environmental realities, and what George Hargreaves has termed "simpler, more receptive compositions and non-compositions." Hargreaves's plan for Byxbee Park on Palo Alto's bay shore, designed in collaboration with artists Peter Richards and Michael Oppenheimer, exemplifies his approach (fig.29). This collaboration points up the influence on landscape architects of artists working at a large scale on the landscape as well as the artistic aspirations of some of this generation.[67]

Byxbee Park is a landfill dump converted into an inviting public space that still expresses its lowly origins. An industrial vocabulary from the surrounding shoreline areas is absorbed into the park's iconography. A methane gas flare burns constantly, releasing gas from the still-decomposing garbage below, and repetitive undulant forms, covered with natural grasses and wildflowers, suggest both garbage mounds and the land-forming forces of nature, expressing the history of the site and creating new hills almost like the natural hills around the bay shore. In a different kind of project, Hargreaves Associates's redesign of the Guadalupe River corridor in San Jose, incorporating the flood control apparatus of the Army Corps of Engineers in a linear park, also expresses the history of the site and the necessary infrastructure of much of contemporary life. Designs for healing gardens by Topher Delaney manifest a different set of concerns (fig.30). Settings carefully orchestrated for direct, personal involvement by patients in harmoniously landscaped "rooms" elicit the therapeutic qualities of nature.[68]

As important as any other development has been the enormous expansion of the systems of regional parks, largely as a result of public pressure and volunteer action. Most significant was the expansion from ten thousand to sixty thousand acres of the East Bay Regional Park District, the establishment of Point Reyes National Seashore in 1962, and the creation of the Golden Gate National Recreation Area in 1972. Together with various state and local parks these areas constitute the largest regional park system for any metropolitan region in the United States.

Conclusion

The landscape of the Bay Area today is a complexly layered creation, resulting from the interaction of natural, economic, artistic, technological, philosophical, and other forces. Overwhelmingly, the landscape is the incidental result of actions that were undertaken for irrelevant reasons. The work of landscape architects and other design professionals has produced innumerable isolated works that enrich human experience of the landscape – such as the gardens of Thomas Church – and others that occasionally affect the landscape on a larger scale – such as Golden Gate Park, the influence of *Sunset Magazine* on the designs of suburban gardens, and the landscape design of Highway 280 and the BART system. Equally important have been the popular efforts to preserve the East Bay hills and Golden Gate National Recreation Area and other regional parks. Massive environmental changes have occurred within the past fifty years, but the origins of much that is visible around us today stretch back considerably longer. The view from a third-floor window in Oakland, San Jose, San Rafael, or Vallejo – or in any of the numerous gold rush-era cities – includes houses built on streets laid out on the grid system of the 1840s and 1850s, utility poles and wires put up early in the twentieth century, and tall palm trees planted as parts of farms or estates in the 1890s. Hillsides that were never built upon because of military occupation or watershed use, which have been protected as parks since the 1930s, might display stands of eucalyptus trees planted for tax reasons before 1905. Different views reveal different, equally multifaceted conjunctions and histories.

The landscape of the Bay Area seemed profoundly uninviting to gold rush-era Americans, but the early realization that anything would grow here has made the Bay Area a kind of blank slate where, unlike almost anyplace else, anything could be tried. Kevin Starr notes that "San Francisco seems a figment of its own imagination. The city should not have been here in the first place – on the edge of a waterless, treeless peninsula,"

fig.28 Lawrence Halprin, Levi Strauss Plaza, San Francisco, 1983

fig.29 George Hargreaves, Hargreaves Associates, with artists Peter Richards and Michael Oppenheimer. View of Pole Field with Land Gate in the distance, Byxbee Park, Palo Alto, 1988-1991

and that San Franciscans, for more than one hundred fifty years, "have been forced to rearrange their environment to make it habitable."[69] The results, in San Francisco and the surrounding nine counties, include all the ugliness, sprawl, and poverty of other cities, but also present a remarkable marriage of the natural and constructed that has been referred to in aggregate as a work of art, which contains an inordinate number of artistic elements.

What will the Bay Area be like tomorrow? Its landscape has never been the focus of more intense pressures or interest than it is today. The birth of a strong environmental movement, the redefinition of landscape architecture fostered in the 1930s, and the export of landscape architecture from the Bay Area after World War II have provided continuing sources of new ideas on the management and enhancement of the environment.

The unprecedented ferment over the landscape today is evident in continuing wide popular support for the regional park system, a new generation of ideas from landscape architects, and a variety of small-scale, sometimes unconventional efforts. These include movements for urban tree planting and creek protection, the establishment of a trail around the bay, the revival of native plants and removal of exotics (such as eucalyptus trees), the appreciation of ethnic and folk gardens, community and healing gardens, and organic gardening as an educational exercise for school children and a therapeutic activity for prisoners. Such undertakings occur against a rich tradition of innovation and accomplishment. The Bay Area of the future will be the product of interaction between the intentional efforts at shaping and improving the physical environment and ongoing forces such as land and housing development, freeways, and interest rates that are indifferent to the landscape. Some of the results will delight us and some will dismay us. All of it will reflect human use of the land.

fig.30 Topher Delaney, Delaney & Cochran, Inc., Healing Garden for Cancer Center, The Marin General Hospital, Greenbrae, 1993

Notes

1. J. B. Jackson, *Discovering the Vernacular Landscape* (New Haven: Yale University Press, 1984), 3-13. In addition to a basic perspective on the landscape from Jackson, this essay has drawn heavily on the writings of others. Especially helpful were David C. Streatfield's many articles, some of which are cited below, and recent book, *California Gardens: Creating a New Eden* (New York: Abbeville Press, 1994); Jere Stuart French, *The California Garden and the Landscape Architects Who Shaped It* (Washington, D. C.: The Landscape Architecture Foundation, 1993); Michael Laurie's writings on the profession of landscape architecture in California, some of which are cited below; Randolph S. Delehanty, "San Francisco Parks and Playgrounds, 1839 to 1990: The History of a Public Good in One North American City" (PH.D. diss., Harvard University, 1992), for San Francisco issues; and Mel Scott, *The San Francisco Bay Area* (Berkeley: University of California Press, 1959), and Charles Wollenberg, *Golden Gate Metropolis* (Berkeley: Institute of Government Studies, University of California, 1985), for a regional perspective. In addition to those cited elsewhere in this book, I have benefited from conversations with Randolph Delehanty, Amy Meyer, and John Roberts. I am especially grateful to Denise Bradley, Robert Bruegmann, Mary Hardy, and Woody Minor for their comments on early drafts of this essay.

2. W. W. Robinson, *Land in California* (Berkeley: University of California Press, 1948), chapters 4-5. Also Paul Groth, "Street Grids as Frameworks of Urban Variety," *The Harvard Architecture Review* 2 (Spring 1981): 68-75.

3. David C. Streatfield, "'Paradise' on the Frontier: Victorian Gardens on the San Francisco Peninsula," *Journal of Garden History* 12, no. 1 (1982): 71-74.

4. Albert Shumate, *Rincon Hill and South Park, San Francisco's Early Fashionable Neighborhood* (Sausalito, Calif.: Windgate Press, 1988), 30-31.

5. Delehanty, "San Francisco Parks," 43-47.

6. Eric Sandweiss, "Claiming the Urban Landscape: The Improbable Rise of an Inevitable City," in David Harris, *Eadweard Muybridge and the Photographic Panorama of San Francisco, 1850-1880* (Montreal: Canadian Center for Architecture, 1933), 27.

7. *The California Horticulturist and Floral Magazine* 6, no. 2 (February 1876): back cover.

8. Spiro Kostof, *America by Design* (New York: Oxford University Press, 1987), 217.

9. S. H. Herring, "Ornamental Agricultural Grounds," *Pacific Rural Press* 1, no. 6 (11 February 1871): 85.

10. Ward Hill and Michael Corbett, "Warm Springs Hotel," Historic American Building Survey, 1991. Remnants of this resort survive in Fremont.

11. Streatfield, *California Gardens*, 262.

12. Streatfield, *California Gardens*, 6. These are both demolished.

13. Charles H. Shinn, *Pacific Rural Handbook* (San Francisco: Dewey & Co., 1879), 9. Streatfield, "Paradise," 76-77.

14. Shinn, *Pacific*, 27-29.

15. Marilyn Ziebarth, "California's First Environmental Battle," *California History* 68, no. 4 (Fall 1984): 274-279.

16. "Benefits of Forests, Woods, and Belts of Trees to California," *California Horticulturist* 6, no. 5 (May 1876): 138-140.

17. "Trees on Goat Island and Elsewhere," *California Horticulturist* 9, no. 31 (March 1879): 315.

18. John Langellier, "San Francisco Presidio: A Chequered History." Funding did not become available for the program until 1889.

19. "Three Striking Trees," *Pacific Rural Press* 69, no. 1 (14 January 1905): 17.

20. David C. Streatfield, "The Arts and Crafts Garden in Califor-

nia," in Kenneth R. Trapp, *The Arts and Crafts Movement in California, Living the Good Life* (Oakland: The Oakland Museum and Abbeville Press, 1993), 40-41.

21. Paul Venable Turner, *Campus: An American Planning Tradition* (New York: The Architectural History Foundation and MIT Press, 1984), 269-274.

22. Paul Venable Turner, Marcia E. Vetrocq, and Karen Weitze, *The Founders and the Architects: The Design of Stanford University* (Stanford University Department of Art, 1976), 23-26. Also Streatfield, "Arts and Crafts," 42.

23. Karen J. Weitze, *California's Mission Revival* (Los Angeles: Hennessey & Ingalls, 1984), chapters 1-3.

24. Dianne Harris, "Maybeck's Landscapes," *Journal of Garden History* 10, no. 3 (July-September 1990): 149; Charles Keeler, *The Simple Home* (San Francisco: Paul Elder & Company, 1904; reprint with intro. Dimitri Shipounoff, Santa Barbara and Salt Lake City: Peregrine Smith, Inc., 1979).

25. Richard Longstreth, *On the Edge of the World: Four Architects at the Turn of the Century* (New York and Cambridge, Mass.: The Architectural History Foundation and MIT Press, 1983), 313-315. Harris, "Maybeck's Landscapes"; Streatfield, "Arts and Crafts," 42-43.

26. See any of several Historic Atlas Maps by Thompson & West or Smith & Elliott for Bay Area counties, 1876-79. Palms and olive trees are often all that remains of more diverse lines of trees, because they can survive without regular watering.

27. Daniel P. Gregory, "A Vivacious Landscape: Urban Visions Between the Wars," in Paolo Polledri, *Visionary San Francisco* (Munich: San Francisco Museum of Modern Art and Prestel-Verlag, 1990), 78-81.

28. Frank Baum, "The Pit River Power and 220,000 Volt Transmission Problem," *Electrical World* 81 (27 January 1923): 205-212. Also Ivan C. Frickstad, "Some Sub-stations of the Pacific Gas & Electric Company," *The Architect and Engineer* 43, no. 2 (November 1915): 54-62. Duncan Hay, *Hydroelectric Development in the United States, 1880-1940* (Washington, D.C.: Edison Electric Institute, 1991), 29-30.

29. John B. McGloin, *San Francisco: The Story of a City* (San Francisco: Presidio Press, 1978), 218-221.

30. Michael Laurie with David Streatfield, *Seventy-five Years of Landscape Architecture at Berkeley: An Informal History* (The Department of Landscape Architecture, University of California, Berkeley, 1988), pt. 1, 10.

31. Stephen D. Mikesell, *Historic Highway Bridges of California* (Sacramento: California Department of Transportation, 1990), 5-6. Charles Wollenberg, *Golden Gate Metropolis: Perspective on Bay Area History* (Institute of Governmental Studies, University of California, Berkeley, 1985), 212-215.

32. Norman T. Newton, *Design on the Land*. Duchêne was the most famous landscape architect of the day, involved in the restoration of Le Notre's gardens at Versailles.

33. Streatfield, *California Gardens*, 83-100.

34. Gray Brechin, "San Francisco: The City Beautiful," in Polledri, *Visionary San Francisco*, 40-60; also Judd Kahn, *Imperial San Francisco: Politics and Planning in an American City*, 1897-1906 (Lincoln and London: University of Nebraska Press, 1979).

35. Michael R. Corbett, *Splendid Survivors* (San Francisco: California Living Books, 1979), 50.

36. Delehanty, "San Francisco Parks," 234-255. Also Joan E. Draper, *Edward H. Bennett, Architect and City Planner, 1874-1954* (The Art Institute of Chicago, 1982), 11-13. Other outsiders brought to the Bay Area in this period were Charles Mulford Robinson, who prepared a multifaceted plan for Oakland; Bion Arnold, a Chicago engineer who addressed the Bay Area as a whole; and Werner Hegemann, a German city planner with an international reputation, who prepared *Report on a City Plan for the Municipalities of Oakland and*

Berkeley. See Mel Scott, *The San Francisco Bay Area: A Metropolis in Perspective* (Berkeley and Los Angeles: University of California Press, 1959), 148, 160-161, 165, 167.

37. The advisory architects of the civic center were John Galen Howard, Frederick H. Meyer, and John Reid, Jr. The adopted plan was based on an 1897 proposal by B. J. S. Cahill.

38. Brechin, "San Francisco," 57-58.

39. Laurie, *Seventy-five Years*, 9.

40. Brechin, "San Francisco," 54-57; Gray Brechin, "Sailing to Byzantium: The Architecture of the Fair," in Burton Benedict, *The Anthropology of World's Fairs* (Berkeley, Calif.: The Lowie Museum of Anthropology and Scolar Press, 1983), 94-101.

41. Brechin, "Sailing to Byzantium," 111-112.

42. "Electric Power on Sacramento Valley Farms," *Sacramento Valley Monthly* (March 1924): 4-5. This discussion about farms along the new transmission lines from the Sierra to the Bay Area applies equally to those Bay Area counties crossed by the lines (Solano, Contra Costa, and Napa) as well as other rural areas served by electricity.

43. Laurie, *Seventy-five Years*, 6, 10.

44. Laurie, *Seventy-five Years*, 21. John Gregg stated in 1930 that more graduates of Berkeley's landscape architecture program were in practice than those of any other school.

45. Phoebe Cutler, *The Public Landscape of the New Deal* (New Haven, Conn.: Yale University Press, 1985), 42-46.

46. Mikesell, *Highway Bridges*, 133.

47. Quoted in Gregory, "A Vivacious Landscape," 96.

48. Christopher H. Nelson, "Classical California: The Architecture of Albert Pissis and Arthur Brown, Jr." (PH.D. diss., University of California, Santa Barbara, 1986), 278; Milton T. Pflueger, *Time and Tim Remembered* (San Francisco: Pflueger Architects, 1985), 27.

49. Gregory, "A Vivacious Landscape," 94; Mikesell, *Highway Bridges*, 139.

50. Efforts to promote regional government were made by the Regional Plan Association, established by Fred Dohrmann in 1925, and by Harland Bartholomew, a planning consultant from St. Louis and advisor to the RPA.

51. Gregory, "A Vivacious Landscape," 98-102.

52. Laurie, *Seventy-five Years*, 17; Norman T. Newton, *Design on the Land* (Cambridge and London: The Belknap Press, 1971), 572.

53. Malcolm Margolin, *East Bay Out* (Berkeley, Calif.: Heyday Books, 1988), 225-226.

54. *Contemporary Landscape Architecture and Its Sources*, (San Francisco Museum of Art, 1937). The state of modern landscape architecture was the subject of two exhibitions at the San Francisco Museum of Art, following the first show in 1937. The catalogue of the 1948 exhibition was a classic statement of modern landscape architecture, emphasizing the role of the Bay Area in its wider development and acceptance, illustrated largely with residential gardens. The catalogue of the 1958 exhibition reflected the movement of the profession beyond the garden to a consideration of the larger environment. *Landscape Design*, ex. cat. (San Francisco Museum of Art and the Association of Landscape Architects, San Francisco Region, 1948); R. Burton Litton, Jr., ed., *Landscape Architecture*, ex. cat. (San Francisco Museum of Art, 1958); Streatfield, *California Gardens*, 35; Michael Laurie, "From Garden Design to Regional Plan: The California Influence on Contemporary Landscape Architecture," *Landscape Architecture* 56, no. 4 (July 1965): 297-298.

55. *Contemporary Landscape Architecture*, 32.

56. French, *The California Garden*, 162.

57. French, *The California Garden*, 154-160; Streatfield, *California Gardens*, 193. Garrett Eckbo, *Landscape for Living* (New York: F. W. Dodge Company, 1950).

58. *Lawrence Halprin: Changing Places*, ex. cat. (San Francisco

Museum of Modern Art, 1986); French, *The California Garden*, 174-182.

59. These included installations for coastal defense, training and supply, shipbuilding, and aircraft.

60. Other major shipbuilding sites were in Vallejo, Sausalito, and San Francisco.

61. Cold War military developments included a radar station whose two white spherical radomes atop Mount Tamalpais are visible from a very wide area, and several Nike missile bases around the bay.

62. This change involved demolition of most finger piers, and construction of enormous new container cranes, themselves prominent features of the landscape. The first container crane in the United States was built and installed in Alameda.

63. Michele Bertomen, *Transmission Towers on the Long Island Expressway* (Princeton Architectural Press, 1991), 4.

64. By traditional measures, pollution in this period was substantially less than it had been when heavy industry flourished and before controls were implemented – air and water were cleaner, for example. By other measures, there were serious problems remaining that weren't always recognized before.

65. Allen Temko, *No Way to Build a Ballpark* (San Francisco: Chronicle Books, 1993), 137.

66. Lawrence Halprin has written *Freeways* (New York: Reinhold Publishing Corporation, 1966). He played a major role in the design of Interstate 280, "The World's Most Beautiful Freeway," including its alignment and controlled vistas.

67. Among the most important artists working in the landscape were Robert Smithson, Michael Heizer, and Robert Irwin. In the Bay Area, Christo and Jeanne-Claude's *Running Fence*, 1976, and Stuart Williams's *Luminous Earth Grid*, 1993, are two examples.

68. Ron Herman, ed., "Landscape Design: New Wave in California," *Process: Architecture* 61 (August 1985); Streatfield, *California Gardens*, 238-241; Anne Raver, "Patients Discover the Power of Gardens," *New York Times*, 29 December 1994.

69. Polledri, *Visionary San Francisco*, 11.

Arthur Mathews, *California*, 1905
Oil on canvas, 26 x 23½ in.
Collection of The Oakland Museum of California,
gift of The Art Guild, *cat.no.108*

Pastoral Visions at Continent's End: Painting of the Bay Area 1890 to 1930

Nancy Boas and Marc Simpson

During the years from 1890 to 1930 Californians looked to their actual and dreamed landscapes as the most meaningful sources for their art. They expected that a specifically Californian language of art would arise and that landscape painting would be its vehicle of expression. As museum director J. Nilsen Laurvik proclaimed in 1918:

[T]he most distinctively national expression in American art [will soon be] produced in California. Especially will this be true, I think, of the landscapes painted out here....

The bold contours of the hills bulging large against the blue vault, the sweeping arms of the bay, the big trees and great streams, the vast expanse of the Pacific, upon which the Californian gazes from birth, give him a bigness of vision that visualizes things and events in their entirety.[1]

The spectacle of the San Francisco Bay and its environs prompted some of the leading landscape artists in the early decades of the period to create tonal reveries and poems.[2] For those active later, the place encouraged bolder gesture and more vibrant color. To a degree, these changing approaches from lyric vision to coloristic expression followed the shifting of the generations, with artists of a given period adapting artistic styles known in other places to the specifics of the region. Whether the artists worked principally as visionaries or as colorists, however, they most often invoked a pastoral ideal, believing that a new culture of high human virtue in concert with nature could arise at that time and in that place. This pastoralism – with its components of reverence for the natural world, appreciation of simplicity and rusticity, and a lyric awareness of the unbridgeable distinction between the real and the ideal – formed a compelling ethos for the region.

Westward the Course of Empire:
Growth of a Regional Art Community

In his monumental *Cities of the Golden Gate*, 1893 (fig.1), Raymond Dabb Yelland combined the role of witness with just an overlay of the visionary, presenting the San Francisco Bay as a heroic panorama bathed in a revelatory light. Yelland's decision to place the viewer in the relatively undeveloped Berkeley hills, dominated by oak trees to the left and identified with the young woman at the center, asserts the painting's point of view as origi-

nating from within the pastoral perspective. The cities that give the work its title are but a small portion of the chosen scene – topographically accurate as they may be. The work reads simultaneously as a paean to the natural wonder of California and as a visual fulfillment of Bishop Berkeley's "Westward the course of empire takes its way."

One element symbolizing and documenting the westward course of empire during the years around 1900 was the continuing attempt to establish a viable regional art community in the San Francisco Bay Area. The hoped-for components were many: dynamic artist associations, educational institutions, museums, exhibition facilities, and commercial galleries, as well as critical and informational periodicals. Although the whole did not come together, moments of solid institutional achievement occurred, including the founding of the San Francisco Art Association (SFAA) in 1871 and its important California School of Design in 1874,[3] and the organization of the two world's fairs that profoundly affected cultural life in the region – the California Midwinter International Exposition (CMIE) of 1894 and the Panama Pacific International Exposition (PPIE) of 1915. From these grew what would become San Francisco's two municipal museums, the M. H. de Young Memorial Museum and the California Palace of the Legion of Honor.[4] Other progress was marked by the establishment of the Stanford Museum of Art in 1894, the Oakland Art Gallery in 1916, and the Mills College Art Gallery in 1925. These expositions and museums brought to many in the local art community their first direct contacts with worldwide advances in the visual arts.[5]

But it was also a time of great trauma. The defining experience of the first decade of the century was the 1906 San Francisco earthquake and fire, in which the fragility of Eden revealed itself. In terms of art, vast reserves in studios and private collections were destroyed. Although many artists started painting again – William Keith reportedly borrowed brushes and paints from a friend in the East Bay as San Francisco burned – others moved instead to Monterey and spots yet more distant.[6]

On a more individual level, one of the era's most promising interludes took place in the spring of 1891,

fig.1 Raymond Dabb Yelland, *Cities of the Golden Gate*, 1893
Oil on canvas, 55 x 96½ in.
University Art Museum, University of California, Berkeley,
gift of the artist, *cat.no.175*

fig.2 George Inness, *California*, 1891 (later dated 1894)
Oil on canvas, 60 x 48 in.
Collection of The Oakland Museum of California,
gift of the Estate of Helen Hathaway White
and the Women's Board of the Oakland Museum Association

fig.3 William Keith, *The Glory of the Heavens*, ca.1891
Oil on canvas, 35¼ x 59¼ in.
The Fine Arts Museums of San Francisco, presented to the City and County
of San Francisco by Gordon Blanding, *cat.no.90*

when the preeminent American landscape painter, George Inness, made a pilgrimage to California. Arriving in early March in San Francisco, Inness worked with and in the studio of William Keith, the area's major landscape talent.[7] The two painted in Monterey and together visited Yosemite. They exhibited the fruits of their local labor in May at the SFAA Spring Annual, notably including a Monterey scene by Inness, probably *California* (fig.2). At the same time, local private collections provided the components for an impressive *Art Loan Exhibition of Foreign Masters*.[8] The works, from Inness's *California* to J.-F. Millet's *Man with a Hoe* (1860-62, J. Paul Getty Museum), were principally French Barbizon in fact or spirit, evocative of a generalized mood and feeling rather than a detailed rendering of specifics. An outpouring of press reviews and manifest public interest caused the painter and writer Charles Dorman Robinson to trumpet the good news of "A Revival of Art Interest in California."[9]

In his own work well before Inness's visit, Keith had shifted from grandly scaled, detailed landscapes to more diffuse and subjective views. But the presence of the eastern artist inspired Keith anew: "I am learning so much from him. . . . I no longer want to die since Inness has come. I have been feeling for a long time that I was just hanging around waiting. Now I want to work."[10]

One of Keith's paintings that probably grew from the inspiration of Inness is the large-scale *The Glory of the Heavens*, ca. 1891 (fig.3).[11] Keith valued the work highly, including it among the six paintings he exhibited in the California Building of the Chicago World's Columbian Exposition of 1893. Considered by many to be the painter's masterpiece, *The Glory of the Heavens* elicited praise as "a song without words such as only a master-hand and spirit can call from the spheres."[12] This recognition of the poetic, visionary element of the work was precisely the effect that Keith desired: "What a landscape painter wants to render is not the natural landscape, but the state of feeling which the landscape produces in himself."[13]

Beauty Passed through Thought and Fixed in Form: Visionaries and Aesthetes

When Keith spoke in later life about his manner of working, he noted:

I cannot paint in the presence of nature. . . . Every flower, every blade of grass cries out, "Put me in; put me in!" . . . The only thing a poor bewildered artist can do is to seize in his mind some flash of sun upon a tree, some light of God in the sky, brood upon it, work it into his soul, and some day – suddenly, before he knows it, he has fixed his thought – God's thought he hopes it may be – upon the canvas.[14]

fig.4 William Keith, *Looking across the
Golden Gate from Mount Tamalpais*, ca. 1895
Oil on canvas, 40 x 50⅝ in.
Private collection, *cat.no.91*

Keith's notion of painting away from the subject, relying on memory and inspiration, and his repeated appeal to the Deity, probably grew in considerable measure from his friendship with the Reverend Joseph Worcester and his interest in the Swedenborgian Church. Inness, too, was Swedenborgian; the two artists and their wives attended church services together and visited Worcester at his Russian Hill home.[15] Keith reportedly was never an unquestioning convert,[16] but the church's tenets informed much of his later aesthetics and interpretation of nature. According to one of Emanuel Swedenborg's key precepts, the doctrine of correspondences, the physical world is but a reflection of the divine idea behind it. Particularly in his later paintings, Keith sought to embody this doctrine on canvas. His dark, moody glades and pools are readily seen to aspire to these spiritual equivalencies. His friendships with Worcester and with the writer and naturalist John Muir enhanced Keith's view of nature as inspiration, guide for conduct, and romantic creed.

And yet, as Muir noted, the painter was also true to the specifics of a given place, "observing a devout truthfulness to Nature yet removing veils of detail, and laying bare the very hearts and souls of landscapes."[17] Among the scenic places that Keith visited frequently was Marin County's Mount Tamalpais. *Looking across the Golden Gate from Mount Tamalpais*, ca. 1895 (fig.4), describes a real site, Bolinas Ridge on Mount Tamalpais near Rock Springs. Keith accurately observed the rosy color of the hills, the curved shore to the south in the distance, the dry grasses of the foreground. And he portrayed the startling climatic conditions, elsewhere unusual but commonplace on Mount Tamalpais, in which one can stand in sunshine while low-lying clouds drift below. Keith's *From Point Richmond Looking toward the Golden Gate*, 1898 (fig.5), presents the view west from mudflats on the eastern shore of San Francisco Bay, the thin mast of a boat marking the Golden Gate. A few small figures and boats aground in the middle distance punctuate the vast scale of the scene. The work contrasts the gritty reality of the wetlands with intimations of spirituality in the sunlight reflected off the breaking fog. Its orientation alludes perhaps to the Pacific focus resulting from the American war in the Philippines that year. Even when Keith is at his most objective in recording natural phenomena, his works seem imbued with allegorical content.

In contrast to Keith's use of landscape as a vehicle for spiritual expression, Arthur Mathews's landscapes were settings for narrative themes, first as history painting, and later as classical allegory. Second to Keith, Mathews most dominated the art world of San Francisco at the turn of the century.[18] He was a guiding force in the SFAA, from 1890 to 1906 directing the California School of Design, where he influenced a

fig.5 William Keith, *From Point Richmond Looking toward the Golden Gate*, ca. 1898
Oil on canvas, 30 x 40 in.
Private collection, *cat.no.92*

fig.6 Arthur Mathews, *Discovery of the Bay of San Francisco by Portolá*, 1896
Oil on canvas, 70¼ x 58½ in.
Courtesy of Garzoli Gallery, San Rafael, *cat.no.107*

fig.7 Arthur Mathews, *View from Skyline Boulevard, San Francisco*, 1915
Oil on canvas, 30 x 40 in.
Collection of The Oakland Museum of California,
gift of Concours d'Antiques, and The Art Guild, *cat.no.109*

fig.8 Florence Lundborg, *The Lark/November*, 1895
Color woodcut, 19¹³/₁₆ x 16³/₈ in.
Courtesy Hirschl & Adler Galleries, Inc., New York

fig.9 Arthur Atkins, *Piedmont Hills, Summer*, 1896
Oil on paper board, 20 x 25⅞ in.
Ruth Vickery Brydon, *cat.no.5*

fig.10 Bruce Porter, *Presidio Cliffs*, 1908
Oil on canvas, 27 x 32 in.
Private collection, *cat.no.130*

fig.11 Giuseppe Cadenasso, *Alameda Marsh*, ca. 1900
Pastel on paper, 12 x 19 in.
Private collection, *cat.no.22*

fig.12 Xavier Martinez, *The Road*, ca. 1907
Oil on canvas, 30 x 36⅛ in.
The Fine Arts Museums of San Francisco,
Museum purchase, Skae Fund Legacy, *cat.no.105*

generation of students through his emphasis on life drawing and anatomy classes, and encouraged many to study in Paris. After 1906, through the medium of his magazine *Philopolis* – "Published for those who care," as announced in its subtitle – and through the crafts work of the Furniture Shop, Mathews dedicated himself to the creation of a complete urban environment, from visionary city planning to the furnishings of a citizen's home integrating art and life.

One of the earliest extant examples of a Bay Area landscape painting by Mathews is *Discovery of the Bay of San Francisco by Portolá*, 1896 (fig.6). Responding to the challenge of soon-to-be-mayor James D. Phelan to envision a creation myth for San Francisco's European settlement, Mathews, Keith, and two other artists created a group of history paintings in 1896 in competition for a cash prize. Both Mathews and Keith chose the moment in 1769 when Gaspar de Portolá, leader of the earliest European expedition to view the bay, first gazed upon the site. Keith set Portolá and his men in the midst of a vast, effulgent swirl of golden light and land; his work won second prize. Mathews instead emphasized the figures, depicting the Spanish soldier explorers grouped on a hill overlooking the bay shore as if they were Old Testament characters within sight of the Promised Land. The painting's grand scale, dramatic costume, and composition prevailed; Mathews received the top prize of eight hundred dollars.

This historical re-creation is unusual in Mathews's outdoor scenes. More typically, he created a storied realm, a landscape distinctly resembling Northern California, inhabited by graceful allegorical figures, as in his *California*, 1905 (page 30).[19] California in this incarnation personifies the region as the contemporary embodiment of Attic-Mediterranean tradition. Her timeless dress is the brilliant gold of the forty-niners, no less than the color of California poppies in spring. Sitting at the continent's edge, she is, as Walt Whitman sang it, "Facing west from California's shores."[20]

On occasion, however, Mathews turned to pure landscape exercises. One of the most handsome is *View from Skyline Boulevard, San Francisco*, 1915 (fig.7). A tonal harmony of grays, purples, ochers, and greens, the work portrays the distinctive hills of the Coast Range with the afternoon clouds so frequently seen there.[21] A small farm sits at the center of the rolling valley, linked to both foreground and distance by a winding dirt road. Mathews has ordered the surrounding countryside by imposing on it a series of chromatic shifts. Somewhat removed from nature, the colors seem sufficiently arbitrary to establish a pattern as readily as they suggest space. The feel of the land is evoked, rather than described, through Mathews's artful treading of the line between illusion and pattern.

This same conscious art making (rather than merely replicating a view) is evidenced in the work of Mathews's prize pupil and wife, Lucia Kleinhans Mathews. Even more than her husband, Lucia Mathews simplified form and reduced a reliance on complex drawing to suggest space. Her reveling in the way in which simple patterns can suggest the truths of nature is boldly seen in the border of her monumental *Dining Table with Decorated Top* of 1918.

The Mathewses' various activities suggest a larger purpose: the creation of an aesthetic and ethical image of San Francisco and its environs as an ideal city-state, integrating art and life and developing an artistic language according to arts-and-crafts precepts. Easel paintings, murals, city plans, publications, and furniture evoked an imaginative civilization drawn from classical antiquity but set in the present and in the actual landscape of Northern California.

While the Mathewses may have been the dominant personalities in developing the so-called California decorative style, helping their patrons to live the good life by bringing the decorative and fine arts together, they were by no means the only such visionaries in the area. Northern California's distinctive Bay Region style first took form and received articulation in the architecture and aesthetics of Worcester. He most notably inspired the collaborative design of San Francisco's Swedenborgian Church of the New Jerusalem, built in 1894-95. That project's creators – Worcester, Keith, Bruce Porter, Bernard Maybeck, A. Page Brown, and A. C. Schweinfurth – dreamed of an indigenous, wholly integrated artistic environment, animated by "an exquisite impatience that [they] must deal with material things at all; yet with supreme intelligence fitting the material to its perfect use."[22] The church sanctuary's unadorned natural wood interior, devoid of paint and plaster, displayed its honest construction. The roof was supported by exposed rough-hewn madrone tree trunks cut from nearby forests. Truth to nature and to undisguised materials reflected divinity; simplicity was an echo of the divine.

A comparable appreciation of simple beauty, coupled with youthful wit, motivated a number of young men and women – some such as Porter and Willis Polk overlapping with Worcester's circle, others such as Gelett Burgess and Porter Garnett, somewhat less reverent – to launch an aesthetic/literary circle called *Les Jeunes*. Proclaiming, "It is the luxuries that are necessary," they founded a stylish magazine called *The Lark*, printed with hand-set type on imported bamboo paper. For the two years of its production, 1895-96, it included literature, some nonsense (including the debut of Burgess's "I never saw a purple cow"), and elegant covers – sometimes converted to advertising posters – such as Florence Lundborg's view of San Francisco Bay (fig.8). Looking back from a perspective of twenty years,

Porter wrote:

It was a charming, brief period, filled with enthusiasm and a quite fresh perception of the city and its romantic beauty and the beauties of California. . . . Writers, painters, sculptors, architects, and musicians communicated their enthusiasms one to the other, in a communion closer and more stimulating than has ever happened locally, before or since.[23]

One of the painters who exemplified the ideal of close artistic communion that this group represented was the English-born Arthur Atkins (relative of San Francisco art dealers W. K. Vickery and Henry Atkins), who came to San Francisco in 1892. He quickly grew to appreciate the Bay Area landscape, especially the empty Piedmont hills.

The landscape sings with colour, as a gem. . . . The grass, almost golden, holding still a lingering note of green, blazes now in the rich light: here and there long shadows steal over it, giving peace. The trees, rejoicing in a wealth of colour, are of green with gold in the green and a broken vibrant violet in the shadows, and opulent gold upon trunks and branches.[24]

Piedmont Hills, Summer, ca. 1896 (fig.9), might serve to illustrate Atkins's rhapsodic text. Both painting and prose are suffused with an almost adolescent intensity of feeling.

Atkins traveled to France, via New York, England, and Wales, for artistic training in 1897. Even while abroad, however, he anticipated the development of a specifically Californian language of art: "My second volume of 'The Lark' reached me a few days ago. How utterly Californian it is and heavens! – how Californian am I!"[25] Atkins returned to California in late 1898. But before he could fulfill his great promise, in the next year he died unexpectedly, a loss mourned by writers on California art over the next three decades.[26] The most moving testimony of loss and the most lucid statement of his contribution came from his friend Bruce Porter, who wrote that Atkins "saw natively and with [his] own eyes, and . . . inevitably spoke his own language. In [his] language we have, perhaps, an intimation of what, ultimately, the speech of California is to be."[27]

For Porter – architect, landscape designer, stained-glass designer, editor, exhibition organizer, connoisseur – the language of California was romantic and visionary. These qualities are evident in one of his best-known paintings, published as *Presidio Cliffs* (fig.10) in 1915 but probably the work called *Taking Horses to Bathe* exhibited in 1908.[28] In the painting's middle ground, the Marin Headlands, radically simplified in form and colored a brilliant flesh tone, rise up across the bay, bringing to mind William James's impression of the area's "atmosphere of opalescent fire, as if the hills that close us in were bathed in ether, milk and sunshine."[29] The pink earth of the foreground, with just a touch of green in the shadowed left corner, is a flattened stage to contain the exuberant horses and

fig.13 Gottardo Piazzoni, *The Land*, 1915
Oil on canvas, 53 x 124 in.
University Art Museum, University of California, Berkeley,
gift of Helen and Ansley Salz, *cat.no.126*

fig.14 Gottardo Piazzoni, *The Sea*, 1915
Oil on canvas, 53 x 124 in.
University Art Museum, University of California, Berkeley,
gift of Helen and Ansley Salz, *cat.no.127*

their riders, their twisting, Leonardesque figures drawn in bold sweeps of paint. In spite of the nudity of the main horseman, Porter's *Presidio Cliffs* is not a wholly idyllic vision. Off to the right a two-masted schooner makes its way toward harbor, a reminder of commerce and society just beyond the edge of the canvas. Porter's oblique reference to the hurly-burly of the modern world in his view of San Francisco is pertinent, for he believed that the visual arts grew only within civilization's boundaries.[30]

Others who evoked the poetic mood as the principal object of landscape art were Giuseppe Cadenasso, Xavier Martinez, and Gottardo Piazzoni, all former students of Mathews. All three were foreign-born but came to Northern California as youths. The eldest of them was Cadenasso. From his Russian Hill studio he sent forth paintings and pastels of the Bay Area, although he concentrated especially on views of Oakland's Lake Aliso (he taught for many years at Mills College),[31] the Alameda marshes (fig.11), and the "soldierly eucalyptus trees that grow so decoratively in 'regiments'" in Golden Gate Park.[32] Such examples found particular favor with critics:
No other artist has painted the eucalyptus with such grace or delicacy, and yet with so much truth. He has put on canvas those spectral trees whose ghostly leaves make silver shadows through the fog. He has made them sister to the misty air in which they thrive.

Martinez was among the best known and most flamboyant of San Francisco artists.[34] Noted for working "under the canon of Whistler," Martinez was admired for his "distinct individuality of manner." "No painter in California," wrote one critic, "has more closely approached universality in his art."[35] After training in Paris at the École des Beaux-Arts from 1897 to 1900,[36] Martinez returned to an active bohemian life in Northern California, first in San Francisco and then, his studio lost in the fire of 1906, in the East Bay's Piedmont hills. Proud of his Mexican and Aztec heritage, he changed one of his given names, Timoteo, to Tizoc. Martinez's early landscape work often shows the generalized landforms of the East Bay in muted, somber tonalities, as in *The Road*, ca. 1907 (fig.12). Contemporary critics appreciated the thin washes of drab colors, heightened with but a touch of rich pink or blue – the "gray effects so noticeable in California scenery."[37] In later years, however, Martinez turned to a somewhat lighter, brighter palette, which he employed on *The Bay*, completed in 1918. The mood of that painting is still overcast, but soft light floods the pastel-colored houses as the viewer gazes to the west from the Piedmont hills.

The acknowledged leader of the tonal school in California, however, was Piazzoni. "What I am willing & eager to do," he wrote in 1929, "is . . . to leave behind in form & color all I know of California."[38] Working with a

fig.15 Charles Rollo Peters, *Houseboats and Wharf Nocturne*, ca. 1925
Oil on canvas, 19¼ x 25⅜ in.
G. Breitweiser, *cat.no.125*

closely toned palette and extreme simplification, he developed a highly reductive style to convey his vision of California as a vast, unencumbered space, its organizing principle the edge separating earth from sky.

The shape of that edge was not caprice but determined by the specific geological facts of the Coast Range. This rolling contour carries a vitality of its own, animating Piazzoni's composition and helping the viewer sense the rhythmic "poetry" so often spoken of by critics of the day: "His pictures are chants. . . . Poetry is the essential quality of his work . . . simple, sincere, and totally spontaneous."[39]

Two of the strongest examples of this sensibility are *The Land* and *The Sea* (figs.13-14), both from 1915. In *The Land*, the undulating and unadorned sweep of golden grasses rises up to a high horizon line. The sheer scale of the work augments the viewer's illusion of being within the landscape. In *The Sea*, the diagonal slice of beach and the swelling of low clouds to the left break the otherwise static rectilinearity of the composition. Gently cresting wave, drifting fog bank – only the most subtle movement intrudes into the stillness of the scene. Off to the west, a single square sail establishes a focus in the limitless expanse, "the human note to be forever present," as the artist later declared.[40]

For over thirty years Piazzoni was considered "spiritual advisor and father confessor to the [San Francisco] art colony."[41] An advocate of new ideas and organizations, Piazzoni, along with Cadenasso, Maynard Dixon, and others, led the effort in 1902 to create the California Society of Artists – an alternative exhibition site to the SFAA.[42] Again in 1907 he was one of several artists who sought to form an exhibiting group – this time at the Studio Building at 147 Presidio in San Francisco.[43] Moreover, in the '20s, Piazzoni was one of the chief

fig.16 Granville Redmond, *Poppies in Marin County*, n.d.
(also known as *Lupine and Poppies, Marin*)
Oil on canvas, 25¼ x 30¼ in.
Collection of Dr. and Mrs. Oscar Lemer,
on loan to State Capitol Restoration Project, *cat.no.132*

fig.17 Arthur B. Davies, *Pacific Parnassus, Mount Tamalpais*, ca. 1905
Oil on canvas, 26¼ x 40¼ in.
The Fine Arts Museums of San Francisco, Museum purchase,
gift of The Museum Society Auxiliary, *cat.no.31*

movers behind San Francisco's Galerie Beaux Arts and Jehanne Bietry Salinger's art periodical, *The Argus*.[44] With his friend the sculptor Ralph Stackpole, Piazzoni helped bring the influential *Exhibition of Contemporary French Art* to San Francisco in 1923. Even though he led an active life teaching, organizing, and exhibiting, critic after critic found in Piazzoni's work a spiritual quiet that plumbed the soul of the land.[45] Piazzoni kept the vision of California ever before him. In 1918 he reportedly said:

This is the country I know better than any other . . . in California I have made my home and here is where my heart and interests lie. In every canvas I produce, whether it is a landscape, a symbolic painting, or figure work, it is always the spirit of California that I am endeavoring to express.[46]

In their portrayals of the Golden State, many of these California painters at the turn of the century used a vocabulary derived from the work of James McNeill Whistler: subtle tonalities, simplified forms, suggestive evocations. Whistler's creations – enticingly called arrangements, nocturnes, harmonies, or symphonies, to lift them further toward the realm of the abstract – and his exceedingly adept use of publicity had served to make him one of the best-known artists of the era. Californians could and did meet him directly and they absorbed his principles in their travels abroad: Lucia Mathews studied at his Académie Carmine in Paris; Arthur Atkins filled his letters home from Europe with both artistic and personal details of Whistler's career; Xavier Martinez was widely reported to have been his student, although it seems that their acquaintance was more casual.[47] Even for those who could not travel to Europe, Whistler's principles were readily available through the teaching and writing of Arthur Mathews – in *Philopolis* one finds direct echoes of the expatriate artist's writings.[48] The intensity of Whistler's influence on art in the Bay Area is perhaps best indicated by the bitterness of the later critical reaction against it. As one example among many, in 1916 a writer railed against "the aesthetic anaemia that emanated from the delicate organism of Whistler."[49]

In spite of critical disdain, Whistler's influence persisted. Such artists as the well-respected Charles Rollo Peters continued to paint nocturnes for at least a decade after the PPIE. Peters's handsome *Houseboats and Wharf Nocturne*, ca. 1925 (fig.15), a romanticizing night scene probably painted in Benicia, shows a dark and ruddy tone that, in addition to the work's title, evokes thoughts of Whistler. In the work of Granville Redmond, too, who studied at the California School of Design and in Paris in the 1890s, there is often a crepuscular mood and preference for atmospheric tonal effects.[50] The opulent patterning of his painting *Poppies in Marin County* (fig.16) relates it further, of course, to the decorative style of Arthur and Lucia Mathews.

The Inevitable Bit of California: Visitors and Travelers

Not all painters of the California landscape lived in the state for extended periods. As one writer observed in 1915, "men who have painted the world over" seemed to "find their repertoire incomplete without the inevitable bit of California."[51] Arthur B. Davies journeyed through the western United States in 1905, recording his direct impressions of the changing landscape on a series of small panels. Some of these, as in *Mount Tamalpais*, are quirkily observed color notes, freely brushed and boldly composed. Others, such as *View of San Francisco*, looking north across Golden Gate Park from Twin Peaks, while as summary in handling are yet topographically accurate to the most precise degree. When back in New York, however, setting about such finished studio works as *Pacific Parnassus, Mount Tamalpais*, ca. 1905 (fig.17), Davies smoothed out his touch and moved his colors toward more expected harmonies. In *Pacific Parnassus* he wrapped Marin County's fabled peak and its northward view of an undeveloped Stinson Beach in lowlying clouds, which dominate the canvas in substance and patterns of light and shadow (comparable with the effect in Keith's view southward in *Looking across the Golden Gate from Mount Tamalpais* of a decade earlier).

Davies was clearly moved by California. Although he never returned to the state, motifs of sierra and sequoia recurred in his works for many years. One of the painter's friends wrote, "[T]he mighty landscape of the West fulfilled his new craving for solemnity and grandeur. . . . It is a primeval country he depicts . . . [;] those whom one sees there are apparitions in human form."[52] Thus Davies (most famous for his painting of unicorns done within a year after his California trip), intent on making art rather than recording his impressions of the Bay Area, provided his vision of Stinson Beach with three tiny, naked figures to frolic on the edges of the hillside – transforming the view into a fogbound pastorale.

When, nearly a decade after Davies, Childe Hassam visited the Bay Area, he too was fascinated by the atmospheric effects of the place. He arrived in 1914, one of the most respected and honored painters in the United States, "the strongest exponent of the school of Monet in America."[53] Although he had traveled west before, Hassam made this trip expressly while preparations were underway for the PPIE.[54] Hassam had reason to be personally interested in the fair-to-be: he was scheduled to be honored with a separate gallery at the Palace of Fine Arts, and he had a commission to paint a mural, *Fruit and Flowers*, for the exposition's Court of Palms.[55] In 1914, however, he focused also on less official activities, painting landscapes from San Anselmo to Carmel. One of the most successful of these is *The Silver Veil and the Golden Gate, Sausalito, California*, 1914 (fig.18).

In the upper two-thirds of the canvas Hassam has evoked the power of the poetically named silver veil, the fog that rolls over the hills, merging with the land in a symphony of cool tones that hymn the mystery of this region's palpable atmosphere. In the Bay Area, Hassam, "an avowed sun-worshiper," found a clouded world in which "outline does not exist . . . form and color are inseparable."[56]

Hermann Dudley Murphy was a Boston-based painter of portraits, still lifes, and landscapes, best known for his oils that were sympathetic to an arts-and-crafts sensibility. It seems likely that he also traveled to the region around the time of the PPIE, where he received a silver medal for works exhibited.[57] One of the few known works resulting from the trip is *Coyote Point, Salt Flats, California*, ca.1916-17 (fig.19). Here, Murphy has turned his attention to the wooded shoreline along San Francisco Bay in San Mateo County, with early morning light flooding the scene. He has simplified the view into patterns that stretch across the canvas. His highly decorative approach to the landscape, accentuated by the artificiality of the triptych format, has led scholars to associate this work with Murphy's known interest in Asian art.[58] Whatever its sources, the work effectively evokes the quiet of the natural scene while reducing the sense of a topographic rendering.

Treasures of Color and Form Untold: The Panama Pacific International Exposition

The PPIE celebrated both the completion of the Panama Canal and the rebuilding of San Francisco. It was a defining moment for the region, a counterpoint to the earthquake, bringing an infusion of energy and optimism to the community. Artists and their works converged in San Francisco from across the world. Although the fine arts display of more than eleven thousand works was overwhelmingly academic, examples by Monet, Gauguin, Cézanne, Munch, Boccioni, Severini, and Kokoschka helped introduce modern ideas. The *Post-Exposition Exhibition* in 1916 was more advanced in spirit, showing several avant-garde works by Picasso, Matisse, and Picabia.

In addition to the attractions the exposition held for artist-visitors, local artists found rewarding motifs in the buildings and environment of the PPIE. One of the most delightful renderings of the fair is E. Charlton Fortune's *Panama Pacific International Exposition*, 1915 (fig.20), a painting of the Colonnade of the Court of the Four Seasons.[59] Poet Edwin Markham described the court as "the heart of the exposition" where there were "treasures of color and form untold."[60] In addition to being a striking memento of the site, the painting displays the high-keyed color and overt brushwork that Fortune helped introduce to Northern Californians.

Ray Boynton came from Spokane to San Francisco specifically for the PPIE. He started to work at the Palace of Fine Arts and stayed for the remainder of his career, painting, writing, and teaching extensively in the Bay Area. *The Bay* (fig.21) was painted in 1920, the year Boynton moved to Mill Valley in Marin County. This work and other paintings executed soon after his move convey the solidity and structure of the hills, using a bold downhill view from Mount Tamalpais. *The Bay*, with its rectilinear houses perched on evenly contoured slopes, foreshadows by a decade or more the comparably schematic landscapes of such regionalists as Grant Wood, and by its broad conception anticipates the resurgence of interest in mural painting.[61]

Color for Color's Sake

Increasingly in the years after 1910 Bay Area painters began to approach the landscape not to create studies of mood but rather to celebrate an overt, in some cases almost exclusive, appreciation of pigment and composition. Their legitimization – especially through seeing examples of European impressionism, postimpressionism, and futurism – came largely at the PPIE. The shift of aesthetic approach to the colorful and objective revealed aspects of the landscape that had been minimized in the decades devoted to quietude and twilight. The colorists' revolution was described most pointedly by J. Nilsen Laurvik in the foreword to the catalogue of the 1918 annual exhibition of the SFAA:

[T]he new spirit was clearly discernible in color and treatment, no less than in subject matter. In these later exhibitions the Whistlerian tonalities and Barbizon romanticism in vogue before the Exposition were conspicuous by their absence. . . .

At last the noble lines of the California hills are being painted without pseudo-idealistic, romantic preconceptions, and gradually the painter and public are coming to realize how much more beautiful are these realistic versions of our grandiose landscape than the vague, characterless echoes of the Barbizon School, which so long passed for true portraits of California.[62]

The change was not uncontested. Arthur Mathews was reported as saying as late as 1925:

The atmosphere of San Francisco – I mean the physical atmosphere – is almost exactly the atmosphere of Venice, where so many great painters worked. And, like Venice, we come in touch here with the Orient, only more directly.

Our sun is not so clear or our colors so intense as away from the bay. So much the better. The atmosphere here is thicker and richer for that reason.[63]

One of the boldest of the new spirits lauded in California was Anne Bremer – San Francisco-born, Mathews-trained, and Paris-educated. Bremer chose to define herself largely through depiction of the California landscape, attracted to the motif of cultivated

fig.18 Childe Hassam, *The Silver Veil and the Golden Gate, Sausalito, California*, 1914
Oil on canvas, 30 x 32 in.
Valparaiso University Museum of Art, Sloan Fund Purchase, *cat.no.79*

fig.19 Hermann Dudley Murphy, *Coyote Point, Salt Flats, California*, ca. 1916-17
Oil on canvas, 17½ x 53¾ in.
Mr. and Mrs. Mason Walsh, Jr., *cat.no.114*

fig.20 E. Charlton Fortune, *Panama Pacific International Exposition*, 1915
Oil on canvas, 12 x 16 in.
Collection of Dr. and Mrs. Oscar Lemer, *cat.no.49*

gardens as well as the natural landscape for the display of coloristic inventiveness. Bremer's artistic viewpoint reportedly was revolutionized in the first decade of the century by seeing two small paintings, a Matisse and a Cézanne, brought from Paris by a San Francisco friend, and, soon thereafter, by attending one of Alfred Stieglitz's first exhibitions of French postimpressionist painting in New York.[64] She was one of the earliest of the California painters to legitimate advanced French modes of seeing, as critic Porter Garnett noted in 1912 upon her return from a two-year Paris sojourn:
Miss Anne Bremer is the most "advanced" artist in San Francisco. She is also one of our best painters. . . . [T]his artist has brought us something with which our public is unfamiliar and for which it is so unprepared that many persons will be found who are disposed to condemn it out of hand without trying to understand it.[65]

In such early landscapes as *Across Carquinez Straits*, ca. 1906, Bremer revealed her appreciation of Cézannesque composition, blond coloration, and her affinity for a pronounced surface of parallel, hatched brush strokes. But she balanced this with a continuous awareness of the specific light and atmosphere (the work was described in 1917 as "finely descriptive")[66] of the hot, sun-bleached terrain near Benicia. Bremer's *An Old-Fashioned Garden*, ca.1915 (fig.22), praised by one critic of the day as "the virile note of the flaming California garden,"[67] exemplifies her bolder, more thickly pigmented style. Flattened forms create a surface patterning almost as if it were a woven tapestry. A contemporary critic discerned Bremer's "objectivity": "The fact is set down with an almost brutal directness . . . as the sophisticated modern mind has learned to see it, the real thing in its essential outstanding form."[68]

Perhaps the most important convert to color at the PPIE was Selden Connor Gile. His embrace of the new vision was immediate and wholehearted. For the next decade he hiked over the Bay Area's hills and along its coves, capturing its rural aspects in a series of plein-air studies: "He paints out of doors entirely. This, he says, accounts for his use of brilliant color, by which he endeavors to catch the spirit of California."[69]

During the '20s Gile (called the "dean of Oakland artists")[70] and five other men collectively known as the Society of Six (William H. Clapp, August Gay, Maurice Logan, Louis Siegriest, and Bernard von Eichman) painted together on weekends and mounted, from 1923 to 1928, annual group exhibitions at the Oakland Art Gallery. Working in plein air, they maintained a vital relationship to nature, their art serving as an arena in which to explore the primacy of painterliness, the force of intuitive expression, and the power of color. On the occasion of their third group show in 1925, they posted a manifesto (probably written by Clapp, director of the gallery) that set forth their collective ambition to celebrate optical delight:
To us, seeing is the greatest joy of existence, and we try to express that joy. Hence the cheer and happiness of the present exhibition. We do not believe that painting is a language. Nor do we try to "say" things, but we do try to fix upon the canvas the joy of vision. To express, to show – not to write hieroglyphics. . . . [W]e are not trying to illustrate a thought or write a catalogue, but to produce a joy through the use of the eyes.[71]

They were markedly successful in their ambition, at least in the eyes of leading Bay Area critics. Joy, in fact, was one of the words that writers especially associated with Gile's work: "'Joyism.' Now, we've coined a word. And Selden Connor Gile inspired it whether he likes it or not. . . . Gile is as much an expressionist as an impressionist, and perhaps more a colorist than either. A 'joyist' – that's it."[72] One of the works that most expresses Gile's joy – of site, vision, and handling of paint – is *Untitled (Cows and Pasture)*, ca.1925 (page xii). It is a painted landscape pared to its essence – all detail suppressed, the buttery pigment stroked over the surface, congealing in patches to suggest animal and plant life but mostly transforming an anonymous California ranch into an abstract rendering of pictorial light and space. This is one of the most forward-looking California paintings of the decade – but one apparently done for the artist and his friends alone, as no document records its public exhibition.

In 1927 Gile retired from his position as office manager at an Oakland tile firm and moved to Belvedere in order to make art full-time. His enthusiasm and productivity were at their peak: "I have been here all the time painting my head off. . . . I too never felt better in my life and never enjoyed things so much before."[73] A number

fig.21 Ray Boynton, *The Bay*, 1920
Oil on canvas, 35⅞ x 48 in.
The Fine Arts Museums of San Francisco,
gift of Albert Bender, *cat.no.12*

fig.22 Anne Bremer, *An Old-Fashioned Garden*, ca. 1915
Oil on canvas, 20 x 24 in.
Mills College Art Gallery, *cat.no.14*

fig.23 Selden Connor Gile, *The Soil*, 1927
Oil on canvas, 30⅛ x 36 in.
Private collection, San Francisco, *cat.no.59*

of large, nearly square landscape paintings clearly intended for exhibition signal the increasing ambition of this time. In its decorative format and intent, Gile's *The Soil*, 1927 (fig.23), is reminiscent of the earlier landscapes of such artists as Mathews and Martinez. But Gile transformed the tradition, pushing significantly further in pattern making and color intensity. Here, for example, his orange-red hill pulls the background to the fore, negating the illusionistic recession suggested by the curve of the pathway in the foreground. Sky, hill, farm – all familiar forms – are unexpectedly removed from the natural world by the force of color. A contemporary critic may have had this or a comparable work in mind when he wrote of the Oakland Art Gallery's fifth annual exhibition: "Selden C. Gile. Oakland – *The Red Hill*, the reddest, in fact, in the show; green trees, yellow foreground; good painting, no matter what color."[74]

In *The Red Earth*, ca.1928 (fig.24), Gile continued to push his large landscapes toward the same level of abstraction found in his plein-air sketches. The vibration of color opposites, red-orange and blue-green, dominates the canvas. The dizzying tilt of the perspective echoes the sharp clash of complementary colors. This is the type of painting that prompted critics to write of the group: "Use due caution in approaching the third annual exhibition of the Society of Six at the Oakland Art Gallery. . . . You will get used to the color, which at first is staggering in its brilliancy. You can see it oozing out the door before you enter the gallery."[75] In all these years, critically admired but commercially ignored, Gile set a path independent of all but his close colleagues: "[C]olor for color's sake, work for the joy of working, and efficiency – the greatest result achieved in the simplest, most direct way."[76]

August François Gay was the first of the Six to join Gile; Gay worked at menial jobs and lived in Gile's house intermittently for over a decade. During the '20s Gay pioneered a view of the California landscape as a mirror of alienation and melancholy. His palette darkened and the forms gained expressive force. His painting of sailboats in San Francisco Bay near Belvedere, *Decoration*, ca. 1927 (fig.25), shows "a group of small sail boats flying before the wind with gracefully curving sails of many colors."[77] The stylized shapes and volumes and decorative use of color indicate Gay's change from a direct, plein-air approach to one in which formal issues predominate, but that nonetheless conveys something of his moody intensity. Critics described the work as "reflecting the Paris art of today," although acknowledging that the artist's contact came from Bay Area exhibitions rather than foreign travel.[78]

For Gile's comrade Maurice Logan, years of study at the Mark Hopkins Institute instilled a preference for a subdued palette – one critic referred to "the old influence of Hopkins seeming to linger, as to the virtue of

fig.24 Selden Connor Gile, *The Red Earth*, ca.1928
Oil on canvas, 31½ x 37½ in.
Private collection

fig.25 August Gay, *Decoration*, ca.1927
Oil on artist board, 22¼ x 24½ in.
Gay Collins, Santa Barbara, *cat.no.56*

fig.26 Maurice Logan, *Point Richmond*, 1929
Oil on canvas, 15 x 18 in.
Collection of The Oakland Museum of California,
gift of Louis Siegriest, *cat.no.101*

fig.27 Louis Siegriest, *Tiburon Buildings*, ca. 1923
Oil on canvas, 11¼ x 15¾ in.
Private collection, *cat.no.147*

dull pigment."[79] This changed by the mid-'20s, when, under the influence of Logan's Society of Six colleagues, he committed himself to the heightened colors that come from painting almost entirely in the out-of-doors. Logan's flowing brushwork – his career as a commercial artist provided him with an easy draftsmanship – served him well in *Point Richmond*, 1929 (fig.26), allowing him swiftly to capture the curve of hills, rocks, and the incoming tides of the bay. This predilection was noted by his critics: "[I]n his marine[s] he is exceedingly happy, attaining a heretical (for this away-from-Cezanne group) adherence to form in his rocky formations."[80]

Gile's colorful approach also set the direction for the group's two youngest members, Siegriest and von Eichman. Born at the turn of the century, the two received the PPIE's artistic offerings unencumbered by trappings of nineteenth-century landscape tradition. Their motifs of small rural and suburban buildings portrayed in an almost childlike manner both reflect the character of the bay region and relate to similar themes in American and European modernist art of the time. Siegriest created extremely simplified compositions, using bold designs in a shallow space. *Tiburon Buildings*, ca.1923 (fig.27), shows the flat patterns, dry paint, and vivid color that characterize his early work. While von Eichman was best known for highly individualized abstractions – critics described him as "leading the ultra-modernists"[81] – on occasion he turned an almost lyric sensibility to portrayals of the land. One of his most sensitive efforts, *The Red House*, ca.1920 (fig.28), might well be the work described in an exhibition review of 1930: *Perhaps the most serious painting in the group is one called "Shacks," a very simple rendering of a couple of shanties against the hills, flanked on one side by a scrubby gnarled tree which seems much akin to the houses in feeling. Here we have an expression for depth and solidity and for full and rich chiaroscuro.*[82]

For C. S. Price (not a member of the Six, but closely allied) the use of vivid color peaked during the mid-'20s and then took a steady course toward abstraction and a more earth-toned palette. During his California years Price arrived at his own expression, which consisted of raw, scraped surfaces and simplified shapes, as a means to capture "the felt nature of things."[83] An artist friend from the '20s remembered that Price preferred *crude, harsh work that showed signs of primitive strength.... [C]olor used not to express form or atmosphere but color that would satisfy some standard he was building up in his own mind.... At times he spoke as if he was trying to get at something that was in himself but usually he spoke as if the thing he was trying to get was in the paint on the canvas.*[84]

Coastline, ca.1924 (fig.29), is the high point of Price's career and one of the most significant works made in California in the decade. Its surface, showing layers and vestiges of color, recalls Price's wish "to get the

fig.28 Bernard von Eichman, *The Red House*, ca. 1920
Oil on board, 15½ x 19½ in.
Mr. and Mrs. C. Richard Kramlich, *cat.no.159*

same effect on a canvas as was got by nature on an old building covered with layer after layer of paints of different colors, cracked, worn, and weathered."[85] The painting is large, its sense of space yet more vast. Its size, wrought paint surfaces, and simplified volumes present a monumental view of the continent's edge parallel to the nearly contemporary poetry of Robinson Jeffers: "I gazing at the boundaries of granite and spray, the established / sea-marks, felt behind me / Mountain and plain, the immense breadth of the continent, / before me the mass and doubled stretch of water."[86] *Coastline* exemplifies Price's austere integrity. The painting captures the geological and emotional sense of demarcation; in color drawn from the natural world and one artist's feelings, great slabs of paint and sculpted form tell how the western slope meets the Pacific. As a colleague noted:
The forms are radically simplified, the space and relationships adjusted to intensify Price's perception of the subject.... [H]is conviction had slowly grown that the earth and all its creatures exist in one great stream of life which has a single spiritual source... what he called "the one big thing."[87]

By the '20s a new relationship to the landscape was evolving; as the city grew, suburbs filled Bay Area hills and valleys and the agrarian land dwindled. More artists came to find the cityscape the compelling motif. It is perhaps revealing that, in the decade following World War I, the most vital work inspired by the rural landscape was produced by Gile and his comrades and Price – painters with stronger allegiance to nature than to the art world. A young painter for whom the urban landscape occasioned displays of formal inventiveness

fig.29 C.S. Price, *Coastline*, ca. 1924
Oil on canvas, 40⅛ x 50 in.
Hirshhorn Museum and Sculpture Garden, Smithsonian Institution,
gift of Joseph H. Hirshhorn, 1966, *cat.no.131*

was Yun Gee, a precocious protégé of Otis Oldfield. Having emigrated from China as a youth, the twenty-year-old Yun Gee successfully overcame cultural and language difficulties and extreme poverty to join a group of young bohemians at the California School of Fine Arts and to found with them the Modern Gallery adjacent to sculptor Ralph Stackpole's stone-yard. Many of his California works (he traveled to France and later settled in New York) are demonstrably urban views. *Camping with Otis Oldfield*, 1926 (fig.30), charmingly, albeit ironically, presents the painter's encounter with a corner of nature as a colorful geometric arrangement, incorporating curious architectural forms – "camping" with his teacher apparently near the top of Telegraph Hill.[88]

Calitopia:
Reconciling the Bounties at Continent's End

The pastoral point of view favored by the region's leading painters at the turn of the century moderated both the sublimity of nature and the transforming power of human culture, positing instead that the world could be a benign realm of comfort and ease. During these years throughout Europe and America, this generalized pastoralism – a necessarily urban construct – held widespread appeal and was manifest in such diverse guises as the arts-and-crafts aesthetic in architecture and interior design, the genteel tradition in literature, and the proliferation of experimental communities of varying social, religious, and philosophical bents.[89] But coastal California laid claim to this tradition with particular justice, by virtue of its nurturing climate and agricultural bounty no less than by the ease and apparent harmony with which human beings could exist there with nature. California, it seemed, was humankind's *Simple Home*, as writer Charles Keeler (a friend of Keith and Worcester and many of those mentioned earlier) named his 1904 text on how one ought live – and, indeed, how some then were living – in the Bay Area.[90] Many writers and propagandists for the state during this era turned to images of Eden or Arcadia in their praise of the region. Frederick J. Teggart, writing in *Philopolis* in 1907, coined the word "Calitopia" to describe this merging of geographic California with the glories of the mythic Utopia.

Teggart, however, while acknowledging the bounties of the state, also sensed a responsibility awaiting Californians in their land at the end of westward migration, the place Robinson Jeffers would later call "Continent's End."[91] Teggart apotheosized Calitopia:

Most favored child of Nature, heiress of all the treasury of man's experience, only descendent of the lineage of Utopia, it is to her that the gods look in expectation, it is around her that all the unrealized hopes of our forefathers throng confidently. Dowered as no other land, reserved from time immemorial to be the seat of the crowning civilization of the European stock,

Calitopia – the beautiful place – having welcomed those upon whom her future depends, now awaits, perchance impatiently, the evidence of their devotion.[92]

He highlighted, in other words, the difficulties of doing justice to the glories of the state. His single phrase "perchance impatiently" underlines his sense that appropriate realization of the quest was yet in the future.

Even without the prodding of *Philopolis*, landscape painters were aware of the challenge. They found themselves in an earthly paradise of agricultural abundance, mineral wealth, and climatic softness, at the end of a celebrated and apparently successful cultural march across the continent. As but one example, from southern France Arthur Atkins wrote that the European scenes were "not as beautiful as the country north of the Cliff House," making more pointed his earlier, Paris-based opinion of California that "from such a land, generous and open-handed, a great art should spring."[93]

But as they turned their gaze upon California, artists found that realities of scale, substance, and light defied transcription. Painters responded variously to this fact. In the 1890s, retreating from his view-painting of earlier decades, Keith claimed he could not paint in front of nature and instead sought to cull a moment of divine insight from the accumulated memories of his outdoor studies.[94] His colleagues after the turn of the century, such as Piazzoni and Martinez, sought the essence of the land by evoking characteristic rather than spectacular beauty – the anonymous eucalyptus rather than the towering redwood – through ever simpler means of color and form. This modesty of outward subject led one critic to write in 1905 of the painters' "tamer themes": "No one would go into polite raptures over these pictures and call them 'pretty,' but they are art. They tell the story. They are California."[95] They were art, that is, to the extent that they revealed a spirit of place that was recognized by the wider culture. By 1915, the year of the PPIE, these poetic and atmospheric renderings of mood dominated the regional art scene.

As enthusiastic as critical response could be to specific works, leading critics of the day still looked to the future for a distinctly Californian landscape art to arise. At a symposium held in conjunction with the PPIE, and later printed in book form as *Art in California*, speakers uniformly and rightly praised individual California artists and works – Keith, Atkins, and the sculptor Arthur Putnam were especially singled out. Equally uniformly, the principal essayists on art in Northern California voiced a concern: "[T]he fact that [artists] are Californians by birth or adoption does not make their art Californian. They may – and many do – *represent* California, but how many of them *express* California?" asked Porter Garnett.[96] Bruce Porter, painter and writer, was the most thoughtful on the point:

fig.30 Yun Gee, *Camping with Otis Oldfield*, 1926
Oil on paperboard, 12 x 17¾ in.
Collection of Helen Gee, *cat.no.57*

Keith and Hill and the painters of their time and later looked upon the actual nature about them with (shall we say) something of the eyes of strangers in a strange land. Their transcripts are undoubtedly of the California scene, but we feel (as we feel in the great majority of works of landscape art) that, set down anywhere on earth, the painters would employ this identical language of transcription. Here and there a great man does speak in the particular terms of the country about him, fits the language to his native theme: Vermeer, Constable, Corot, Titian, Velasquez, and the Chinese masters thus speak. It would seem to mean that the artist and his theme had become mutually penetrative, and it is this interchange and perfect transfusion that we must wait for in California's art. [97]

In spite of their sense of present disappointment, all of these men had sincere hope for the establishment of a particularly Californian landscape voice in the future. Everett C. Maxwell declared that "out of this land of silent places will come a native art as strong, as vital, and as colorful as the land that inspired and fostered it," a sentiment the others echoed. [98]

Younger painters, those coming to maturity after the PPIE, sought to effect the mutual penetration of self and subject not through a lyric reverence toward the land that animated the earlier generation but by an emphasis on the materials and practice of art making. Critic Willard Huntington Wright recognized this as soon as he arrived in San Francisco in 1919. [99] Wright saw that the Bay Area lacked an entrenched art community and he praised the resultant openness that allowed painters to "exhibit a more spontaneous and genuinely emotional reaction in front of nature." Central to his appreciation of the art he saw in San Francisco was color, "bold, resounding color on all sides." [100]

The landscape art that found favor from the advanced critics of the 1890s through the 1920s moved progressively from veristic depictions of California's glories toward ever freer expression of the artist's response to those glories. In other words, when landscape painters thought less self-consciously of California and more of the fundamental elements of painting, they seemed to touch the soul of the place. Expression and broad gesture – often, in the case of artists such as Gile and Price, achieved in the open air and in vivid colors – allowed painter and subject to approach the "interchange and perfect transfusion" that Bruce Porter yearned for. The fusion of feeling, paint, and motif showed a way forward. It was a lesson that would endure.

Notes

1. J. Nilsen Laurvik, "Foreword," *Catalogue of the 1918 San Francisco Art Association Annual Exhibition*, exh. cat. (San Francisco: Palace of Fine Arts, 1918), 11-12.

2. San Francisco was the principal art center of the region. For an insightful review of the relation between the city and the region, see James E. Vance, Jr., *Geography and Urban Evolution in the San Francisco Bay Area* (Berkeley: Institute of Governmental Studies,1964),55.

3. The SFAA, dedicated to both teaching and exhibition, maintained a series of annual exhibitions throughout the period that engaged the region's leading artists. The California School of Design was renamed the Mark Hopkins Institute and, later, the California School of Fine Arts; it is now known as the San Francisco Art Institute. A majority of artists discussed in this essay participated as students and teachers in the CSD/Mark Hopkins Institute; Yelland and, later, Arthur Mathews served as the school's directors. Across the bay, the California School of Arts and Crafts, now in operation as the California College of Arts and Crafts, was founded in 1907. Male artists had the exhibition opportunities and camaraderie of the Bohemian Club, founded in 1872. For women painters, the Sketch Club was founded in 1887; by 1897 it had nearly 200 members.

4. The CMIE gave the city its first public institution, leaving its Fine Arts Building in Golden Gate Park as the Memorial Museum, which became in 1921 the M. H. de Young Memorial Museum. The PPIE was the most significant cultural event of its era. The exposition's French Pavilion inspired Adolph B. and Alma de Bretteville Spreckels to found San Francisco's second city-owned museum, the California Palace of the Legion of Honor (CPLH), dedicated in 1924 in Lincoln Park to California's fallen in World War I. The CPLH and the de Young merged in 1972 into The Fine Arts Museums of San Francisco. In the meantime, a complicated series of alliances and reorganizations established the San Francisco Museum of Art, a private exhibition organization initially growing from the SFAA, in the PPIE's Palace of Fine Arts. Now in its new home on Third Street, it is known as the San Francisco Museum of Modern Art. The name shifting of these and other San Francisco-based visual arts organizations seems indicative of their continually evolving sense of mission and identity.

Crucial for the local art scene, several of these institutions sought specifically to promote local art and artists. At the Memorial Museum in Golden Gate Park, for example, with an annual attendance averaging half a million people a year, galleries of California painting and sculpture were dedicated in 1904, again in 1910, and renewed in 1915.

5. The response to a 1914 exhibition consisting largely of reproductions was unenthusiastic: "The Art of Matisse, Picasso, Duchamp, Van Gogh and others of similar ilk is upon us; at least a sufficient reproduction of it to give a perfectly adequate idea of the originals, and one is an original – the noted, or notorious, *Nude Descending a Staircase* perpetrated by Marcel Duchamp [acquired from the Armory Show by Frederick C. Torrey of Vickery, Atkins & Torrey], which is idiotically funny when it is remembered that anyone could take it seriously" (Anna Cora Winchell, "Specimens of the New Art at Hand," *San Francisco Chronicle*, 16 April 1914). But the region was primed, and in the 1920s a rich survey of advanced contemporary painting was shown in the Bay Area. Modern European painting, for example, was seen in San Francisco at the Civic Auditorium's *Exhibition of Contemporary French Art* in 1923; the inaugural exhibition of contemporary French art at the CPLH in 1924; *Henri Matisse and Contemporaries*, organized by Pierre Matisse, at the CPLH in 1926; the *Blue Four* at the Oakland Art Gallery in 1926; the *Foreign Section of the Twenty-Sixth International Exhibition of Paintings from Carnegie Institute*, at the CPLH in 1928; and *Thirty European Modernists*

at the Oakland Art Gallery in 1928.

6. See Ruth Lilly Westphal, ed., *Plein Air Painters of California: The North* (Irvine, Calif.: Westphal Publishing, 1986); Helen Spangenberg, *Yesterday's Artists on the Monterey Peninsula* (Monterey, Calif.: Monterey Peninsula Museum of Art, 1976).

7. Marjorie Dakin Arkelian and George W. Neubert, *George Inness Landscapes: His Signature Years, 1884-1894*, exh. cat. (Oakland, Calif.: The Oakland Museum Art Department, 1978),23-25,33. For discussion supporting the 1891 date for *California*, see 25 and 30, n.70.

8. These were lent by Irving Scott and Mrs. W. H. Crocker and included examples by Eugène Boudin, John Constable, Camille Corot, Gustave Courbet, Charles Daubigny, Gustave Doré, Jules Dupré, Jean-François Millet, Claude Monet, and Théodore Rousseau. Keith and Inness later showed their works at a commercial gallery in San Francisco; the *Art Loan Exhibition of Foreign Masters* had first been shown at Shreve's Art Rooms before moving in large part to the SFAA.

9. C. D. Robinson, "A Revival of Art Interest in California," *Overland Monthly* 17, no.102, ser.2 (June 1891): 649. Emil Carlsen, the great painter of still life and for two years head of the California School of Design, failed to sense a comparable optimism and declaimed, on the eve of his departure for New York: "I am going where people buy pictures, where there is an opportunity to exhibit them, and where a name means something. After two years, I find it unpleasant to be a pioneer in a place where the wealthier people get their pictures from Europe and the East, and the class of people that might like to purchase local paintings cannot well afford it" (*San Francisco Examiner*, 27 September 1891; quoted in *California Art Research* [San Francisco: Works Progress Administration,1937], vol. 4:39).

10. Notes recorded by Joseph Worcester and dated 9 April 1891; quoted in Brother Cornelius, *Keith: Old Master of California* (New York: G. P. Putnam's Sons, 1942), 216. Two years later, after Keith visited the art exhibition at the Chicago World's Columbian Exposition, he wrote to Worcester: "In the American exhibit there was a loan collection. – a dozen of Inness, Wyant, Corot, Daubigny, Rousseau, etc., and I sincerely think that Inness stands at the head" (Keith to Worcester, 21 May 1893, Keith-McHenry-Pond papers, The Bancroft Library, University of California, Berkeley).

11. Brother Cornelius wrote of the work as "a Keith with a striking Inness feature. It is the fiery crimson intensity along the horizon that is Inness-like; the rest is Keith, especially the magnificent simple arrangement of the broad light and shade masses and the sublime grandeur; already in this painting, it seems to the author, the grandeur is of a quality and degree that Inness never reached" (*Keith*, 220).

12. *The William Keith Collection of Paintings*, exh. cat. (San Francisco: Golden Gate Park Museum, 1912), cat.no.11. See also Emily P. B. Hay, *William Keith as Prophet Painter* (San Francisco: Paul Elder and Co., 1916), 38.

13. William Keith, "Lecture on Art" delivered in the mid-1890s to the Sorosis Club, quoted in Brother Cornelius, *Keith*, 271.

14. Quoted in Mary Bell, "William Keith," *The Keith Number: University of California Magazine* 3, no.3 (April 1897): 98.

15. Brother Cornelius, *Keith*, 215.

16. Alfred C. Harrison, Jr., *William Keith: The Saint Mary's College Collection* (Moraga, Calif.: St. Mary's College, 1988), 25.

17. Quoted in Bell, "William Keith," 97. Recent scholars have emphasized this point, writing that Keith "may have come to the theoretical belief that the glories of factual nature were insignificant compared to the glories of the imagination, but he never gave up painting objective scenery in his late career" (Harrison, *William*

*Keith,*33).

18. The best discussion of Arthur and Lucia Mathews's career is Harvey L. Jones, *Mathews: Masterpieces of the California Decorative Style* (1973; Santa Barbara and Salt Lake City: Peregrine Smith, 1980).

19. A contemporary writer described the work (or a close variant then called *History*) as portraying a "woman, tall, slender, and long limbed . . . seated beneath a tree. Just back of her, at her shoulder, stands a second figure, that of a youth, half in shadow. The woman's figure, clad in a rich yellow robe, and girdled with the same color, is the one note of glowing splendor in the composition. She holds an open book and the youth leaning over her appears to point to certain words. . . . A simple nobility, grandeur and impressive reticence pervade the work" (unidentified clipping, Mathews collection, The Oakland Museum).

20. Walt Whitman, *Complete Poetry and Collected Prose* (New York: Library of America, 1982), 266-267.

21. Mathews wrote: "It takes a delicate skill to paint a gray picture, and it does not often happen that a full colored one escapes the garish" (*Philopolis* 1, no.8 [25 May 1907]: 30).

22. Bruce Porter, "The Beginning of Art in California," *Art in California* (San Francisco: R. L. Bernier, 1916), 22.

23. Porter, "The Beginning of Art in California," 32.

24. Arthur Atkins, "On Landscape: Piedmont, 1895," in Bruce Porter, ed., *Arthur Atkins* (San Francisco: A. M. Robertson, 1908), 53.

25. Atkins, August 1897; in Porter, ed., *Arthur Atkins*, 6.

26. See "The Memorial Exhibition of the Landscapes of Mr. Arthur Atkins," *The Mark Hopkins Institute Review of Art* 1, no. 1 (December 1899): 31; Porter Garnett, "California's Place in Art," *Art in California* (San Francisco: R. L. Bernier, 1916), 42-43; Eugen Neuhaus, *History and Ideals of American Art* (Stanford, Calif.: Stanford University Press, 1931), 242.

27. Porter, "The Beginning of Art in California," 32.

28. The exhibition was held in April 1908 – a nine-person show in the Studio Building – and included Emil Carlsen, Gottardo Piazzoni, and Porter. It was praised as being "apart from the usual exhibit in that it preserves the true integrity of the artists' domain. . . . All suggestion, even, of commercialism, is eradicated; there are no catalogues, no opportunities within the hall to ascertain the monetary value of any piece of art, and one is not inclined to think of that side of the exhibit" ("Local Artists Show Canvases," *San Francisco Chronicle,* 19 April 1908).

29. William James, letter of 1898, quoted in Kevin Starr, *Americans and the California Dream, 1850-1915* (New York and Oxford: Oxford University Press, 1973), 316.

30. This is the main theme of Porter's essay "The Beginning of Art in California."

31. The fullest source on Cadenasso is *California Art Research*, vol. 11, 1-33. See also Jovanne Reilly, *Cadenasso, Cuneo, Piazzoni: Painters of the California Landscape,* exh. cat. (San Francisco: Museo ItaloAmericano, 1990).

32. "About Local Studios," *San Francisco Chronicle,* 28 May 1905.

33. Hortense Russell, *Town Talk,* 13 August 1910, quoted in *California Art Research*, vol.11,22.

34. The fullest source on Martinez is George W. Neubert, *Xavier Martinez (1869-1943),* exh. cat. (Oakland, Calif.: The Oakland Museum, 1974).

35. Garnett, "California's Place in Art," 44.

36. "Mr. J. Martinez, who has been studying in Paris, under Gerome for some time past, returned to this city December 15th." ("Local News," *The Mark Hopkins Institute Review of Art* 1, no.3 [December 1900]: 32).

37. *San Francisco Daily News,* 7 February 1909.

38. Piazzoni to Albert Bender, 3 January 1928, Piazzoni files, no. 580, Albert Bender papers, Mills College, Oakland, Calif.

39. Pio Vanza, in *Sancho Panza* (Rome); quoted in Josephine Mildred Blanch, "A Western Painter," *Overland Monthly* 54, no.5, ser.2 (November 1909): 461.

40. Piazzoni to Albert Bender, 3 January 1928, Piazzoni files, Albert Bender papers, Mills College, Oakland, Calif. When *The Land* and *The Sea,* along with two companion paintings, were exhibited at Helgesen's Gallery in May 1915, critic Michael Williams said of them that "rarely, if ever, has the unique individual character of the State been more faithfully and poetically rendered," and declared, "Happy California, to stir such reverent love in the breasts of your artist children" ("Piazzoni's Mural Decorations," *The Wasp,* 22 May 1915).

41. Laura Bride Powers, *Oakland Tribune,* 7 June 1922. Maxwell Armfield wrote of Piazzoni as the "recognized leader of Californian painting, so far as the younger men are concerned" (*An Artist in America* [London: Methuen & Co., Ltd.,1925],116).

42. While newspapers of the time portrayed the Society as a rebellion against the "stifling attitudes" of the SFAA (i.e., Arthur Mathews) and while the Society organizers issued a boldly headlined "MANIFESTO," in fact the manifesto did little more than invite participation of all area artists to a new show, "bringing them into closer contact with the public" and "closer and friendlier contact with one another" (broadsheet, private collection). Mathews even encouraged the Society: "The younger artists who are inclined to look askance at our methods have a right to their separate organization. I am in favor of any advance in the standard of art, and we will help and not hinder the new association" ("New Art Movement Takes Form and Tests Its Wings," *Evening Post,* 18 March 1902). The Society was in fact short-lived, and the members were soon participating again in the SFAA annuals.

43. "Local Artists Show Canvases," *San Francisco Chronicle,* 19 April 1908.

44. Jehanne Bietry Salinger, "Editorial," *The Argus* 3,no 6 (September 1928): 2.

45. "It is not the outward garb that Nature wears that attracts him, but the underlying spirit or elemental force of Nature that his pictures reveal, its vastness, its silent voice, and above all its perfect peace – one stands silent and prayerful before them" (Blanch, "A Western Painter,"462).

46. Louise E. Taber, "Gottardo Piazzoni and Rinaldo Cuneo Discuss Art," *The Wasp,* 5 January 1918.

47. See Jones, *Mathews,* 22; Porter, *Arthur Atkins,* 6, 9, 13, 14 (Whistler "seems to me, more and more, one of the greatest artists, and perhaps the greatest painter, I know"), 46; in his memoirs, *As I Remember,* Arnold Genthe wrote, "Xavier Martinez, or 'Marty' as he was known to all of us was a pupil of Whistler" (quoted in *California Art Research*, vol.10,54). In an interview with Martinez's widow and daughter, Marjorie Arkelian reported that Martinez's contact with Whistler was far more limited: "Marty was making a Velasquez (portrait) copy in The Louvre one day; Whistler came along and watched him. He said, 'You have great talent, young man.' Marty was not Whistler's pupil" (Arkelian to George W. Neubert, 21 June 1973, Paul C. Mills Archives of California Art, The Oakland Museum, Martinez artist file).

48. Mathews wrote, "The horrid side of the tableau was forgotten when we were under the spell of the mysteries of the twilight. The many-storied buildings down town appeared in sharp silhouette against the sky like huge campanilli [*sic*], and seemingly arose from still more ponderous structures lost in the heavier atmosphere of the earth" (*Philopolis* 1, no.1 [25 October 1906]: 4). This descrip-

tion of San Francisco after the 1906 fire is a clear echo of Whistler's famed evocation of the Thameside from his "Ten O'Clock Lecture" (James McNeill Whistler, *The Gentle Art of Making Enemies* [1890; New York: G. P. Putnam's Sons, 1953], 144).

49. Christian Brinton, "American Painting," *Impressions of the Art at the Panama-Pacific Exposition* (New York: John Lane and Co.,1916), 98.

50. *Granville Redmond*, exh.cat. (Oakland, Calif.: The Oakland Museum, 1988).

51. Jessie Maude Wybro, "California in Exposition Art," *Overland Monthly* 66,no.6 (December 1915), 517.

52. Bryson Burroughs, *Arthur B. Davies Memorial Exhibition 1930*, exh. cat. (New York: The Metropolitan Museum of Art, 1930), xiv.

53. Leila Mechlin, "Contemporary American Landscape Painting," *The International Studio* 39, no.153 (November 1909): 6.

54. The other American painters so honored included James McNeill Whistler, Howard Pyle, John Singer Sargent, Gari Melchers, William Merritt Chase, Frank Duveneck, Edward Redfield, Edmund Tarbell, William Keith, and John Twachtman. Arthur Mathews and Francis McComas shared one gallery.

55. The mural, which at least one critic of the time called "anaemic" and "frugal in every sense" is currently rolled in storage at The Fine Arts Museums of San Francisco (Eugen Neuhaus, *The Art of the Exposition* [San Francisco: Paul Elder and Company, 1915], 60-61).

56. J. Nilsen Laurvik, "Childe Hassam," in John E. D. Trask and J. Nilsen Laurvik, eds., *Catalogue de Luxe of the Department of Fine Arts Panama-Pacific International Exposition*, 2 vols. (San Francisco: Paul Elder and Company, 1915), 1:30, 32.

57. Works by Murphy of California subjects appear in exhibitions from about 1920 onward. A Boston critic noted: "Mr. Murphy has painted a great deal in the tropics, in Porto Rico and in California, and he is especially fond of the beautiful half-lights of evening and early dawn, and above all of cloud effects and the open sea" (M. F. B., "Mr. Murphy's Paintings," unidentified clipping, Hermann Dudley Murphy papers, Archives of American Art, Smithsonian Institution, roll 4039, frame 232).

58. *Hermann Dudley Murphy (1867-1945: "Realism Married to Idealism Most Exquisitely")*, exh.cat. (New York: Graham Gallery, 1982), 25.

59. The *Inaugural Exhibition* of the Art Gallery of the Oakland Public Museum in 1916 included almost 160 objects by thirty-two artists showing views of the fair. Among them were two by Fortune, nos. 111, *The Columns*, and 112, *Court of Four Seasons*, either of which could be the present work.

60. Edwin Markham, "Court of the Four Seasons, The North Colonnade by Night," in Louis Christian Mullgardt, ed., *The Architecture and Landscape Gardening of the Exposition* (San Francisco: Paul Elder and Company, 1915), 136.

61. For all his success in these relatively reportorial works, Boynton in the 1930s repudiated his earlier landscape concentration, saying: "I have painted more landscape than anything else, but I have come to feel that landscape is a limited medium. Landscape is largely a technical performance, not an emotional expression. . . . [P]ainting must have greater human value than is possible in the painting of the natural scene" ("San Francisco Artists," *San Francisco Chronicle*, 15 September 1935).

62. Laurvik, "Foreword," *1918 SFAA Annual Exhibition*, 11-12, 14.

63. Quoted in George P. West, "Secluded S.F. Painter Revealed as State's Most Famous Artist," *San Francisco Examiner*, 28 March 1925.

64. Undated, unidentified clipping, Albert Bender papers, Archives of American Art, Smithsonian Institution, roll 2293, frame 832.

65. Porter Garnett, "News Notes of the Artist Folk: Miss Bremer Pronounced One of San Francisco's Most Talented Painters," *San Francisco Call*, 15 September 1912. Bremer was later honored for "the

courage with which she introduced to this country and to this coast the new art which has come to be almost so common to you now that you think it has always existed" ("Tribute Paid Memory of Art Apostle," *San Francisco Chronicle*, 21 March 1924).

66. *The Brooklyn Daily Eagle*, 4 November 1917.

67. *The Brooklyn Daily Eagle*, 4 November 1917.

68. Phyllis Ackerman, "A Woman Painter with a Man's Touch: Anne Bremer Builds Up Her Paint in Solid and Unsentimental Forms," *Arts & Decoration* 18, no. 6 (April 1923): 20. Ackerman closes her article with one of the many considerations of gender in art prompted by Bremer's work: "In method as well as in attitude the work is decidedly masculine in character. And it might be expected that it would be a western woman who would break away from the point of view and the habits of her sex. For in a country like California with its huge, untamed spaces and its social quality still reminiscent in some respects of pioneer days, the conventional assumptions drop away and women cease to be primarily women and become first of all persons, so that when they approach a job they can do it unself-consciously in a workmanlike spirit."

69. "Gile Has One-Man Show in Elder Galleries," *San Francisco Chronicle*, 18 May 1930.

70. Florence Wieben Lehre, "Artists and Their Work," *Oakland Tribune*, 2 September 1928.

71. Source of the manifesto is Edward Doro's Docent Guide, unpublished manuscript, 1957-58, Society of Six file, Paul C. Mills Archives of California Art, The Oakland Museum, Oakland, Calif. For a discussion of the Society of Six, see Nancy Boas, *The Society of Six: California Colorists* (San Francisco: Bedford Arts, 1988). See also Terry St. John, *Society of Six*, exh. cat. (Oakland, Calif.: Oakland Museum, 1972).

72. Florence Wieben Lehre, "Artists and Their Work," 2 September 1928. Earlier in the year, the same critic had written, "In this land of modernism Gile dares to love the light, the winds, the air, the color, that make life – that make life worth while. For form, be it significant or otherwise, he cares not a jot. He admires it in others, to be sure. But color–! For life and the joyous opportunity that it offers to splash color on canvas! That is something quite different, something worthy of such an apostle of joy" (*Oakland Tribune*, 22 April 1928).

73. Gile to Nellie Gile McGuigan, 26 July 1928; Louis B. Siegriest and Edna Stoddart papers, Archives of American Art, Smithsonian Institution.

74. H. L. Dungan, "Artists and Their Work," *Oakland Tribune*, 6 February 1927.

75. H. L. Dungan, "Artists and Their Work," *Oakland Tribune*, 3 May 1925.

76. Florence Wieben Lehre, "Artists and Their Work," 2 September 1928.

77. H. L. Dungan, "Artists and Their Work," *Oakland Tribune*, 15 May 1927.

78. *Decoration*, and the closely related work by C. S. Price called *Boats* (ca. 1928, Seattle Art Museum), seem compelling illustrations of this reliance on art more than nature. Both works relate closely to Jean Dunand's *Seascape*, which was the cover of the catalogue – and the sole color reproduction – for the *Exhibition of Contemporary French Art* at San Francisco's Civic Auditorium in 1923. *Decoration's* provenance tells of the difficulties of patronage Gay experienced. One of his few painting commissions, the work was declined and, instead, the artist gave it to a member of his family.

79. Laura Bride Powers, "Artists and Their Work," *Oakland Tribune*, 11 March 1923.

80. Laura Bride Powers, "Artists and Their Work," 11 March 1923.

81. Laura Bride Powers, "Artists and Their Work," *Oakland Tribune*, 7 January 1923.

82. "Notes of Art and Artists," *San Francisco Chronicle*, 8 June 1930.

83. Price, quoted in Robert Tyler Davis, *C. S. Price Retrospective Exhibition of Paintings, 1920-1942*, exh. cat. (Portland, Ore.: Portland Art Museum, 1942).

84. Robert V. Howard, "Remarks on Price," unpublished manuscript, 11 December 1950; photocopy of manuscript in the American Art Study Center, The Fine Arts Museums of San Francisco.

85. Howard, "Remarks on Price."

86. Robinson Jeffers, "Continent's End," *Roan Stallion, Tamar, and Other Poems* (New York: Boni & Liveright, 1925), 252.

87. Rachael Griffin, "C. S. Price, Maverick of Western Art," undated, unidentified article in the American Art Study Center, The Fine Arts Museums of San Francisco.

88. Yun Gee and Oldfield camped in earnest later in the year at Muir Woods and during an extended car trip from Monterey to Lake Tahoe.

89. One of the best discussions of this phenomenon is T. J. Jackson Lears, *No Place of Grace: Antimodernism and the Transformation of American Culture 1880-1920* (New York: Pantheon Books, 1981).

90. Charles Keeler, *The Simple Home* (San Francisco: Paul Elder & Company, 1904).

91. Robinson Jeffers, "Continent's End," 252-253.

92. Frederick J. Teggart, "The Education of the Adult," *Philopolis* 1, no. 9 (25 June 1907): 3-4.

93. Atkins, October and August 1897; in Porter, ed., *Arthur Atkins*, 19, 6.

94. And he reveled when his colleague George Inness returned from Yosemite overwhelmed, admitting that nature there was too much to be encompassed on canvas (see Brother Cornelius, *Keith*, 217).

95. "Striking Pictures Exhibited by Art Society," *San Francisco Examiner*, 31 March 1905.

96. Garnett, "California's Place in Art," 39.

97. Porter, "The Beginning of Art in California," 30.

98. Everett C. Maxwell, "The Structure of Western Art," *Art in California* (San Francisco: R.L. Bernier, 1916), 36.

99. Willard Huntington Wright, "Exhibit Shows New Impulse: California Artists to the Fore," *San Francisco Bulletin*, 25 January 1919.

100. Willard Huntington Wright, "Local Exhibit Excels All N.Y. Displays," *San Francisco Bulletin*, 27 March 1919. Porter Garnett saw this exhibition and praised its "intelligent emancipation" and "refreshing vitality in pleasant contrast to the academic catalepsy of a few years ago" ("Painting in California," *The Nation* 108, no. 2809 [3 May 1919]: 702).

José Moya del Piño, *Chinese Mother and Child*, 1933
Oil on canvas, 40 x 30 in.
Mrs. John Dowling Relfe, *cat.no.112*

Celebrating Possibilities and Confronting Limits: Painting of the 1930s and 1940s

Patricia Junker

Certainly California is a Paradise. . . . In a sense, together with all its joys, that is the defect that California presents, because paradise is an impossibility for men to construct on earth, and the Californian is no exception to the rule. Furthermore, the excellences of Paradise are in the long run deficiencies in the "real world," which is of necessity constituted of possibilities and limitations, facilities and difficulties, urgency and constraint. To live in this world means to be always between the swordpoint and the wall, to have to make the right choice with every moment, to have infinite resources at one's disposition but a counted number of days, to live and to die.

> Julián Marías[1]

If ever a place can be said to represent the ultimate irony of human existence, it is the San Francisco Bay Area, a landscape of surpassing physical beauty, natural bounty, and ease of living – ample virtues that serve to remind us of the short time we have on earth to embrace them. It is a place where visions of possibility are tempered by a keen sense of human limitation. By geological accident, inhabitable space is confined to discrete land masses, each bounded by the bay or one of its inlets; it is a circumscribed world of human beings and nature. The blessings of a mild climate and a long growing season are checked by the difficulty of securing and maintaining arable land. And that urgency to meet the ever-expanding needs of modern urban society is constrained by recognition that this ever-shifting landscape is fundamentally at odds with the building of cities.

Although the inhabitants of the Bay Area were awakened to these ironies in 1906 at the time of the devastating earthquake and fire, it took the cataclysmic events of the Great Depression to give them human face and form – to present us with clear images of aspiration and failure, hope and despair, which have remained a part of our vision of California. In Bay Area landscape art of the 1930s and '40s, it is the human element that gives the region its distinctive shape, color, texture, and meaning. During this period, the city and the cultivated landscape took on new meaning to artists. For some, human intrusion lent to the local scene a unique kind of plastic rhythm, and they delighted in its contours – in the geometric edge of the modern city, in the dynamic pattern of land and water masses. Landscape served a developing formalism, and it was favored as a vehicle of revelation and artistic invention. For others, however, the inescapable shoreline that is the distinctive feature of this region suggested more than just formal tension – it became the focus for ruminations on the social and psychological consequences of living within a delimited space.

The Landscape of Possibility

Considering the state of the regional landscape school in 1932, *Los Angeles Times* critic Arthur Millier observed: *In California . . . we still have the group of mature painters who deal with our landscape. Untroubled by the age of speed and change they continue to interpret nature in terms of light and atmosphere. A younger element which has grown up here evinces more interest in what man has done to the landscape. They begin to see the forms, cities, and people as art material.*[2]

Millier's "younger element" is exemplified in San Francisco by a small group of forward-thinking artists who, through the decade of the '20s, expanded the concept of landscape painting in the Bay Area. Their new focus on the cultivated landscape and urban life may be explained in part by their deep roots in the region and their awareness of how the human presence had shaped the state's landscape during the first decades of the twentieth century. Otis Oldfield, Rinaldo Cuneo, and Charles Stafford Duncan – among the most innovative and expressive painters of the local scene by the middle of the decade – were all raised in or around San Francisco, and their lives were shaped by an essentially urban experience.[3] A closely knit group, with their studios clustered, at least initially, on Montgomery Street, they shared as well a synthetic vision that had been conditioned by keen interest in and assimilation of French modernist painting. Having experimented with postimpressionist color and the radically distilled cubist forms and condensed space, they brought to landscape painting a new sense of design – a keen eye for the essential patterns and colors of the kaleidoscopic world around them. That world was distinctly modern, undeniably American, and uniquely Californian; it was, moreover, emphatically human-centered.

fig.1 Otis Oldfield, *Telegraph Hill*, ca. 1927
Oil on canvas, 40 x 33 in.
The Delman Collection, San Francisco, *cat.no.121*

Otis Oldfield's *Telegraph Hill*, ca.1927 (fig.1), is a rich tapestry of images derived from the artist's daily experiences within the carefree bohemian community that sprang up atop San Francisco's signal hill. Oldfield had taken up residence and established his studio there in 1926, shortly after returning to the city following thirteen years of living abroad. The composition dramatically conveys the unusual high vantage point from which Oldfield could survey the city and the unobstructed view he enjoyed from the hill's eastern slope. The viewer looks down the steep hillside onto the artist's topsy-turvy world of simple houses and tenements, seemingly built one upon another, all standing tenuously on rickety wooden stilts, and all connected by a network of sidewalk staircases, porches, and clotheslines. A sense of community, of the ease of human interchange, permeates the painting.

Unveiled in 1927 at his first show of California subjects held at San Francisco's still new cooperative space, the Beaux Arts Gallery, *Telegraph Hill*, by its allusions to Cézanne, proclaimed literally and symbolically Oldfield's triumphal return from Paris. In it he revealed the extent to which he had absorbed French modernism, employing expressive color, intuitive brushwork, and spatial distortions to heighten visual and emotional impact. But, more important, he also demonstrated the success with which he could apply an international style to the American landscape without sacrificing a sense of place, and he further declared his immense satisfaction with the pictorial challenges and vital energies presented by the local scene. The painting was praised as much for its subject as its treatment, suggesting the concerns of his audience at the time. "All the picturesque sites of Telegraph Hill, those which are known to everybody, have been registered with the flavor of a true devotee and the candor of an unsophisticated artist whose vocation seems to him as sacred as that of a religious order to a monk," declared Jehanne Bietry Salinger in the *San Francisco Examiner,* commending the artist's serious but unpretentious treatment of a subject with broad appeal.[4] While such an art was refreshingly nonelitist, it was also thoroughly native, and, more to the point, wholly local, a depiction of the "picturesque" charm of an American Montmartre for an audience more accustomed to seeing Parisian scenes in contemporary painting than views of this equally delightful American city. "To those who always clamor for true San Francisco work, by San Francisco artists, this picture should be beloved and it should be held here as a city treasure for the outsiders to come and admire," Salinger continued.[5] The canvas was subsequently hung for special viewing in the Mark Hopkins Hotel, possibly through the year-end holidays.[6] For San Franciscans in 1927, Oldfield's *Telegraph Hill* stood as a measure of their cultural distinction, and it could be celebrated as such.

Oldfield's landscapes are detailed records of a painter's life – sites visited with family or friends, for instance, or, as in the example of *Telegraph Hill*, familiar spaces that denote "home." His eye is typically on the near ground, on revealing details of the here and now. By contrast, Rinaldo Cuneo and Charles Stafford Duncan both took a much broader view of their landscape in these years and, in doing so, discovered aspects of the region that were timeless and transcendent.

The lush farmlands and orchards of Northern California have been to the twentieth century what the gold fields were to the nineteenth. Indeed, the fecundity of the region has defined California for much of the nation throughout the modern era. The landscape of the Bay Area encompasses the rolling vine-covered hills of Napa and Sonoma counties and the flat vegetable fields of the Santa Clara Valley. Planting and harvest are among the essential rhythms of life here. Yet, despite the omni-presence of these cultivated lands from the late nineteenth century onward, it took a modern eye to recognize and articulate their formal structure and innate beauty within the region's landscape and to reveal their singular economic significance to the world at large.

Cuneo's feeling for the cultivated landscape as a subject for painting stemmed from a formalist's concern

fig.2 Rinaldo Cuneo, *California Landscape*, ca. 1928
Oil on canvas, three-part screen, 66 x 66 in.
Zora and Les Charles, *cat.no.28*

with design. The geometry of the agricultural landscape appealed to his taste for pattern in color and line. But Cuneo also embraced the idea of cultivation on a conceptual level, finding in it a natural process of shaping and ordering nature that was akin to – and, indeed, helped to explain – the ideals of modern art. "He saw that man makes patchwork of the earth in the mere routine of living and must do formal things in a significant way, such as in sowing alfalfa fields or planting square miles of sugar beets," his biographer wrote in 1936.[7]

The cultivated landscape was celebrated time and again in Cuneo's paintings, but perhaps never so impressively as in the painted screen now known simply as *California Landscape* (fig.2), probably dating to 1928 or 1929. The monumental format was certainly appropriate to his expansive theme – a boundless red clay field of lettuce stretching from well outside the picture frame to the great golden California hills in the far distance. But the screen conceit could serve other artistic aims as well, especially as it suggested the venerable tradition of architectural arts and mural painting, then enjoying a tremendous resurgence of interest in the Bay Area; a screen provided means to integrate painting with architecture and, by extension, to connect the arts inexorably with modern life. And, perhaps most important, Cuneo was able to take the screen's decorative function and use it as an appropriate means for expressing the vision of a landscape that existed in his imagination, rather than one simply transcribed from nature, a landscape rich in graphic qualities and expressive forms.

From their first appearance at San Francisco's Beaux Arts Gallery in 1928, Cuneo's innovative screens were highly acclaimed. Local critics generally agreed that Cuneo had, through the process of reinventing what were familiar scenes, captured the essential spirit of the Northern California landscape in these new works. "Now he has made use of a decorative scheme . . . which has all the creative expression and design that could be desired while translating into fixed forms the breadth of the big hills," observed Robert Wilson in the *San Francisco Bulletin*.[8] The following year, Aline Kistler, in the *San Francisco Chronicle*, wrote in praise of another of the resplendent new works, "Cuneo's screen is of the fields that spread out toward brown California hills. He has kept his whole canvas pregnant with the feeling of productivity."[9] "Most of these are far from literal views of the mountains," Kistler wrote again in 1930, "but the character is so well given that one feels these are definite places – groups of real hills. . . . Cuneo has painted these hills as though he knew every foot of them – as though he had tramped up and down their sides, feeling their contours and knowing their spirit."[10]

Unlike Cuneo, whose principal medium of expression was landscape painting, Charles Stafford Duncan devoted far more energy to figure painting and still life

than he did to painting the local scene. But when he did turn his attention to landscape, he brought to it an intense feeling for pictorial design that owes its strength to the artist's mastery of the other genres, to his experience as a typographer and illustrator, and to a clear affinity for the hard-edged art of his modernist contemporaries. *The Dark Hills of Saratoga*, ca. 1929 (fig.3), is one of Duncan's earliest landscapes, and it is one of the most abstract compositions in his entire body of work. Like an exercise in still life, Duncan has reduced his subject – the long ridge of high hills leading to the Santa Cruz Mountain range – to a series of sculptural shapes modeled in light and shadow, and he has ordered them in a shallow, rational, planar space. As in portraiture, he has studied the attributes of these hills and has presented their most distinctive features with the utmost clarity, in profile against the yellow sky. In his emphasis on design Duncan has here experimented with format, stretching the view horizontally to an extreme. Reinforcing that horizontality are the bands of color that are the brown field and green orchard along the composition's bottom edge. The picture suggests a kind of long ornamental frieze, a continuous rhythmic pattern of color and shape. Seeing it at the Beaux Arts Gallery group show in September 1929, one critic summed up its striking visual effect: "It is an original and baffling canvas, decorative in the most sophisticated manner."[11] In the process of creating art from nature, Duncan had in fact defined a particular locale in the simplest of terms: as a land of boundless fertile fields, majestic hills, and golden sky, all described with a clarity that reminded viewers that they lived in a machine age.

For Mexican painter Diego Rivera, Northern California represented both progress and promise, and by the late '20s he had come to view it as a region uniquely suited to his art: "[T]he larger experiment in mural painting, of which all my work since 1921 had been a part, could not be completely realized in Mexico," Rivera recalled in 1934, adding:
it was urgently necessary for me to continue it in a highly industrialized country, under conditions impossible to find in Mexico. Only by testing the action and reaction between my painting and great masses of industrial workers could I take the next step towards my central objective – that of learning to produce painting for the working masses of the city and country.[12]

Rivera understood that California was distinctly different from the urban industrial centers of the country, but he nevertheless saw it as "the ideal intermediate step between Mexico and the United States." He elaborated:
Although it is also more agricultural than industrial, its agriculture is highly advanced and mechanized; its mining districts are very like the part of Mexico where I was born,

fig.3 Charles Stafford Duncan, *The Dark Hills of Saratoga*, ca. 1929
Oil on canvas, 19 x 50 in.
Private collection, *cat.no.44*

*even though the primitive mining technique of my boyhood
days bore little relation to the methods in use here; and the
state as a whole is a rich land intimately bound up with the
remains of its earlier Mexican character, forming a transition stage between the industrial East and primitive, back-
ward Mexico; a region whose mountains and deserts are the
connecting link between the strong, bitter, rugged landscape
of Mexico and the flat plains and lake dotted rolling hills
of the Middle West, North, and East, the cradle of America's
industrialization.*[13]

Economically, culturally, and physically, California was
connected to Rivera's Mexican past, and by those connections it revealed to him as no other locale could the
promise of the future. Therefore, when he was offered
commissions to create murals for San Francisco's new
Pacific Stock Exchange and for the California School of
Fine Arts, he eagerly accepted, seeing in them the long-
awaited opportunity to experience American culture.

Rivera's arrival in San Francisco in November 1930
represents a defining moment for Bay Area art. His presence shook the Bay Area art community as no other
event ever had. As one of the world's most acclaimed
practitioners of public mural art, he brought renewed
attention to what were already the substantial contributions of local artists to that art form, and he helped to
encourage its further development here. His impact on
public art was immediate and direct. Rivera employed

local assistants, disseminated his techniques through
them, and offered painters the most significant models
of contemporary mural art to be seen anywhere in the
region. Unintentionally, Rivera also helped to politicize
civic art in San Francisco, his Stock Exchange commission prompting public debate over the artist's leftist
reputation and the slighting of local muralists who
were passed over for the job.

A sense of place is expressed symbolically in the two
public mural projects Rivera completed in San Francisco during his eight-month stay in 1930-31: California
as earth mother, in the Stock Exchange mural, and as
the domain of the great city builder, as it is represented
in the loggia of the California School of Fine Arts, now
the San Francisco Art Institute. The only pure landscape
he produced during his first visit was a small mural in a
private residence on the Peninsula. Yet, as this mural
shows, even when he responded directly to his immediate surroundings, he regarded landscape as a symbol of
human progress toward civilization.

In April 1931, having completed his work at the
Stock Exchange and looking ahead to the mural for the
California School of Fine Arts, Rivera enjoyed a brief
respite at the country home of Mr. and Mrs. Sigmund
Stern in Atherton, south of San Francisco. Mrs. Stern's
proposal for a fresco for the house had met with Rivera's
enthusiastic acceptance. Neither patron nor artist had

any preconceived notion of what the subject of the mural might be, but the elements of the design were soon revealed to Rivera on the drive from the city through the lush springtime landscape of the Peninsula. Mrs. Stern's daughter, Elise Haas, recalled of that trip: *I remember driving down with my mother and Rivera. . . to Atherton. In those days, there were vast fields of fruit trees, which were then in blossom. It was when the Japanese had this tremendous industry down there. He [Rivera] also saw a mechanical plow for the first time. When we got down to my mother's home, the gardeners were turning up earth to put in a new lawn. All this he must have retained in his inner eye.*[14] The subject evolved through three sketches (figs.4-6), from a simple, open view of the almond orchard, with two children and a fruit bowl set among the trees and the mechanical tractor in the distance, to a design that was compositionally and symbolically more complex. In the finished mural, entitled *Still Life and Blossoming Almond Trees* (fig.7), three children – a Caucasian boy and girl and their mestizo friend – occupy the foreground, where they partake of the contents of a magnificent bowl of fruit that sits atop an illusionistic wall. Behind the children, light- and dark-skinned workmen till the soil and a mechanical tractor cuts a swath through the well-ordered grove of almond trees in full blossom. As he had in his Stock Exchange mural, Rivera here celebrated the fruits of human labor and the importance of modern technology in the reaping of those rewards. The scene is made especially poignant by Rivera's references to the unity of the Mexican and Californian people. Such a bucolic scene seems especially appropriate for a mural intended for an outdoor dining area.[15]

The painting actually includes portraits of the Stern grandchildren, but documentation clearly shows that Rivera conceived his subject in the broadest of terms and not as a vehicle for the singular purpose of honoring his patron. Upon reviewing Rivera's preliminary design, it was Mrs. Stern who suggested that her grandchildren might serve as models for the central figures, and Rivera agreed. Rhoda and Peter Haas appear in the foreground, along with Rhoda's imaginary companion, "Dega." Their brother Walter sat for the figure of the young laborer at left.[16]

When we look at some of the most progressive painting being produced in the Bay Area in 1930 – the work of local artists Otis Oldfield, Rinaldo Cuneo, and Charles Stafford Duncan, for instance, and the San Francisco murals of Diego Rivera – we find no hint of the social and economic problems that had gripped the region even before the stock market crash. Their collective view of the Bay Area landscape is one of natural fecundity, of infinite possibilities that accommodated humankind with ease.

fig.4 Diego Rivera, *Study No. 1 for "Still Life and Blossoming Almond Trees" (The Stern Mural)*, 1931 Charcoal on paper, 18⅝ x 23½ in. Private collection, *cat.no.136*

fig.5 Diego Rivera, *Study No. 2 for "Still Life and Blossoming Almond Trees" (The Stern Mural)*, 1931 Charcoal on paper, 17½ x 23½ in. Private collection, *cat.no.137*

fig.6 Diego Rivera, *Study No. 3 for "Still Life and Blossoming Almond Trees" (The Stern Mural)*, 1931 Graphite, charcoal, and watercolor on paper, 18⅝ x 23½ in. Private collection, *cat. no.138*

fig.7 Diego Rivera, *Still Life and Blossoming Almond Trees (The Stern Mural)*, 1931
Fresco, 62¼ x 105 in.
University of California, Berkeley,
gift of Rosalie M. Stern (Mrs. Sigmund Stern), *cat. no.139*

A Fascination with Configuration

In spring 1930, months before Diego Rivera came to San Francisco, another visiting artist arrived in the Bay Area to teach a summer session at the University of California. Hans Hofmann, renowned painter and teacher and master of the most advanced art school in Europe, had come to the United States from Munich for the very first time. He traveled to Berkeley at the invitation of a former student, Worth Ryder, a professor in the university's art department. His presence was little noticed outside Berkeley at the time, but his impact on the Bay Area art scene was significant. Hofmann introduced a new formalist vision into Bay Area art, and he influenced the teaching of art at the University of California for more than fifty years.

Ryder's invitation came at a most propitious time. Although he hated to leave his homeland and feared the difficulty of establishing himself in New York, Hofmann also knew that he could not stay in Hitler's Germany. His assistant and confidant, the American Glenn Wessels, had known Worth Ryder at the Hofmann Schule, and Wessels saw the Berkeley appointment as a convenient "stepping stone," as he called it – a spot where Hofmann's ideas were known and respected and where, because of the presence of Ryder and visiting artist Vyclav Vytlacil, his pedagogic method was already in use. "Worth Ryder had laid the grounds and this was a very comfortable place for Hofmann to land," recalled Wessels. As he explained it:

Two years before this [1928], Vyclav Vytlacil had played John the Baptist to Hofmann, had talked Hofmann and taught Hofmann.... And so you might say, here was a kind of soft spot ready to land in so we put Hofmann in a nest already feathered and he was able to go on from there.[17]

Because Hofmann's ideas on the foundations of art were radical and because he spoke little English, Wessels and Ryder sought to ease the transition from Munich to the United States by providing their mentor with the kind of environment where he might be easily understood.

That spring Wessels and Hofmann traveled by train from New York to California. Along the way they stopped to present lectures to the painting students of Hofmann's friend and protégé Cameron Booth at the Minneapolis School of Art, lectures drawn from Hofmann's "Creation in Form and Color," a textbook-in-progress that Wessels was translating for publication in the United States; among the attendees were John Haley, who would, coincidentally, follow Hofmann to Berkeley that fall, and Erle Loran, both painters whom would become Hofmann's most enduring champions on the West Coast. The cross-country train trip revealed to Hofmann the vastness of his new surroundings, and he saw in the wide-open landscape an image of promise. Wessels recalled:

He kept saying, 'Ein reichesland: a rich land, a rich country.

You have everything. In Europe we have exhausted everything. A rich land, a place where things can grow and will grow. A place where there is place to put down roots for art....' So he reacted to America as a new land, as virgin territory artistically speaking; instead of thinking of it as ignorant and provincial, he thought of it as an opportunity.[18]

The contours of the California landscape inspired Hofmann's most visual terms of praise. Wessels remembered that "When he first saw the Berkeley hills... he said, 'This is a feminine landscape. In Germany we have masculine hills. These are feminine hills.' He said that he had never seen such a gentle land."[19]

Landscape was a special focus of Hofmann's teaching at Berkeley (fig.8). He transplanted to the East Bay the landscape course he had offered every summer, first in the Bavarian Alps and then at Capri and St. Tropez, almost since the inception of the Hofmann Schule.[20] Drawing and painting from nature provided Hofmann with the simplest means of introducing the fundamentals of composition: line, plane, volume, and formal complexes. The class notes of a student in Hofmann's first Berkeley landscape course reveal the master's vision. He taught that one should look at nature and feel nature and then begin to draw. Contours were all important, for he taught space as volume, not perspective. "Only volume makes positive and negative space. We cannot see volume, we must feel it, and feel movement in opposition to volume." To understand form, Hofmann implored his students, "Feel the character of your objects – the mountain looks like a lion, a beast. Make it monumental. Arrange the foreground to make the immensity of the background possible."[21]

Hofmann himself went into the landscape and drew with the vigor of an artist on a voyage of discovery. The ink brush was his medium of expression, and he produced a large body of spare, almost wholly abstract contour line drawings that nevertheless convey the shapes and rhythms of unmistakable Bay Area sites. He was fascinated by the configuration of the region – by the positive volume of hills and islands and the negative volume of the bay, by the dynamics of those land and water masses in opposition, and by the rhythms created by such forms in space. He was drawn to a certain kind of vital landscape that one sees looking out upon the North and East Bay hills. "When he began to draw and paint around here," Wessels recollected, "he said, 'I am used to angles; I am used to a more masculine type of landscape.' This is the way he expressed it. 'It is very hard to fasten onto a positive thing here. The landscape undulates and flows.'"[22]

Hofmann's landscape studies figured prominently in his first exhibition in the United States, which was actually two concurrent shows of drawings held at the California Palace of the Legion of Honor in San Francisco and at Haviland Hall on the Berkeley campus in

fig.8 Hans Hofmann teaching his landscape drawing class,
Berkeley, California, summer 1930 or 1931.
Hofmann Archive, The Bancroft Library, Berkeley

August 1931 at the close of Hofmann's second summer
session.[23] Bay Area subjects made up one-third of the
exhibition in San Francisco, but the show also included
recent drawings made at Lake Tahoe and earlier
sketches from St. Tropez. Figure drawings were more
numerous in the Berkeley component. Ryder, writing to
Legion of Honor director Lloyd LePage Rollins, felt certain that Hofmann's works would find an enthusiastic
audience in the Bay Area and would sell easily, but only
one drawing – a local subject – was purchased from the
Legion of Honor exhibition.[24] Both shows were ignored
by the San Francisco art press. "So Hofmann's first
appearance here affected a select group of people, but on
the whole it was overlooked and rejected, particularly
since the wave of Mexican Revolutionary art was hitting
San Francisco at that time," Wessels lamented.[25]

John Haley arrived in Berkeley in fall 1930 with a
thorough command of Hofmann's ideas, having studied
with the master at his summer landscape school on the
island of Capri in 1929, and in Munich. In 1936 Haley
was joined at the University by his old classmate at the
Minneapolis School of Art, Erle Loran. Unlike Haley,
Loran had only a passing knowledge of Hofmann's ideas
at this point, but he had recently returned from a three-
year stay in Cézanne's studio at Aix-en-Provence, where
he had steeped himself in the French master's late landscapes and gained fresh insight into the means by which
Cézanne had distilled abstract form from nature. Their
approach to painting landscape proved remarkably similar, and Haley and Loran eventually became the leading
figures of the so-called Berkeley School of landscape
watercolorists.[26]

Haley's *Lawrence House, End of Ocean Avenue, Point
Richmond*, 1936 (fig.9), shows his highly graphic style
fully evolved, his assimilation of Hofmann's teachings
complete, and it represents the hallmarks of Berkeley
School painting. A view taken near the artist's studio
in Point Richmond, a small spit of land jutting into San
Francisco Bay, the painting captures the unique lay of
the land as a series of interwoven planes. The design is
strongly linear, employing the kind of bold ink drawing
that Hofmann favored. And like Hofmann, Haley has
characteristically used color in a purely formal way –
not to describe, but to create spatial complexes. Loran,
who recalled the experience of painting with his colleague in those early years, explained Haley's unusual
technique: "[H]e would draw with a brush rather thin
lines and describe objects and forms so that the three-
dimensional character of forms was developed with line
entirely, and the color was always there. Now this
avoided modeling."[27] Watercolor, Haley's principal
medium of expression through the next decade, served
what was his intuitive approach to plein-air painting.

Loran's much later *Victory Shipyards I*, 1945 (fig.10),
demonstrates how far he was able to push the basic

fig.9 John Haley, *Lawrence House,*
End of Ocean Avenue, Point Richmond, 1936
Watercolor on paper, 15 x 20 in.
Private collection, *cat.no.76*

fig.10 Erle Loran, *Victory Shipyards I*, 1945
Watercolor and gouache on paper, 15½ x 22½ in.
Anne Schechter and Reid Buckley, *cat.no.102*

technique of Hofmann and Haley. Loran conceived his subject – the otherworldly Kaiser shipyards, then looming monuments on the Richmond shoreline – as an intricate mosaic of pure unmodulated color. There is no modeling of the forms; space and volume are created by color relationships alone, hence the composition has been rendered extremely flat. We see the great ship hulls behind weblike scaffolds as line and color pattern. Such complexity in Loran's gouaches is the product of the studio, and not open-air painting. Although his initial ideas were often worked out on the spot, he frequently repeated compositions in the studio – this subject exists in at least one other earlier version, for example – refining them, and working ever closer to complete abstraction.[28]

In 1932 Worth Ryder invited his friend Chiura Obata to teach a summer course at Berkeley on the Japanese technique of drawing and painting. Obata, who had been in San Francisco since 1903, had recently begun to attract attention with his distinctly Japanese interpretations of the Bay Area and Yosemite landscapes – traditional sumi paintings and watercolors on silk – that he exhibited for the first time in 1928. One enthusiastic critic explained:

Working on the theory that an artist must know his material thoroughly, even to the extent of sleeping on the ground and eating the products of the earth underlying the landscape he wishes to interpret, Obata has studied California and made himself at home in its different regions until his brush expresses what California means to him.[29]

Obata's was an art based on memory, intuition, and formal discipline, and his work held great appeal for the Hofmann-trained painters Ryder and Haley. Such was their regard for his teaching that after the 1932 summer session Obata was offered a permanent position on the Berkeley faculty.

Obata had been trained in the traditional Japanese manner of re-creating the essential experience of a place from memory. In his native city he had earned the title of artist through a grueling "public examination" in which he was required to sketch from his "mind's eye" any aspect of local scenery that his audience might propose.[30] In San Francisco, his formal demonstrations of his technique enraptured those who witnessed them:

Obata, robed in the black garment of the Japanese artist, kneels before the specially prepared silk on which he is to paint. . . . He holds himself erect, in an almost buddhistic attitude, and contemplates the naked silk.

Then, with sure deft strokes he starts to paint. Brushes and colors are handed to him by his wife who always assists with his work. Without a moment of hesitation or a single gesture, he applies the color, first in broad sweeps for the background, then, timing the spread of drying with a nicety, he paints in the figures of a composition, depending on the degree of wetness to give diffused or definite outlines.

The audience holds its breath. For those few moments everything is centered on the artist and the picturization of his concept. It has become more than painting; it has become a rite.[31]

Obata's deep feeling for the local landscape and his sure technique are exemplified by two ink paintings, his *Rolling Hills*, 1946 (fig.11), a site near Walnut Creek; and a striking, atmospheric view of San Francisco as seen from a ferry under the Oakland Bay Bridge (fig.12). The latter is an especially poignant statement. Dated 30 April 1942, it was created on the day Obata was taken to the detention camp for so-called enemy aliens set up at Tanforan racetrack just outside the city; eventually he would be interned at the Topaz Relocation Center in Utah. Writing in the *Topaz Times* on 1 January 1943,

fig.11 Chiura Obata, *Rolling Hills*, 1946
Sumi on paper, 15 x 20½ in.
Collection of the Obata Family, *cat.no.120*

fig.12 Chiura Obata, *View of San Francisco*, 30 April 1942
Sumi on paper, 15 x 20½ in.
Collection of the Obata Family, *cat.no.119*

Obata recalled the moment: "While buses carried us across the great San Francisco Bay Bridge, we caught a glimpse of the San Francisco skyline silhouetted in the rain. We felt a tug in our hearts as we bid farewell to the familiar surroundings to which we had become so attached."[32]

Berkeley was not the only center for European modernism in the Bay Area in the '30s. In Oakland, Mills College, the oldest women's college in the West, hosted an extraordinary group of modern artists every summer from 1930 onward. Alexander Archipenko, Lyonel Feininger, Max Beckmann, Fernand Léger, Laszlo Moholy-Nagy – all accepted appointments to teach in the college's coeducational creative arts summer session. Lyonel Feininger, who had lived in Germany since 1887, returned to the United States for the first time since his youth to teach at Mills for two summers, in 1936 and 1937. Thus, the San Francisco Bay Area played an important part in Feininger's rediscovery of his native land and in the development of American themes in the artist's late work.

Although Feininger did not know California, the bay art community knew his work. In 1926 his paintings had been exhibited at the Oakland Art Gallery with those of Wassily Kandinsky, Paul Klee, and Alexej von Jawlensky – the famous Blue Four – in what was their first museum exhibition in the United States. In 1931 the Blue Four were exhibited again at the California Palace of the Legion of Honor in a show that was held under the official auspices of Diego Rivera as well as Galka Scheyer, the representative for the Blue Four group in America.[33]

The years 1936 and 1937 were difficult ones for Feininger, despite the efforts of Alfred Neumeyer, director of the Mills College Art Gallery, to reintroduce Americans to his work.[34] Neumeyer's invitation to join the summer faculty at Mills had been Feininger's first significant acknowledgment from America. And Hitler's denigration of modernism had made the climate impossible for him in Germany; in 1937, Feininger's work was exhibited by the Third Reich in Munich as "degenerate art." That year he was forced to settle permanently in the United States. At age sixty-five Feininger faced starting over.

By all accounts, Feininger's summers in the Bay Area were immensely satisfying. His teaching and his exhibitions helped to ease him into American art life. And the landscape itself left an indelible impression. In 1939, when Feininger returned for the first time to painting, he created from sketches a series of San Francisco and Oakland scenes that he had been re-forming in his imagination for two years.[35] *Bay*, a highly imaginative view of the San Francisco coastline along the Presidio cliffs and Marin Headlands, is from that group of Bay Area recollections.

The watercolor together with a rare pencil sketch of the Embarcadero made on the spot in 1937 (fig.13), clearly show that it was the edge of the city and the openness of the bay that defined San Francisco in Feininger's mind. These compositions remind us that this city of steep hills has been felicitously designed by nature to afford revealing bird's-eye views of vast expanses of shoreline. Feininger's San Francisco is not the sensuous female form of Hofmann's vision. For him, it is a site that has been engineered. Even natural forms of the landscape are architectonic. "The world of architecture, in the fullest and widest sense of the term, concerns him completely," wrote San Francisco critic Alfred Frankenstein after meeting Feininger in 1936; "His pictures are composed in block, line, and angle. It is no accident that his favorite composer is Bach."[36]

Throughout this era, the city and its environs appeared in the work of a number of artists whose contacts with the region were only brief. The Bay Area as destination for the casual traveler in search of a change of scene and a milder climate is an aspect of place that has also contributed to the region's art life. For many of the artist-visitors, it was the topography and the quality of light that distinguished the locale and that presented interesting artistic challenges. Those painters who were naturally inclined toward a formalistic approach created some of the most original and transcendent interpretations from their brief encounters with the Bay Area landscape. Los Angeles watercolorist Millard Sheets, for example, in his view entitled *Church of Saints Peter and Paul, San Francisco* of 1933 captured the sculptural quality of the architectural landscape – a quality manifest through the play of brilliant light across the city's densely settled hills. Even Edward Hopper, whose *House in San Mateo*, 1941 (fig.14), evokes the region's Victorian past, focuses on the formal qualities of light and shadow to convey the spirit of this locale. For the New York precisionist painter Ralston Crawford it was as well the optical experience of light, shape, color, and texture that inspired one of his most wholly abstract late works, his *Fisherman's Wharf, San Francisco*, developed over three years, from 1947-50 (fig.15). In 1954 Charles Sheeler turned his photographer's eye to the monumental towers of the Golden Gate Bridge, and found in the patterns of light across its brilliant orange surface and forms a vast, abstract landscape. His *Golden Gate*, 1955 (fig.16), is a highly refined but unmistakable emblem of modern San Francisco that needs no grounding in topography.

The abstract art of the Berkeley group that emerged in the mid-'30s, which was inspired by a close connection to Hans Hofmann, a keen interest in traditional Japanese painting, and a strong current of European modernism that ran through the East Bay, stood in sharp contrast to the social realism that characterized

fig.13 Lyonel Feininger, *The Embarcadero, San Francisco*, 1937
Pencil and colored crayon on paper, 6 x 8 in.
Collection of Cathy and Tom Creighton

fig.14 Edward Hopper, *House in San Mateo*, 1941
Watercolor on paper, 13¾ x 19¾ in.
Private collection, *cat.no.83*

fig.15 Ralston Crawford, *Fisherman's Wharf, San Francisco*, 1947-1950
Oil on canvas, 30 x 40 in.
Private collection, *cat.no.27*

fig.16 Charles Sheeler, *Golden Gate*, 1955
Oil on canvas, 25 x 34 in.
The Metropolitan Museum of Art, New York,
George A. Hearn Fund, 1955, *cat.no.143*

much of the painting in San Francisco in the depression years. Although painters like Glenn Wessels, John Haley, Chiura Obata, and Erle Loran took their inspiration from the local scene, their art was concerned with the physical configuration of the landscape and not with its social and political character. "Nature knows no depression," Obata told a critic in 1931.[37] To those who argued that depiction of modern life constituted the only truly meaningful contemporary art, Glenn Wessels offered an eloquent defense of the Berkeley group's formalism:

Painting is no longer a servant, but an art with its own lyric purpose. . . . To insist, as many do, that art must have some other meaning is like insisting that music must always be associated with words. . . .

This is not a popular view for the moment among the most popular American painters. The "American Scene" school is laying great emphasis upon the subject, which is all very well, but the beauty of a painting resides in its formal relations after the "meaning" drops away. The eternal and universal quality of art resides in its plastic rhythm.[38]

Confronting Limits

You who construct the iron road of "progress,"
gleaming-hard and ruthless,
laid upon girders of injustice,
spiked in toil and mortared in men's pain, –
building from blind causes to blind
      consequences in men's minds, –
how do you make traffic in men's lives?
Do you effect a transportation of men's souls
in shuttling their bodies back and forth?
      Maynard Dixon, "The Iron Road," ca.1920[39]

Maynard Dixon, San Francisco poet and painter, thus gave voice to the steadily growing anxiety of his age – an anxiety of change, of a national migration born not of hope but of despair. "A half million people moving over the country; a million more restive, ready to move; ten million more feeling the first nervousness," as John Steinbeck described it.[40] The uprooted generation of the dust bowl and the depression became acutely aware of the limits of space. For them, California's position at the continent's end suddenly took on a new and sobering meaning, expressed succinctly by Steinbeck's migrants in *The Grapes of Wrath*:

    Well, California's a big State.
    It ain't that big. The whole United States ain't that big. It ain't that big. It ain't big enough. There ain't room enough for you an' me, for your kind an' my kind, for rich and poor together all in one country, for thieves and honest men. For hunger and fat.[41]
San Francisco by the '30s seemed to many to epitomize

a circumscribed world, and the city provided a powerfully symbolic setting for the pictorialization of what one contemporary writer has called "the pressures unique to cultivated life in a bounded space."[42]

"Like other artists, I had dodged the responsibility of facing social conditions," Maynard Dixon told the *San Francisco Chronicle* in 1935; "The depression woke me up to the fact that I had a part in this as an artist."[43] Dixon's forays into the western landscape had offered little relief from what he described as the overwhelming sense of impending doom, a "sense of being surrounded by vague ominous threatening forms," that gripped him in the months following the stock-market crash.[44] The hopelessness of the unemployed who gathered along San Francisco's waterfront, the leagues of homeless men on California's roadways, and the events of Bloody Thursday and the San Francisco General Strike of 1934 – all captured in the photographs of Dixon's wife, Dorothea Lange – fixed in his mind and gave rise to an extraordinary series of highly charged depression subjects. Four of the paintings dealt specifically with the city's violent longshoremen's strike, but three were designed to give form to President Franklin Roosevelt's "Forgotten Man."[45] The entire series was reproduced in the leftist journal *Survey Graphic* in 1935, but Dixon understood that these were paintings that "nobody wants to own."[46] They represented a personal need to externalize rage. As Dixon told an interviewer in 1937, once his "burst of anger over these conditions had died," he never again returned to social themes.[47]

No Place to Go (fig.17) is the only painting in Dixon's *Forgotten Man* series that utilizes landscape to convey essential meaning. It offers a vivid picture of the despair that accompanied the first sudden realization that this broad country had its limits, and that westward migration, historically the solution to the country's economic ills, was no longer an option. When it was shown with Dixon's other depression subjects at the Artists Cooperative Gallery, *No Place to Go* was singled out for "making the most appeal to popular sympathy," a testament clearly to the potent conjunction of the figure of the lost man and the unmistakable California coastline.[48]

It is locale that also supplies the tension in John Langley Howard's *Embarcadero and Clay*, 1935 (fig.18). Although today the picture is somewhat difficult to read, in 1936 Howard's references were so apparent that the canvas was proclaimed a "frankly propagandizing picture."[49] The intersection of Embarcadero and Clay is near the Ferry Building and the center of San Francisco's wharf activity. Therein lies the meaning of this distinct urban landscape. According to the artist, the painting depicts the ominous hours before the longshoremen's strike in the summer of 1934. At left are men of the union committee on their way to a meeting. The businessman at right eyes the group with fear.

fig.17 Maynard Dixon, *No Place to Go*, 1935
Oil on canvas, 25⅛ x 30 in.
Museum of Art, Brigham Young University, *cat.no.42*

fig.18 John Langley Howard, *Embarcadero and Clay*, 1935
Oil on canvas, 35⅞ x 43½ in.
Mr. and Mrs. Norman Lacayo, *cat. no. 84*

fig.19 Ray Stanford Strong, *Golden Gate Bridge*, 1934
Oil on canvas, 44⅛ x 71¾ in.
National Museum of American Art, Smithsonian Institution, transfer
from the U.S. Department of Interior, National Park Service, *cat.no.151*

Quite uncharacteristically, dark clouds hang over the city, and in the background Howard adds an important symbolic note: a figure in the top floor window of the Bay Hotel holds his hand out to check for rain; "Is there a storm brewing?" he asks.[50]

For all the charges of propagandizing that surrounded *Embarcadero and Clay*, Howard's picture is in fact strangely ambiguous. Howard himself had been deeply involved in the struggle on the labor side, as his brother-in-law was one of the striking longshoremen. And he had not shrunk from injecting his leftist politics into his controversial government-sponsored mural in Coit Tower in 1934, as the public well remembered.[51] Yet this picture includes no such overt signs of Howard's sympathies. All the figures impart equal amounts of hostility and vulnerability. Reaction to this picture would seem to be tied to whatever interpretation one chose to make of the events of 1934 themselves, and there were, indeed, many conflicting points of view: "To most Americans there is something foreign about a general strike, and a bit ominous – like the . . . storm troopers, socialists, communists, fascists, and a host of other things that used to seem farther away than they are now," wrote Paul Taylor and Norman Leon Gold in *Survey Graphic* in September 1934,

But to many on the Pacific Coast, experience has made the general strike at least real, however differently they may interpret it – as a splendid demonstration of the strength and "solidarity of labor," a victory for the "real soldiers of labor," a "sell-out," by labor "fakirs," a "strikers' dictatorship," or an "insurrection."[52]

It is the idea of human conflict that Howard pictorializes and deplores – man's tragic flaw manifest again in this particular situation.

Ray Strong was another painter who was drawn to landscape and the urban scene by his social conscience. He had come down to San Francisco from his native Oregon in the early 1920s in his words, "to paint the West." He found little encouragement at the California School of Fine Arts, where he sought enrollment. "I want to paint West of the Rockies and I want to do it with integrity and sincerity, and you're telling me I'm going to be fifteen or twenty years behind the time?" he has recalled asking the school's director, impressionist painter Lee Randolph. Still, he persisted:

I had my sights set on trying to paint light, form, geology – the works – of Western landscape, in the tradition of Thomas Moran particularly, but in the great tradition of Homer, Eakins, the whole Hudson River School. You just name 'em.[53]

With his close friend Maynard Dixon, he founded an Art Students League on Montgomery Street and there advanced the ideal of art for life's sake. Landscape was an important element of that aesthetic: "Look at the land! Get out, live in it! Sleep in it! Paint it!," Strong exhorted his students.[54]

fig.20 Maxine Albro, *Women Picking Flowers*, detail from *California* (left panel), 1934
Fresco, 10 x 42 ft. (total mural)
Collection of the City and County of San Francisco, Coit Tower, Telegraph Hill, San Francisco

fig.21 Lucien Labaudt, *Bathers*, detail from *San Francisco Scenes*, 1936-37
Fresco, 1500 sq. ft. (total mural)
Collection of the City and County of San Francisco, Beach Chalet, San Francisco

Strong's view of his environment was colored by his leftist politics and shaped in part by his friendship with the group of documentary photographers who in the '30s were recording the local scene with frankness and clarity. In the corridor leading to the Artists Cooperative Gallery, which Strong initiated in a space on Maiden Lane, he studied the changing displays of the photography forum that included Imogen Cunningham, Dorothea Lange, Ansel Adams, Roger Sturtevant, and Peter Stackpole –"The best emerging *Life Magazine* talents in the West;" he said; "Their blood is strong with Steinbeck. . . . God, we were alive."[55]

Strong's monumental canvas, *Golden Gate Bridge*, 1934 (fig.19), painted under the auspices of the Public Works of Art Project, the federal government's pilot relief program for artists, suggests the great enthusiasm he felt for the bridge-building enterprise and for the PWAP effort, which employed artists at craftsmen's wages to create art for public buildings. The subject was one that appealed to Strong on several levels: it was distinctly western, emphatically modern, and powerfully symbolic. His painting commemorates in extraordinary detail the construction of the massive pylons on the San Francisco side, which began in January 1933. The magnitude of the endeavor is captured in Strong's sweeping view of the extensive excavation undertaken to set the pylons and to anchor the bridge's suspension cables.[56] As landscape, the scene celebrates human endeavor on an unprecedented scale. It also suggests the artist's personal devotion to "mining deeper toward earthknowing," as he called it, a lifelong objective that led him to explore geology, geomorphology, and paleontology.[57]

Exhibited in the 1934 landmark exhibition of PWAP art held at The Corcoran Gallery of Art in Washington, D.C., *Golden Gate Bridge* was selected by President Roosevelt to hang in the White House. Strong successfully elevated the local scene to a powerful national symbol. His painting still stands as the perfect embodiment of the New Deal: a glorious product of government patronage and an inspiriting display of American enterprise.

Strong envisioned on a heroic scale a subject he thought worthy of the grand social experiment that was the New Deal. He was not alone. The Bay Area landscape is perhaps nowhere more brilliantly celebrated in paintings of the '30s than in the great government-sponsored murals of San Francisco's Coit Tower, 1934, and the Golden Gate Park Beach Chalet, 1938-39. These monumental projects attest to the importance of mural commissions generally to Bay Area artists working under the New Deal and to the accomplishment of local painters in fresco painting and other means of architectural embellishment. The local scene was, of course, a favorite theme for many Bay Area muralists, and fine examples of landscape art exist in murals throughout

the region. Yet the Coit Tower and Beach Chalet murals stand out for their physical scale, conceptual breadth, and technical achievement. The Coit Tower project, was, moreover, the highly important prototype for the New Deal art program and had a significant impact on the tenor of the programs that followed. At Coit Tower, urban, industrial, and agricultural landscapes all describe *Aspects of Life in California, 1934*, the common theme that unifies twenty-seven separate murals by twenty-five different artists (fig.20). Within the structure, landscape also unites the architecture with its site, as painted views are strategically placed to appear as windows onto the San Francisco Bay scene. At the Beach Chalet – the work of a single artist, Lucien Labaudt – the focus is specifically on San Francisco at the water's edge, and the mural offers a splendid tour of the colorful sites along the city's distinctive shores (fig.21).[58]

The practice of mural painting did much to shape the look of all landscape and view painting produced in San Francisco through the decade of the '30s. "A mural can't be impressionistic," Charles Stafford Duncan told the *San Francisco Chronicle* in 1935; "It must be architectural and therefore mathematical. We are learning for ourselves how to build pictures on the basis of principles of design and structure that we are organizing for ourselves."[59] Duncan's large canvas, *San Francisco Bay – Alcatraz*, ca.1935 (fig.22), is a case in point. The composition owes a debt to the formula established by Diego Rivera and popularized in the landscape designs on the walls of Coit Tower and the Beach Chalet. A clearly defined foreground – a view of what is today Ghirardelli Square and Aquatic Park – brings the viewer into the space. Other planar forms – Alcatraz Island, Angel Island, and the Headlands beyond – move the viewer back through space while actually moving the eye up the picture plane to the high horizon, thus reinforcing the surface of the canvas and the artifice of the scene. Each register – foreground, middle ground, and background – is painted with the same hard outline and bright, even light, so that each detail can be read and understood with equal clarity. Even Duncan's subdued palette suggests a mural painting, a fact that was noted by at least one critic at the time:

The manner in which the work is executed is reminiscent of a fresco or tempera style – which handling, by the way, is insidiously affecting most of our painters. It is as though they were tired of the lush freedom of oil paint and were instinctively seeking a more ascetic style. . . . Mr. Duncan seems better than most – perhaps because ever since I can remember he has been an assiduous experimenter – to have achieved his own, rather than a borrowed convention.[60]

Some of these same devices – clearly defined foreground, planar space, carefully described detail, and uniform light – also inform the easel paintings of the

fig.22 Charles Stafford Duncan, *San Francisco Bay – Alcatraz*, ca. 1935
Oil on Masonite, 38¾ x 50½ in.
Private collection, *cat.no.45*

Spanish-born painter José Moya del Piño, who today is best known as a muralist. Yet in the early '30s he produced one of his most arresting views of the city in a portrait: a penetrating study of a *Chinese Mother and Child*, 1933 (page 60). Before the depression, Moya del Piño had built his reputation locally by his society portraits and scenic decorative murals, and social realism never really characterized his art. But as an immigrant himself, he must have had a special affinity for this particular subject, the difficulty of transplanting one's native culture in a foreign land. The Chinese population in the city represented the most obvious example of the conflict of cultures. Ostracized by the very society that had exploited their rush to the "Golden Mountain" in the nineteenth century, the Chinese were confined to those jobs that American laborers did not want and were sequestered in a separate community by discriminatory housing restrictions and by their own withdrawal from the hostile world outside the borders of Chinatown.[61] Remarkably, avoiding the conventions of most painters of San Francisco's Chinese people, Moya del Piño has placed this mother and child not in the setting of Chinatown, but within the city at large, a firm reminder that by 1930 a large portion of the Chinese living in San Francisco were California-born. He has presented his sitters with remarkable equanimity – as a study of the basic human identification with family, home, and community, and of the inner strength that enables the dispossessed everywhere to endure.[62] The artist's uncommon command of Spanish baroque portraiture and history painting – he had painted celebrated copies of the Velázquez paintings in the Museo del Prado in Madrid – is revealed in his brilliant colors and bravura brushwork, in his well-modeled figures, and in the complex composition, incorporating still life and landscape as essential components. However, the personal experience that lends strength to this portrait could be seen by some contemporary critics as Moya del Piño's weakness:

*It has been noted lately, that he is confusing his heritage with his painting, for, in his painting exhibited here [*Chinese Mother and Child, *shown with the Albert Bender collection in 1936], an obvious attempt to be Spanish in design and execution is becoming too noticeable, including the posed and stilted position of his group set against a bay background.*[63] The distinct tone of the artist's realism seemed somehow out of place in contemporary American art.

In the '30s realism was the dominant mode of expression for Bay Area artists who wished to address the most pressing social and political issues of their day and region in a visual language that all could understand. They were the chroniclers of the moment. But the feelings of urgency and constraint that were so forcefully expressed through landscape in the art of the social realists required for others a metaphorical or symbolic language to convey the true force of upheaval. These artists might be called the pictorial poets, and nature and the local landscape also served their expressive needs as well.

In the darkest days of 1934, when the Bay Area was rocked by the massive and violent General Strike, Maynard Dixon composed these lines to describe a time and place:

1934
Horrible – to wake up in the night
and feel time pressing slowly,
the silent hours sliding through the dark
as the dumb world turns, –
slowly pressing the dim dawn
inexorably against defenseless window-panes;
to feel the deep earth shudder
in unimaginable agony,
slowly, slowly being forced asunder;
to feel the perfect buildings of our pride,
clean-cut and small, tilted off-balance,
reel toward darkness;
and in the torn gap helpless myriads
struggling like maggots in a wound;
and clear above
a pitiless cold blade of cosmic light. . . .[64]

The tumult of that year was for him measured only by the most violent forces of nature – the trembling earth, the lighting bolt, the consuming black of night. Nature alone could be capable of inflicting such destructive blows. In representing the essential character of this same time and place, the painters Edward Hagedorn and Irving Norman independently evolved a nearly identical language of expression.

Edward Hagedorn remains an elusive figure in the history of Bay Area art. A lifelong resident of the area, he nevertheless had little connection to the local art community. "Ed was an outsider, a 'loner,' a tall thin man who walked down the street looking like a question mark; he had no use for success," recalls his friend and painting companion, Paul Carey.[65] Galka Scheyer, champion in America of the Blue Four, whose work Hagedorn admired, reportedly wished to include him as the fifth member of her modernist group, but he refused her offers. Having received a large inheritance, Hagedorn was financially independent from the '30s onward, and he worked through the rest of his life in seclusion in his Berkeley studio.[66]

Landscape was an important vehicle of expression for Hagedorn. And while painting the local scene was of no interest to him, his consistent vision of the mysterious realm of nature as one of beach, sea, and hills seems clearly to have evolved from his experience of the distinct Bay Area landscape. Specific references

fig.23 Edward Hagedorn, *Blue Mountains, Large 3-Forked Bolt*, 1937
Graphite, ink, and watercolor on paper, 19^{13}/$_{16}$ x 26 in.
Courtesy Denenberg Fine Arts, Inc., San Francisco, *cat.no.72*

fig.24 Irving Norman, *City Rush*, 1941
Graphite on paper, 30 x 24 in.
Courtesy Jan Holloway Fine Art, San Francisco, *cat.no.117*

to real, observed events are suggested by Hagedorn's precise dates: included in this exhibition are examples dated August 1935 and January 1937 (fig.23). Yet his images are purely of the imagination. "Where these were done, it would be hard to say," Alfred Frankenstein wrote of Hagedorn's landscapes on view at the Vera Jones Bright Gallery in San Francisco in June 1938; "They seem to reflect some brilliant but grim and extreme land of jagged capes and boiling sea such as Sibelius might celebrate in a tone poem."[67]

For the Polish-born artist Irving Norman, who came to San Francisco in 1923 and practiced art while making his living as a barber, the city provided ample evidence of the dehumanizing urban experience. In one of his earliest compositions – *City Rush*, 1941 (fig.24) – wartime San Francisco was the setting for a nightmarish view of the press of modern life. A consummate draftsman, Norman imagined chaos in minute detail. In *City Rush*, two of San Francisco's architectural landmarks, the Italianate Masonic Auditorium on Van Ness Avenue and the neoclassical Pacific Stock Exchange, are rendered with extraordinary precision and clarity and establish the specific locale of this living hell beyond any doubt.[68]

"We the visionaries, will look straight / and see the world with honest candid eyes, / beholding the flow of seasons and of centuries," Maynard Dixon wrote in 1930; "And out of the grandeur of the earth and stars / and man's terrible aspiration toward truth / we will make our vision manifest awhile."[69] Indeed, as Dixon suggests, landscape over the next twenty years would become the principal means by which artists sought to convey the complexities of life in the Bay Area in the era of the depression and World War II. Some found in the changing scene images of hope and redemption in desperate times, and they celebrated the remarkable cultivated landscape. Others absorbed the vital rhythms of a dynamic environment and expressed them as abstract ideas. Still others considered the human condition and lamented a distinctive landscape of despair. Despite their varying points of view and the differing visual languages they employed, all shared a perception of the region as a powerful symbol of a new modern age.

Notes

1. Julián Marías, "California as Paradise," in Leonard Michaels, David Reid, and Raquel Scherr, eds., *West of the West: Imagining California* (New York: Harper Collins Publishers, 1989), 15. Originally published in *America in the Fifties and Sixties: Julián Marías on the United States*, trans. by Blanche DePuy and Harold C. Raley (State College, Pa.: Pennsylvania State University Press, 1972).

2. Arthur Millier, "California Trend," *The Art Digest* (1 November 1932): 13.

3. For biographical information on Otis Oldfield see "Otis Oldfield," *California Art Research*, vol. 19, no. 2, ed. Gene Haley (San Francisco: Works Progress Administration, 1937), 29-73; and *Otis Oldfield, 1890-1990: Centennial*, exh. cat. (San Francisco: Jan Holloway Gallery, 1990). For Rinaldo Cuneo see "Rinaldo Cuneo," *California Art Research*, vol. 11, no. 3, 61-100; and Monica E. Garcia-Thow, *Rinaldo Cuneo: An Evolution of Style* (Carmel and Santa Monica, Calif.: William A. Karges Fine Arts, 1991). For material on the life and work of Charles Stafford Duncan, I am indebted to the artist's granddaughter, Nicole Back, who has generously provided copies of documents in her possession.

4. Jehanne Bietry Salinger, "Telegraph Hill Painted by Otis Oldfield," *San Francisco Examiner*, Sunday, 6 November 1927. Other reviews with extended commentary on this picture are: Louis J. Stellman, *San Francisco Bulletin*, 5 November 1927; Gene Haley, *San Francisco Chronicle*, Sunday, 6 November 1927; Florence Wieben Lehre, *Oakland Tribune*, 6 November 1927; Jehanne Bietry Salinger, *The Argus*, December 1927; Jehanne Bietry Salinger, *San Francisco Examiner*, 28 January 1928.

5. Salinger, *San Francisco Examiner*, 6 November 1927.

6. The artist's copy of the Beaux Arts Gallery catalogue includes a pencil notation alongside the entry for *Telegraph Hill*: "Hold for exhibition at Mark Hopkins Hotel," presumably sometime shortly after the exhibition closed at the Beaux Arts Gallery on 16 November; see Otis Oldfield papers, Archives of American Art, Smithsonian Institution, microfilm roll 1023, frame 167. United States Senator James D. Phelan of Saratoga, who was an enthusiastic collector of the work of San Francisco artists, purchased the painting, as was announced by Jehanne Bietry Salinger in her column in the *San Francisco Examiner*, 13 February 1928. One might assume that the painting remained on public view at the Mark Hopkins for some significant period of time prior to that acquisition.

7. "Rinaldo Cuneo," *California Art Research*, vol. 11, no. 3, 69.

8. Robert W. Wilson, *San Francisco Bulletin*, January 1928, quoted in *California Art Research*, vol. 11, no. 3, 82.

9. Aline Kistler, "Fine Work of California Artists Shown," *San Francisco Chronicle*, 22 September 1929.

10. Aline Kistler, "Rinaldo Cuneo Paintings on Exhibition," *San Francisco Chronicle*, 23 February 1930.

11. Jehanne Bietry Salinger, (Review, Beaux Arts Gallery Group Show), *San Francisco Examiner*, 22 September 1929.

12. Diego Rivera, *Portrait of America* (New York: Civici Friede, Publishers, 1934), 12.

13. Rivera, *Portrait*, 14.

14. Elise Stern Haas, "The Appreciation of Quality," oral history conducted by Harriet Nathan, 1972, Regional Oral History Office, The Bancroft Library, University of California, Berkeley, typescript, 145-146. I wish to thank Derrick Cartwright for bringing the Stern mural to my attention.

15. Haas, "Appreciation," 146. Both the artist and his patron showed great foresight in conceiving of the fresco as a portable work. The plaster support is mounted on a metal frame separate from the actual wall. After Mrs. Stern's death in 1956, the mural was moved to the central stairhall of the women's dormitory she estab-lished at the University of California, Berkeley. For detailed discussion of the project see *Diego Rivera: A Retrospective*, exh. cat. (Detroit, New York, and London: Detroit Institute of Arts and W. W. Norton and Co., 1986), 281; and Laurance P. Hurlburt, *The Mexican Muralists in the United States* (Albuquerque: University of New Mexico Press, 1989), 109-113.

16. Haas, "Appreciation," 146-147.

17. Glenn Anthony Wessels, "Education of an Artist," oral history conducted by Suzanne B. Riess, 1967, Regional Oral History Office, The Bancroft Library, University of California, Berkeley, typescript, 160-161.

18. Wessels, "Education," 141.

19. Wessels, "Education," 145. The deep impression made by the Bay Area landscape manifested itself decades later in Hofmann's *California: Land of Bliss and Wonder*, of 1960 (private collection), painted as a tribute to Worth Ryder. Hofmann wrote to Erle Loran of his conception: "The original idea for the proposed memorial painting for Worth Ryder was as follows: The picture should symbolize California—there should be no figurative reference to any specific places in California but the work should be carried by a personal pictorial idea of mine about California. . . . the large flat colourplane serve through their plastic relation to the entire picture area as pillars to create the immensity of California as colourful saturated space. In the same time they symbolize through the colour that brought them into existence a feeling of luminous fertility and voluminous saturation. The picture is intended to suggest physical and spiritual Health as I have experienced it through my staying in California with the Art department of the University in Berkeley in the summer of 1931 and 1932 [*sic*: actually 1930 and 1931]. This event was initiated by Worth Ryder."; Hans Hofmann to Erle Loran, 7 November 1960, Hofmann Archive, The Bancroft Library, University of California, Berkeley.

20. The printed flyer announcing the special landscape course at Berkeley, held 11 August-30 September, noted that it would be "similar to his Summer Landscape School in Europe." The class was offered "to meet the desire of many artists and students whom it has been impossible to accommodate in the University classes" and was open to members of the general public as well as to Berkeley students; see course flyer in John Haley papers, Archives of American Art, Smithsonian Institution, microfilm roll 1355, frame 1217.

21. Christina Lillian, "From the Notebook of Christina Lillia – The Classes of Hans Hofmann, 1930-1931," manuscript, the Hofmann Archive, The Bancroft Library, University of California, Berkeley, 1.

22. Wessels, "Education," 145.

23. San Francisco, Palace of the Legion of Honor, *Hans Hofmann*, August 1931; and Berkeley, University of California, Haviland Hall, *Hans Hofmann*, 5-22 August 1931. The catalogues carry the same introductory note by Worth Ryder and statement by the artist, the latter dated July 1931.

24. The correspondence is in the Hans Hofmann exhibition file, 1931, Museums archive, The Fine Arts Museums of San Francisco.

25. Wessels, "Education," 163.

26. Critic Alfred Frankenstein coined the term in a review of the second annual exhibition of works on paper sponsored by the San Francisco Art Association and held at the San Francisco Museum of Art in November 1937; see Alfred Frankenstein, "Schools of Watercolor," *San Francisco Chronicle*, 7 November 1937.

27. Erle Loran, interview conducted by Herschel Chipp, Berkeley, California, 18 June 1981, California Oral History Project, Archives of American Art, Smithsonian Institution, typescript, 73.

28. The related gouache was in the collection of the artist in 1993.

I am grateful to Professor Loran for providing me access to works in his studio. I am also indebted to Elisabeth Cornu for her assistance with locating Professor Loran's early paintings. For information on the career of John Haley see Gregory Ghent, "John Haley, Artist and Teacher, 1905-1991," in *John Haley: A Retrospective*, exh. cat. (Richmond, Calif.: Richmond Art Center, 1993), 11-25; and the scrapbook compiled by the artist's widow, Monica Haley, a photocopy of which is in the American Art departmental files, The Fine Arts Museum of San Francisco, a gift of Mrs. Haley. I wish to acknowledge the generous assistance of Mrs. Haley and Gregory Ghent in my researches.

29. *San Francisco Chronicle*, 14 March 1928, quoted in "Chiura Obata," *California Art Research*, vol. 20, pt. 2, no.5, 144. Additional biographical material and a full discussion of the artist's technique can be found in essays by Janice T. Driesbach and Susan Landauer in *Obata's Yosemite* (Yosemite National Park, Calif.: Yosemite Association, 1993). Susan Landauer has linked Obata's intuitive approach to landscape painting and affinity for abstract design to his association as a young artist with the Japanese *nihonga* movement, which decried Western realism, and to the traditions of Zen painting: "Literal transcription was an alien concept in Japan, as it was to the European modernism embraced by many *nihonga* artists. . . . He [Obata] liked to relate to his classes a story he had heard in Japan of a blind man who could paint with unsurpassed feeling and imagination. Obata espoused a fundamental ideal of Zen Buddhist painting known as *kiin-seido*, meaning 'living moment,' the immediate, intuitive expression of the subject's essential nature. *Kiin-seido*, much like the German expressionist tenet of Einführung (empathy), requires a close identification with the thing depicted. Before attempting to paint natural subjects, the Zen artist typically spent many hours in solitude clearing his mind and studying the minute particulars of nature's forms. Only after lengthy preparation, in some cases lasting a lifetime, could the artist hope to achieve an intuitive understanding of the 'life movement' or 'spirit harmony' at the essence of all living things." (Susan Landauer, "Obata of the Thousand Bays," in *Obata's Yosemite*, 28-30.)

30. *California Art Research*, vol. 20, pt. 2, no. 5, 124.

31. *San Francisco Chronicle*, 18 March 1928, quoted *California Art Research*, vol. 20, pt. 2, no. 5, 137-138.

32. I wish to thank my colleague Nancy Boas for bringing these works to my attention and the artist's granddaughter, Kimi Kodani Hill, for sharing information about them. Obata's comment appeared as a caption accompanying an illustration in the Topaz encampment newspaper, which was transcribed for me by Ms. Kodani Hill.

33. Oakland, Calif., Oakland Art Gallery, *The Blue Four: Feininger, Jawlensky, Kandinsky, Paul Klee,* intro. by William Clapp, 2-31 May 1926. The 1931 exhibition at the California Palace of the Legion of Honor is documented in Diego Rivera, "Diego Rivera Introduces Blue Four," *San Francisco Examiner,* Sunday, 19 April 1931; according to the newspaper account, the exhibition, which ran through 17 May, was "held under his [Diego Rivera's] auspices as well as those of Mme. Galka E. Scheyer."

34. Alfred Neumeyer had come to Mills College from his native Germany in 1935, and his interest in and knowledge of contemporary German art was deep. During Feininger's tenure at Mills, Neumeyer mounted two exhibitions, one held June-July 1936, Feininger's first retrospective exhibition in the United States (which was also seen at the San Francisco Museum of Art), and another held July-August 1937. I am grateful to Dr. Katherine B. Crum, Director, Mills College Art Gallery, for sharing Gallery scrapbooks and exhibition files with me. Feininger's experience at Mills is detailed in Hans Hess, *Lyonel Feininger* (New York: Harry N. Abrams, Inc., 1961), 134-135 and 139-140.

35. The exhibition of Feininger's recent watercolors that was held in 1940 at the San Francisco Museum of Art and, subsequently, at the Mills College Library included five Bay Area scenes, four entitled *San Francisco* and one called *On the Campus at Mills College*; see shipping receipt in exhibition file, Mills College Art Gallery. Feininger wrote to his Mills College friends, Professor Gus Breuer and his wife, Professor Alice Erskine, of his return to painting in 1938 after he had settled in Connecticut: "I started painting at the end of December, after purchasing an easel which takes up all the remaining space in my little bed-and-workingroom, and began to patiently build up once more what I had almost forgotten since I last painted in Germany two years ago – how to paint." Elaborating further, he suggested that his enthusiasm for the Bay Area and his recollections of the place were still strong within him, stating, "I should have been glad to see those 'handsome piles of blonde sand' you write about. No doubt I should have made some notes of them, and by this time have incarnated them into an Aquarell at the very least. Sure, Gus! We'll let you take us to them sometime – the sooner the better!" Finally, he wrote of his struggle to maintain a sense of space, which clearly he felt strongly in the Bay Area: "I twist and turn in my overcrowded rooms, in helpless appeal for S P A C E to keep liberal order in. . . . And with this all, I struggle to retain my artistic sense of wideness and simplicity: So imagine a species of spiritual torture that never lets up." Feininger to Gus Breuer, Falls Village, Connecticut, 12 July 1939, collection of Alice Erskine, Piedmont, California. Even as late as 1951, the painter was still recalling his California experience with affection: "Those first weeks in America, (in California for full measure) were just a wonderful experience for Julia and myself; it seemed like a dream come true, for us to be right there, all the way from Germany. We had such days full of adventure, not only out on the 'skyline' or crossing the Ferry into S-F, but also in the class room with my students whom I dry-nursed into enthusiasm for drawing still life." Feininger to Gus Breuer, 20 January 1951, collection of Alice Erskine. I am deeply grateful to Professor Erskine for sharing with me these and other letters from her close friend Feininger.

36. Alfred Frankenstein, "Impressions of the Feininger Exhibition Installed at Mills," *San Francisco Chronicle*, 28 June 1936.

37. Obata, quoted in *California Art Research*, vol. 20, pt. 2, no. 5, 149.

38. Glenn Wessels, quoted in "San Francisco Artists," *San Francisco Chronicle*, 7 July 1935.

39. Maynard Dixon, "The Iron Road," ca. 1920, typescript, Maynard Dixon papers, Archives of American Art, Smithsonian Institution, microfilm roll 822, frame 1365.

40. John Steinbeck, *The Grapes of Wrath* (New York: The Viking Press, 1939), 207.

41. Steinbeck, *Grapes of Wrath*, 163.

42. David Wyatt, *The Fall into Eden: Landscape and Imagination in California* (Cambridge, England: Cambridge University Press, 1986), 133.

43. "The Art of Maynard Dixon," *San Francisco Chronicle*, 18 August 1935.

44. Maynard Dixon, in an interview with Grant Wallace, who was preparing the artist's biography for *California Art Research*; see Grant Wallace, "Chronology Outline for Maynard Dixon Biography," 1936, typescript, Maynard Dixon papers, Archives of American Art, Smithsonian Institution, microfilm roll 823, frame 324.

45. "The Forgotten Man" was the theme of an address by Franklin Delano Roosevelt that was broadcast by radio on 2 April 1932 during the first presidential campaign.

46. Maynard Dixon, quoted in "Maynard Dixon," *California Art Research*, vol. 8, no. 1, 80.

47. Wallace, "Chronology Outline for Maynard Dixon Biography," frame 333; also *California Art Research*, vol. 8, no. 1, 82.

48. "Dixon Portrays the Waterfront Strike," *The Art Digest* 11, no. 2 (15 October 1936): 14.

49. Stephen C. Pepper, "Propagandizing Art," *San Francisco Art Association Bulletin* 2, no. 11 (9 April 1936): 1. For information on John Langley Howard, see "John Langley Howard," *California Art Research*, vol. 17, no. 4, 54-92; Stacey Moss, *The Howards: First Family of Bay Area Modernism*, exh. cat. (Oakland, Calif.: The Oakland Museum, 1988), 58-62; *John Langley Howard: A Life in Art*, exh. cat. (San Francisco: The Fine Arts Museums of San Francisco, 1991); and Ruth Lilly Westphal and Janet Blake Dominick, eds., *American Scene Painting: California, 1930s and 1940s* (Irvine, Calif.: Westphal Publishing, 1991), 182-187.

50. Details of the picture as described by John Langley Howard in a telephone conversation with the author, 26 August 1994. I am grateful to Mr. Howard for helping me to locate other of his early works and for sharing his recollections about them.

51. In his telephone conversation with the author (26 August 1994), John Langley Howard explained the influence of his brother-in-law and his own involvement with the strike. At Coit Tower, Howard included in his mural *California Industrial Scenes* a group of militant unemployed workers gathering for a May Day demonstration and a miner who conspicuously reads the left-wing newspaper *Western Worker*.

52. Paul S. Taylor and Norman Leon Gold, "San Francisco and the General Strike," *Survey Graphic* 23, no. 9 (September 1934), 405.

53. Ray Strong, interview with Paul J. Karlstrom, Santa Barbara, California, 14 September 1993, Archives of American Art, Smithsonian Institution, draft typescript, 3. I am grateful to Paul J. Karlstrom, West Coast Regional Director, Archives of American Art, for sharing with me his draft typescript of his tape-recorded interview, and I wish to thank Ray Strong for permitting me to quote from it.

54. Strong, interview, 12.

55. Strong, interview, 13

56. For details, I have relied upon the Bridge Plan and Elevation as submitted in the final report of Chief Engineer Joseph B. Strauss, 1937, reproduced in *Golden Gate Bridge*, a brochure of the Golden Gate Bridge District, undated. I am grateful to Robert David of the district office for providing me with this information.

57. Ray Strong, "Painter and Patron, Public and Private," typescript, in miscellaneous correspondence of Walter Heil, Northern California Regional Chairman, Public Works of Art Project, lent by the M. H. de Young Memorial Museum, Archives of American Art, Smithsonian Institution, microfilm roll NDA3, frame 829.

58. For details on the Coit Tower project see Masha Zakheim Jewett, *Coit Tower, San Francisco: Its History and Art* (San Francisco: Volcano Press, 1983); and Gladys Hanson, "Last Stop," *San Francisco Examiner*, *Image* section, 19 September 1993.

59. "San Francisco Artists," *San Francisco Chronicle*, Sunday, 28 April 1935.

60. "Alcatraz" (review of the artist's exhibition at Courvoisier Gallery, San Francisco), unidentified newspaper clipping, 1937, Charles Stafford Duncan papers, collection of Nicole Back.

61. I have relied upon the brief discussion in James D. Hart, *A Companion to California* (New York: Oxford University Press, 1978), 80-81.

62. One is tempted to interpret the begonia symbolically, but the artist's daughter asserts that her father had no interest in such symbolism; I am grateful to Clementina Kun, who shared many insights into her father's art in a telephone conversation, 15 September 1994. Therese Bartholomew of the Asian Art Museum, San Francisco, has noted that the tuberous begonia has no significance in Chinese culture and has pointed out that the child's green cap is an attribute that in fact carries a derogatory connotation in Chinese society; hence, the artist's use of these elements seems to have been for purely formal interest. Ms. Bartholomew shared her reading of the picture in a telephone conversation with the author, 16 September 1994. For information on Moya del Piño see "José Moya del Piño," *California Art Research*, vol. 13, no. 4, 100-140; and "Interview with José Moya del Piño," by Mary Fuller McChesney, undated, typescript, Archives of American Art, Smithsonian Institution, microfilm roll 3949, frames 806-820.

63. *The [San Francisco] News Letter*, 26 December 1936, quoted in *California Art Research*, vol. 13, no. 20, 124.

64. Maynard Dixon, "1934," 1934, typescript, Maynard Dixon papers, Archives of American Art, Smithsonian Institution, microfilm roll 823, frame 44.

65. Paul Carey, quoted in *Edward Hagedorn, 1902-1982*, exh. cat. (San Francisco: Denenberg Fine Arts Gallery, 1992), n.p. I owe special thanks to Mr. Carey for his assistance with my researches on Hagedorn and other painters of this period.

66. *Edward Hagedorn*, n.p.

67. Alfred Frankenstein, "Art," *San Francisco Chronicle*, 26 June 1938.

68. For information on the artist see R. H. Hagen, "Irving Norman – Artist who paints in Anger," *San Francisco Chronicle*, 9 November 1956; "Two S.F. Artists and Their Rebellious Works," *San Francisco Chronicle*, 1 May 1959; Alfred Frankenstein, "Norman's Swarming Humans," *San Francisco [Sunday] Examiner and Chronicle*, 11 November 1971, *World* section, 41; *Irving Norman: San Francisco Art Commission Award of Honor Exhibition*, exh. cat. (San Francisco: Capricorn Asunder Gallery, 1980); Thomas Albright, "Different Views from Two Painters," *San Francisco Chronicle*, 2 October 1980; and Michael S. Bell, "Irving Norman – Social Surrealist," in *Irving Norman: The Human Condition*, exh. cat. (New York: Alternative Museum, 1985), 5-8.

69. Maynard Dixon, "Visionaries," typescript, Maynard Dixon papers, Archives of American Art, Smithsonian Institution, microfilm roll 823, frame 36.

James Weeks, *Looking North, Baker Beach*, 1962
Oil on canvas, 48 x 49 in.
Mrs. Pierre Etcheverry, *cat.no.163*

Nature and Self in Landscape Art of the 1950s and 1960s

Steven A. Nash

When asked by an interviewer in 1959 to what extent his large and dramatic abstractions were linked to the natural environment, Clyfford Still replied, "I paint only myself, not nature."[1] Such devotion to personal vision was basic to the doctrines of abstract expressionism that Still had been so instumental in promoting in San Francisco during the late '40s. It also represented one side of an ongoing artistic and ontological tug-of-war that characterized and helped give special vitality to a particularly fertile period for landscape art in San Francisco during the '50s and '60s: the conflict between abstraction and representation, culture and nature, or internal and external sources. For many of the leading artists, this tension remained a critical issue and, in certain cases, helped compel wide variations of stylistic inquiry.

That nature generally held strong sway, however, is one of the distinguishing signifiers of the region and its art. Formulations of landscape responses were many and varied, from the naturalistic to the poetically metaphorical. In most general terms, it was a Mediterranean tradition of *luxe calme et volupté* that prevailed. Gone was the social realism and urban consciousness of the '30s and '40s, replaced by pastoral ideals that recalled the Society of Six and early-twentieth-century tonalists. It was an art more complex than is often credited, however, and expressions also arose of darker, more deeply psychological strains. Artists such as David Park and Elmer Bischoff may have participated in the common lyrical voice, but they also hinted at trouble in paradise with figures and landscapes conspicuous for the alienation they projected or their exposure of the humbling and mysterious sides of nature.

Starting Over in the 1940s

The story of Bay Area landscape painting of the '50s and '60s actually begins with the abstract expressionist movement that played so vital a role in San Francisco art circles starting in the mid-'40s, a movement now much better understood thanks to the scholarly attention it has recently received.[2] Although abstract expressionism had its first stirrings in San Francisco before Clyfford Still arrived on the scene in 1945, it was Still who provided the main driving force behind its devel-

opment and dissemination. The importance of other influences have become well known; these include Mark Rothko's teaching stints in San Francisco in 1947 and 1949, the expanding knowledge of work being done in New York – especially by Willem de Kooning, Robert Motherwell, and Arshile Gorky – and Douglas MacAgy's reforms of curriculum and procedures at the California School of Fine Arts (now the San Francisco Art Institute). A key aspect of the appeal of the movement as it gained momentum in San Francisco was the invigorating sense it provided of new beginnings by sweeping aside outmoded traditions and pioneering a visual language based on deeply seeded emotions and intuitions released by an aggressively gestural handling of paint. In a shift symbolic of the changing fate of landscape art, Hassel Smith, who continued from 1947 to 1951 to teach a popular course on plein-air painting at CSFA, by 1948 had abandoned his energetic and painterly realist style in favor of the new expressionism.

The movement's cohesiveness ultimately proved fragile, however, due in large measure to the underlying struggle between nature and abstraction that helped set San Francisco's expressionist school apart from New York's. Even from within the movement's most orthodox camp came views of the viability of nature in artistic inspiration opposed to Still's professed onanism. Edward Corbett, Still's friend and colleague at CSFA and an accomplished painter in his own abstract idiom, later spoke of the importance of environment for his work: "My visual imagination is not autonomous. . . . I never have believed that any painter has escaped this kind of effect on his work, that is, of his visual experience."[3] Looking back in 1957 over his own, largely abstract body of work, Richard Diebenkorn confided that "temperamentally, perhaps, I had always been a landscape painter,"[4] while Walt Kuhlman, a student at CSFA in the late '40s, characterized the seductive strength of the area's natural beauty for even a determined nonobjectivist: "Of course, the flavor of the land gets into it, the environment. It has to creep in."[5]

Even Clyfford Still, with his doctrinaire insistence on self and imagination, may have failed to expunge completely the influence of landscape on his abstract vocabulary. And it has been conjectured that luminist effects

fig.1 John Hultberg, *San Francisco Bay*, 1948-49
Oil on canvas, 47½ x 63¾ in.
The Fine Arts Museum of San Francisco,
gift of the Richard Florsheim Art Fund
and the artist, *cat.no.86*

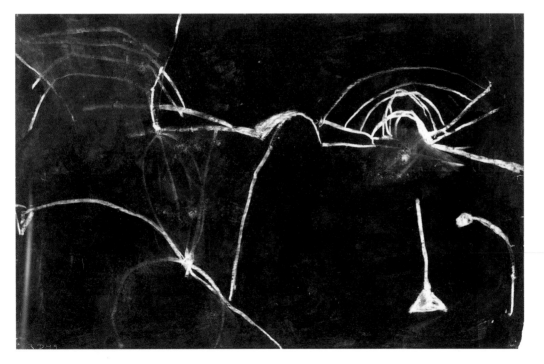

fig.2 Richard Diebenkorn, *Untitled (Sausalito)*, 1949
Gouache and chalk on paper, 18 x 28⅛ in.
Collection of Phyllis Diebenkorn

fig.3 Richard Diebenkorn, *No.3*, 1948
Oil on canvas, 27 x 38 in.
San Francisco Museum of Modern Art,
gift of Charles Ross, *cat.no.37*

in San Francisco's distinctive climate helped generate the billowy, glowing atmospherics that Rothko developed in his art precisely at the time of his teaching visits to CSFA. More concretely verifiable are traces of landscape imagery in the work of San Francisco abstract expressionists such as Lawrence Calcagno, Jack Hultberg, and John Saccaro. Calcagno freely admitted that indelible memories of his boyhood experiences in the natural splendor of the Big Sur region filtered continually through his later art, as, for example, in his *Sun Forest*, 1948.[6] Before leaving to pursue further training in New York in 1949, Hultberg contributed to the local expressionist movement a number of particularly tough and robust works, which did not prevent him from introducing in his *Untitled*, ca.1949,[7] suggestions of plant life, a basket, and a picnic, or from conflating the deep blues and gestural strokes of his *San Francisco Bay* of 1948-49 (fig.1) into a visual poem on the serene beauty of the bay viewed over shoreline piers and tree trunks. Saccaro's *Rock, Branch, and Winter* from 1952[8] applies the prismatic breakup of form and color that became typical of his mature style to a landscape motif, while Corbett's *Untitled* of 1949[9] falls more in the cate-

gory of a visual equivalent to natural experience, suggesting in its Rothko-inspired gray mists the silvery fog that he enjoyed watching as it rolled across the bay toward his Point Richmond house.

Closer readings of other paintings in the orbit of abstract expressionism will undoubtedly yield further evidence of the bifocal approach of some of its key contributors, in which sensitivity to the natural environment helped condition their own gestural and textural styles. Certain artists who more single-mindedly pursued the world of nature soon branched off into what rapidly became known as the Bay Area figurative school. About the same time, Richard Diebenkorn was producing a lengthy series of paintings and drawings that mark a crowning achievement in the integration of landscape and abstraction and invite comparison with similar alliances in the work of certain East Coast artists, including de Kooning and Joan Mitchell.

Diebenkorn's Berkeley Paintings
Diebenkorn's intimation that he had perhaps "always been a landscape painter" is revealing even for his early, seemingly fully abstract work. Following a period of

fig.4 Richard Diebenkorn, *Berkeley No. 53*, 1955
Oil on canvas, 49½ x 47½ in.
Anonymous loan, *cat.no.39*

Edward Hopper-inspired realism during his college years, Diebenkorn opened his work to modernist influences ranging from Matisse and Bonnard to Motherwell and Baziotes. By the time of his enrollment at CSFA in 1946 and his appointment to the faculty the following year, he had developed his own distinctive mode of abstraction. Characterized by a somber palette that shows the preference of San Francisco abstract expressionists for the tough and gritty, his paintings of the period generally feature flattened, interlocked shapes suggesting both surrealist and cubist derivations and a fluid painterliness allied with the strong play of structural or calligraphic line. Diebenkorn refined and expanded the same formal vocabulary through productive years in the MFA program at the University of New Mexico (1950-52) and on the faculty at the University of Illinois at Urbana (1952-53) before returning to the Bay Area in 1953, where he established a home and studio in Berkeley and brought this early line of development to its full consummation.

At no time in this or subsequent phases of his stylistic evolution, however, did a doctrinaire division obtain between the abstract and representational. Elements from one side of Diebenkorn's stylistic range subtly intermixed with and strengthened the other. His early work, for example, owed much to the rugged, darkly expressive compositions of Clyfford Still as well as to such artists as Motherwell, Baziotes, and de Kooning. But while Still was searching for transcendent qualities of the sublime and universal, Diebenkorn's abstractions frequently introduced personal notes drawn from everyday observation and activities. His 1949 drawing called *Untitled (Sausalito)* (fig.2) features the type of spidery, meandering line typical of many drawings and paintings of the period in a pattern that may appear totally free and nonobjective but actually is based on a scene Diebenkorn encountered regularly as he drove past the Golden Gate Bridge northward into Marin County, where he was living: the twin tunnels on Highway 101 just north of the bridge.

It is not surprising that so monumental and beautiful an insertion into the landscape as the Golden Gate Bridge should resonate in the visual memory of even an abstract painter. Diebenkorn said around this time, "Everyday I drive across the Golden Gate Bridge from Sausalito to San Francisco and I'm painting that bridge,"[10] which may seem a mysterious statement until one looks more closely at his work from ca. 1948-49. In a large, untitled ink drawing from around 1948,[11] suspended and trussed forms highly reminiscent of the superstructure of the bridge dominate the image, and echoes of these forms are found in paintings such as *No. 3* from 1948 (fig.3). The geometry of the bridge clearly influenced the linear infrastructure of a number of different works from the period.

Diebenkorn later noted, "When I was working abstractly, everything kept reducing itself to a horizon line."[12] He also pointed out that he tried to eliminate the color blue from his palette because it reminded him of the spatial relationships of sky and landscape, and yet it just "kept popping back,"[13] a further indication of the stronghold that landscape had on his imagination even as he tried to avoid it. Such referencing may have been largely intuitive but became increasingly conscious during Diebenkorn's sojourn in Albuquerque, where experiences such as viewing southwestern topography from the aerial perspective of an airplane window helped inspire more deliberate quotations from nature in his art. He began at this time a long series of works commonly termed abstract landscapes. These are paintings made in the studio that nevertheless have a genius loci quality of the immediate environment although interpreted with the expressive handling of Diebenkorn's abstract-expressionist style, which had become increasingly high keyed and lush in color and more attuned to the richness of natural light. He was well prepared to capitalize on the splendid vistas of the hills from his home and studio in Berkeley.

Diebenkorn's Berkeley series eventually numbered over sixty paintings, ranging in size from 24 x 21 inches to 72 x 64 inches, but generally large in scale and all completed in a twenty-month interval from 1953 to 1955. The extraordinary productivity of this period is signaled in the paintings themselves by the energy and rapt involvement with both nature and paint that they convey. Although Diebenkorn sometimes worked on different paintings simultaneously, and his numbering system for the titles cannot be relied upon for an exact chronological sequence, a stylistic progression is discernible, proceeding generally from simpler, more broadly compartmentalized compositions and a choice of colors reminiscent of the Urbana and Albuquerque groups to more complexly interwoven and textured designs with moist earth colors directly tied to the landscape of San Francisco.

Berkeley No. 44 (page xviii) and *Berkeley No. 53* (fig.4), 1955, are both representative of the later, fully developed phase of this progression. Typical are the steep aerial perspectives, with the landscape rising up to the picture plane in a stacked banding of forms, the high horizon lines, and the slice of blue sky that projects deep into space at the top. Rolling contours suggest hilltops, clumps of vegetation, or the sides of plunging valleys. Masses of gray, frothy fog in certain other pictures envelop parts of the compositions, contrasting with sunstruck blues of water or the greens and golden browns of land. The naturalist impulse behind the paintings can be judged perhaps most clearly from some of the drawings connected with the series, which convey direct, on-the-spot observation. But the spontaneity

fig.5 Jerrold Ballaine, *Abstract Landscape*, 1961
Oil on canvas, 66 x 72 in.
Courtesy Carlson Gallery, Carmel

and free invention that are also basic to the making of the paintings give them a life of their own in which the sensuousness of Diebenkorn's technique and coloration can be fully felt. As Fred Martin, one time associate of Diebenkorn's at CSFA, put it:
The point of the pictures was their wide sweep, the tender balance of warm yet cool, sour yet sweet color, the mind numbing satiety of sensual texture and the sudden violence of a harshly gouged line.[14]
Undisguised by the freedom of handling in these works is their place-specific quality and the sense they convey of the artist's honest pleasure with his lush Arcadian surroundings.

Diebenkorn noted a debt in these works to Chaim Soutine,[15] and acknowledgment must also go to de Kooning for the influence of both his pungent colors and splintery brushwork in which painting and drawing were fully integrated. Although Diebenkorn never included figures in his Berkeley paintings, the presence of the artist himself is always felt through their quality

of personal, enthusiastic response to nature. They seem to follow Max Ernst's advice to artists to "listen to the heartbeats of the earth."[16] Both in form and message, the Berkeley series set a tone for abstract landscape painting that echoes through the work of numerous other Bay Area artists during the '50s and early '60s. Jerrold Ballaine, Sonia Gechtoff, William Morehouse, Walter Snelgrove, Nell Sinton, and Paul Wonner in the early "abstract impressionist" phase of his work are a few of the painters who extended the life of the idiom.[17]

Ballaine's *Abstract Landscape*, 1961 (fig.5), for example, features thick slabs of luscious paint that, in their assertive physicality, nearly muscle out all references to identifiable landscape. Sinton's *Ideas for a Landscape #1*, 1959 (fig.6), is far more lyrical in feeling. Its flowing, calligraphic line recalls Chinese ink-brush painting while with minimal and nearly abstract means it conjures a lovely summertime setting.

Jay DeFeo and Joan Brown responded differently to the legacy of the abstract expressionist landscape.

94

fig.6 Nell Sinton, *Ideas for a Landscape #1*, 1959
Ink and gouache on board, 13¾ x 59¼ in.
Private collection, *cat.no.149*

fig.7 Jay DeFeo, *Mountain No. 2*, 1955
Oil on canvas, 46 x 36 in.
The Fine Arts Museums of San Francisco,
Museum purchase, gift of the 20th-Century Art Council, *cat.no.34*

DeFeo's *Mountain No. 2* from 1955 (fig.7), for example, grapples with more powerful natural forces. While dealing with a recognizable image, her dark colors and rough, gravelly surface invoke the precedent of Clyfford Still. The sensuousness of her thick paint application, however, is a personal trait. Its encrusted surface suggests the flow of lava and heaving movement of geologic processes as well as the sand- and gypsum-loaded pigments with which Louis Siegriest re-created actual earth textures in abstract desert and mountain landscapes a few years later.

Brown's *Things in a Landscape II*, 1959 (fig.8), represents the forceful abstract style in which she worked prior to the emergence in the early '60s of her better-known figurative mode. It was painted while she still attended CSFA (she received her BFA in 1959 and MFA in 1960), where she studied with Elmer Bischoff and Frank Lobdell, and it reveals its roots in Bay Area abstract expressionism both in its challengingly dark palette and thick, muscular brushwork. The unidentifiable but vaguely organic forms in the foreground not only recall some of Lobdell's imagery of prehistoric or metamorphic creatures but also have a slightly whimsical quality that lightens this otherwise mysterious marriage of fantasy and nature.

Refiguring the Landscape

Diebenkorn's Berkeley series provided a means of renewing and redefining abstract expressionism. For David Park and Elmer Bischoff, however, the potential of working abstractly had exhausted itself by the early '50s. Both sought new avenues of approach by turning to historical figurative traditions. Park was the first to make the break with his *Rehearsal*, 1949-50, and *Kids on Bikes*, 1950,[18] works that sent shock waves through the San Francisco art community as critics and fellow artists grappled with the issue of whether they were definitely adventuresome or mindlessly *retardataire*. Bischoff followed suit with such works as *Blues Singer* and *Landscape with Green Trees*, both of 1954,[19] and Diebenkorn also was working figuratively by 1956. Landscapes with and without figures became an important part of these artists' respective repertoires.

By instinct and finally by intellectual decision, David Park was a figure painter. His contribution to abstract expressionism in San Francisco had not been insignificant, but unlike Diebenkorn, he was not able to develop a personal style with which he was fully at ease, nor was he resigned politically to the favoritism and influence that Clyfford Still enjoyed at CSFA as a kind of guru of the movement. In a symbolic act expressing deep frustration, Park piled all the nonobjective paintings from his studio into his car in 1949 and unloaded them on the Berkeley city dump. His earlier work had drawn upon Italian Renaissance art, the neoclassicism of Pablo Picasso, and the modern mural movement. He now turned again to figuration, finding inspiration in the work of Edouard Vuillard and Milton Avery as well as the zany urban scenes from the '40s by Hassel Smith, also maintaining his expressionist use of thick textural paint and raw color.

Park painted a few pure landscapes during this final decade of his career (he died at age 49 in 1960), but they are small, relatively casual productions that recall again some of Hassel Smith's earlier plein-air paintings.[20] They are among only a handful of works by Park that seem to be done directly from nature. Landscape nevertheless played a key role as environmental context for many of his figure scenes and contributed importantly to the overall mood or expressiveness of his work, particularly in its last phases. The urban and social themes that dominated the first years of his return to figuration gave way more and more as the decade progressed to bathers and other figures seen out-of-doors. Intimacy and picturesque narrative were sacrificed in favor of increasingly stark monumentality. At the same time Park's painting style became broader and looser so that near the end of his life the bold handling especially apparent in his landscape backgrounds ironically approached abstract expressionism.

Park's landscape settings rarely have enough topographical specificity to allow identification of a particular locale. One has the sense that they could only have been painted in Northern California because the strength of light and lushness of color and vegetation seem generic to the region. Some of the scenes (e.g., fig.9), however, feature ponds and wooded glens that could derive from Park's boyhood recollections of rural Massachusetts and New Hampshire. That he was beguiled by the Bay Area landscape is shown by one of the earliest known paintings he made in the region, a small oil on hard board executed in 1931 (fig.10), in

which he turned a scene of three boys relaxing à la Picasso's somnolent neoclassical figures into a Mediterraneanlike idyll that clearly recreates the geography of the bay. His work from the '50s, however, is far more generalized in its treatment of nature. His naturalism came not from observation but from memory. Park's landscapes and seacoasts became timeless and placeless as part of his increasingly universalized treatment of the figure. They also contain something of the portentous quality that the poet Robinson Jeffers, for one, saw beneath the Edenic beauty of the California coastlands.

In a work such as his *Riverbank*, 1956 (fig.11), Park reprised a theme that had been popular since Gustave Courbet's studies of nude women bathers. In Park's interpretation, the figures stand in solemn, uncommunicative isolation. Their heavy proportions are made all the more weighty and tactile by the thick strokes with which they are almost sculpturally constructed. Similar latherings of paint in the water and landscape create a dense color-space surrounding the bathers and an equivalence, visual and thematic, between figure and ground and woman and nature. Comparison with André Derain's *Bathers* of 1907 (fig.12) underscores important shared traits, not only in the sculptural modeling but also in the overall sense of humankind, stripped of all appurtenances, sharing in a druidlike, elemental relationship with the natural surroundings. Picasso's primitivized visions of nudes in a landscape from 1908 and 1909 are not far removed.

Park's hulking figures sometimes project a stolid neutrality as if, in Bill Berkson's phrase, they were bred from primordial clay.[21] In other situations they display an all-too-human, melancholic consciousness. Men sometimes stand alone and still at the edge of the sea, gazing outward, numbly self-aware of the loss of which America's western shores and the end of the continent are the paradigm. Trepidation seems to plague some of Park's figures, conveyed by head-bowed immobility or a gesture of self-restraint, where a figure stiffly grips its own arm.[22]

Such intimations provide ample evidence of thoughtful intent or psychological meanings to refute the critical claims against Park and other Bay Area figurative artists that natural description was only a structure on which to hang a coat of abstract expressionist brushwork and color and that their use of the figure was without true necessity. As Dore Ashton then put it, "they do not seem to believe in [the figure's] singular efficacy."[23]

The artists themselves, however, gave considerable testimony to their interest in figure and landscape painting for more than just formal reasons. Park wrote that "even the very fine non-objective canvases seem to me so visually beautiful that I find them insufficiently troublesome, not personal enough."[24] Elmer Bischoff stressed the importance of his paintings as vehicles of

fig.8 Joan Brown, *Things in a Landscape II*, 1959
Oil on canvas, 73½ x 71½ in.
Private collection, courtesy Campbell-Thiebaud Gallery,
San Francisco, *cat.no.17*

fig.9 David Park, *Four Men*, 1958
Oil on canvas, 57 x 92 in.
Collection Whitney Museum of American Art, New York,
purchase, with funds from an anonymous donor, 59.27

fig.10 David Park, *Three Male Bathers*, 1931
Oil on hardboard, 20⅛ x 23⅞ in.
Private collection, gift of Nancy Storm

feeling and the emotional involvement he had for his subjects as "something that exists out in the world that I think is worth dealing with, that I have certain responses to, that I have a certain love for, possibly, and I want to show. . . in a canvas."[25] Bischoff and Diebenkorn both spoke disparagingly of the "hyper" or "supercharged" emotionalism that was a necessary part of abstract expressionism.[26] While they chose a more dispassionate approach, they remained sensitive to the emotional and psychological shadings possible within the figurative and landscape idiom and to the potential of subjective meanings, even if they were ambiguous or not fully articulable. What was identified as an ineffective use of landscape and figure was partly the consequence of formalist criticism's insensitivity to this expressive dimension.

Of all the artists in the figurative movement, Bischoff is the one who most consciously sought to achieve a personal landscape style by aligning himself with traditions of the past, especially those of northern romanticism. The work of Edvard Munch was an important formative influence, as was that of the German expressionists, particularly Emile Nolde. Most impressive for Bischoff were the dramatic aspects of nature, and humanity's interaction with nature, which the northern romantics responded to so poignantly. In his painting entitled *Breakers*, 1963, for example (fig.13), the sea is treated with the same heaving power found in many of Nolde's seascapes and coastal views from Northern Germany. Nolde sought to express explicitly the awesome strength and scale of nature, a message that Bischoff underscored by placing a solitary figure among

massive rocks and crashing waves, a device recalling Caspar David Friedrich's scenes of diminutive figures lost against immense ocean or mountain backdrops. The *Seascape* of 1967[27] again invokes Nolde's example, both in the theme of a small ship menaced by powerful seas and the emphatically thick crusts of paint and glowing red and orange colors. Bischoff sometimes played music by Wagner while painting, and this work has a particularly Wagnerian drama to it. One thinks of Nolde's description of the blustery landscape at Utenwarf as "a place where the heavy storm clouds terrify weaklings."

The nude bather in an expansive or luxuriant landscape was also, of course, a favorite German expressionist theme by which artists stressed the healthiness of outdoor life and the primal harmony between humanity and environment. Bischoff's many bathing scenes carry some of these same meanings,[28] although he often introduces loneliness, solitude, and pointed sexual distance between partners, infusing the natural experience with a sense of angst. The beautiful *Two Figures at the Seashore* of 1957 is an important example (fig.14). In this mysterious encounter of two nudes at ocean's edge, particularities of identity and personality are lost in a generalizing drama in which extremely sensuous color and brushwork yield to an undertow of psychological malaise. One figure turns his back to us while the other's face is obliterated by shadow. Their stances embody tension. A deep sunset glow not so much lights as irradiates the scene, releasing a delicious mix of hot reds, pinks, and purples. Although we cannot know the precise narrative, we are swept up fully in the scene's dark mood.

Bischoff was reluctant to talk about the symbolic side of his work; not all of his landscapes, to be sure, had a psychological edge. He painted numerous views of nature that reveal in their exuberance an honest delight with both process and subject, and many of the smaller works in particular have the vividness of plein-air sketches. Virtually all of these studies, however, were done indoors essentially as inventions (Bischoff confided that he had trouble working directly from nature, with its superabundance of detail),[29] and cannot be tied to specific motifs. Though mixed with generalized references to nature, clearly for Bischoff the psychic and sensuous rewards of pure painting outweighed any concern to describe a particular place. His was a naturalism of emotion, committed to a search for the universal rather than any interest in the merely picturesque.[30] The representational landscapes of Richard Diebenkorn, while admitting references to Bay Area environment and sites, also entered the realm of personal invention.

As Diebenkorn became dissatisfied with the abstract expressionism of his Berkeley series – "I came

fig.11 David Park, *Riverbank*, 1956
Oil on canvas, 59⅝ x 69¹¹⁄₁₆ in.
Williams College Museum of Art,
bequest of Lawrence H. Bloedel,
Class of 1923, 77.9.75, *cat.no.124*

fig.12 André Derain, *Bathers*, 1907
Oil on canvas, 52 x 76¾ in.
The Museum of Modern Art, New York
William S. Paley and Abby Aldrich Rockefeller Funds
©1995, The Museum of Modern Art, New York

fig.13 Elmer Bischoff, *Breakers*, 1963
Oil on canvas, 61 x 70 in.
Archer M. Huntington Art Gallery, The University of Texas at Austin,
gift of Mari and James A. Michener, 1968

to mistrust my desire to explode the picture and super-charge it in some way"[31] – he painted a few small and quite descriptive landscapes as a way of starting over stylistically. These relate views in and around Berkeley and Oakland.[32] This return to the fundamentals of realism soon found expression in a number of intimate still-life paintings from 1955 and 1956 and then in paintings of figures in interiors. Because Diebenkorn had made life drawings from models soon after his return to the Bay Area, this was not, however, as revolutionary a transition as might be assumed.

Like Bischoff, Diebenkorn rarely painted out-of-doors. Landscapes, nevertheless, continued to play an important role in his work, whether as settings for figures, views out of windows, or pure studies of nature. *Seawall* from 1957 (fig.15 and front cover) is an outstanding example of the latter category. Small in scale, it packs into its brusque but lucidly brushed surface a tremendous sense of fresh, immediate outdoor experience, even though it was produced in the studio, as Phyllis Diebenkorn has confirmed. Although simplified into wedged and angled blocks of color, the forms of the painting unmistakably project the essentials of a Northern California coastline view, looking across a verdant hillside that drops steeply to beach and water below. This type of faceted design of vibrant hues and contrasting light and shadow would recur in Diebenkorn's work over the next decade and eventually lead into the Ocean Park series beginning after his move to Santa Monica in 1966.

This painting helped announce a cool, rationalizing order that became increasingly important in Diebenkorn's landscapes. As with Park and Bischoff, however, he was attuned to more than just formal values. Interior scenes with figures quietly looking out at the landscape, for example, play on oppositions of inside versus outside and the domestic and cultural versus the freedom of nature. It should quickly be added that Diebenkorn greatly enjoyed in such works the compositional opportunity of exploring a cool interior light against strong exterior lighting or the angled foreground of interior architecture against rolling organic shapes outside a window, the figure often playing a formal role as a visual stop or transition. But whether it was consciously intended or not, these figures also project quiet reverie as they sit, alone and often with their backs toward us, contemplating a distant view. In the well-known *Girl on a Terrace*, 1956,[33] the woman stands in head-bowed quietude, her arms held tentatively behind her back, an emblem of pensiveness that shifts our own thoughts to the blue and green abstraction of nature beyond. Diebenkorn went out of his way to avoid the anecdotal or sentimental, but he was also highly sensitive to "the effect that a represented human presence had on the mood and flavor of my work."[34]

fig.14 Elmer Bischoff, *Two Figures at the Seashore*, 1957
Oil on canvas, 56 x 56¾ in.
Collection Newport Harbor Art Museum, museum purchase
with additional funds provided by the NEA, *cat.no.11*

fig.15 Richard Diebenkorn, *Seawall*, 1957
Oil on canvas, 20 x 26 in.
Phyllis Diebenkorn, *cat.no.40*

View from the Porch, 1959 (fig.16), eliminates the figure in a more abstract investigation of an angled, manufactured form jutting into the landscape. The porch divides the picture in half horizontally and in quarters vertically, locking into the simplified planes of the surrounding topography to form a grid against which Diebenkorn's heavy brush strokes and vivid if sometimes earthy colors push and pull in an invigorated field of responsive touch. One feels here a definite rising of emotions inspired as much by the subject as the act of painting itself.

The intensity inherent in such a picture, however, became increasingly tamed in succeeding works by the classicizing side of Diebenkorn's style, exemplified by *Cityscape (Landscape No. 2)*, 1963, a San Francisco street scene that would later influence Wayne Thiebaud's cityscapes, and *Recollections of a Visit to Leningrad*, 1965, in which the underlying influence of Matisse during this period rushes to the surface.[35] In these compositions the groundwork had been laid for the Ocean Park series soon to follow. More thoroughly abstracted that his earlier works, and more based on invention than on spontaneous process, these famous paintings nevertheless continued to incorporate responses to the light, atmosphere, and colors of Diebenkorn's new natural surroundings. If the formal side of his work triumphed, it did not eliminate the natural.

Although Diebenkorn, Bischoff, and Park all resisted the notion of a local "school," their combined influence helped foster figurative and landscape painting as primary pursuits in Bay Area art of the '50s and '60s. Numerous other artists developed their own combinations of expressive handling and natural description, although few of them followed the path of urban viewpainting taken by one particularly notable artist-visitor working briefly in the Bay Area. The famous German expressionist Max Beckmann, who spent time in San Francisco while teaching a summer course at Mills College in 1950, made drawings that resulted in the large oil *San Francisco* (fig.17). Carving the scene in harsh black contours with typical aggression, Beckmann translated his view from near the Presidio past the Palace of Fine Arts toward downtown San Francisco into a pulsing matrix of angled forms and colliding movement. For the most part, local landscape painters of the period quite literally turned their backs on Beckmann's urban perspective, concentrating instead on the bucolic with an insistence that speaks on the one hand of escapism from modern society and on the other of an abiding love of nature. James Weeks, Paul Wonner, and William Theophilus Brown are three who contributed importantly to this tradition.

Weeks was the most single-minded realist of the group, working from the late '40s until his move to Los

fig.16 Richard Diebenkorn, *View from the Porch*, 1959
Oil on canvas, 70 x 66 in.
The Harry W. and Mary Margaret Anderson Collection, *cat.no.41*

fig.17 Max Beckmann, *San Francisco*, 1950
Oil on canvas, 40.8 x 56 in.
Hessisches Landesmuseum Darmstadt

Angeles in 1967, in a descriptive style that embraced not just landscapes but figure painting and still lifes as well.[36] In the first category are numerous views out to sea and across the bay from city beaches, sailing scenes against the backdrop of the bridges, and more intimate views of parks and people at leisure out-of-doors. Although his paintings are often large in scale, Weeks worked almost always from sketches made directly from nature.[37]

Looking North, Baker Beach, 1962 (page 88), which shows the view from San Francisco's northern shoreline across the bay to the hills of Marin, typifies Weeks's broad landscape technique. Nature's forms are simplified into masses built up in thick strokes that give even beach vegetation and water a weighty, sculptured heft. Weeks is much less free in his painterly improvisations than, for example, Bischoff or Diebenkorn, but exaggerations of hue often lend the paintings a brilliant, somewhat unnatural light, and his brushwork at its loosest adds an abstract dimension to his naturalism.

In Paul Wonner's slightly earlier landscapes with figures, celebrations of nature merge with personal, biographical content. Wonner had moved from the Bay Area to Davis in 1956 to work as a librarian at the University of California, and in 1957 William Theophilus Brown joined him there. A series of landscapes reflects on experiences shared by Wonner and Brown – swimming trips together to the American River, views from the back of their house, and moments of mutual relaxation.[38] *River Bathers*, 1961 (fig.18), is an especially fine example, showing Wonner's development of a figurative mode that, although influenced by Park and Bischoff, features a distinctively high-keyed palette, an

intense quality of light, and a particularly thick, even frothy, manipulation of paint. As in many works by Park and Bischoff, the figures lack interaction and are portrayed anonymously; indeed, the face of the one looking outward is obscured by an eerie mask of shadow, recalling in expression the memento mori still lifes Wonner produced at about this time.[39] Yet the overall mood is not sinister or strained but conveys instead a diaristic intimacy.

With William Theophilus Brown the personalization of landscape is taken a step further. The work of Edvard Munch and other European symbolist artists provided a strong influence through which Brown filtered his impressions of nature. *River Bathers*, 1968/71 (fig.19), for example, with its portentous mood and stylizations of form, transforms landscape from the particular to the conceptual, diminishing its identity with any regional locale.[40]

The distinctive approaches of Weeks, Wonner, and Brown to the California landscape provide further evidence of the expressive range attained within the Bay Area figurative movement at its height. The work of other artists could also be cited: Roland Petersen's joyous interpretations of figures outdoors, for example, or Nathan Oliveira's invocations of landscapes of an otherworldly sort. By the late '60s, however, the vitality of shared exploration that linked the diverse artists contributing to the figurative movement had subsided. Park was dead, Diebenkorn was painting abstractly again, and Bischoff would soon follow suit. Popularity too often resulted in academic imitation, giving rise to a need for new directions. Nevertheless the movement had yielded one of the most distinctive chapters in the region's art history and a wide range of vivid descriptions of, or reactions to, the natural environment. Much of the work, as we have seen, has a generalized and metaphoric quality not tied to optical fact. It does not just record the landscape but adds a strong personal note, even though it was still the stimulation of the immediate environment that helped prompt these investigations into broader meanings of landscape experience. As Bischoff said of the land around him, he felt "kind of wedded to it." [41]

Expanding the Options

Even at its height, the figurative movement was far from hegemonic. Especially as its influence waned, other stylistic strategies with ramifications for landscape art became more dominant. The independent or even defiant spirit characteristic of Bay Area artists during the '50s manifested itself as these artists' new directions proceeded largely outside of national trends. With increasingly pluralistic approaches, Bay Area landscape art ranged from the glowing, stylized country scenes of Wayne Thiebaud and the funky pictorial ceramics

fig.18 Paul Wonner, *River Bathers*, 1961
Oil on canvas, 50 x 50 in.
Roselyne and Richard Swig, *cat.no.171*

fig.19 William Theophilus Brown, *River Bathers*, 1968/71
Acrylic on canvas, 48 x 72 in.
Collection of Martha and Allen Koplin, Los Angeles, *cat.no.19*

fig.20 Wayne Thiebaud, *Diagonal Ridge*, 1968
Acrylic on canvas, 72 x 72 in.
Private collection, courtesy of the Allan Stone Gallery, New York, *cat.no.152*

of Richard Shaw and Robert Arneson to visionary mindscapes by Peter Saul, Jess, and Bill Martin and the cooler formalist explorations by David Simpson and Sam Richardson.

Wayne Thiebaud has been recognized as one of the dominant landscape painters of the region since the '60s. Best known in this genre for the San Francisco cityscapes that later became such a signature theme, he concentrated in his early landscapes on views of beaches, rivers, and rural hillsides and bluffs, all presented with a deadpan matter-of-factness that linked them to his well-known still lifes as celebrations of the ordinary and all-American. Works from the early '60s have a brushiness combined with strong light and color that show the influence of the Bay Area figurative movement,[42] but gradually he developed a more rationalized approach, parallel to the formalization of his still lifes. *Diagonal Ridge*, 1968 (fig.20), exemplifies this trend.[43]

Depicting in huge scale and simplified, iconic directness the type of dramatic gradient so common to the region, this work also shows Thiebaud's use at the time of a clever stylistic invocation-cum-parody of some of the latest developments in East Coast art, namely, the geometric abstractions of Kenneth Noland and stained compositions of Morris Louis. Thiebaud's intellectual gamesmanship speaks to art-world insiders, but his results appeal on purely visual grounds. Skeins of paint and pastel are laid down in thin veils that run together in controlled "accidents," producing not only nuances of color and light with the feel of earth but also an excitingly independent, luminous quality.

If Thiebaud's art is grounded in the here and now, a countervailing trend toward the fantastic and visionary also arose during the '60s, deriving in part from the surrealism that remained a factor in West Coast painting from the '30s. Although distinct in style, the work of Bill Martin, Jess, and Norman Stiegelmeyer shares a commitment to this otherworldliness that twists the sunfilled visions of their peers into intricately detailed mindscapes. Martin's paintings are filled with a profusion of brilliantly illuminated flora and fauna that idealize nature in a way reminiscent both of the nineteenth-century Pre-Raphaelite Brotherhood and the nature worship so strongly a part of contemporary California pop culture.[44] Stiegelmeyer's surrealism loses all trace of specific locale in his teeming cosmic scenarios.[45]

fig.21 Jess, *If All the World Were Paper and All the Water Sink*, 1962
Oil on canvas, 38 x 56 in.
The Fine Arts Museums of San Francisco, Museum purchase: Roscoe and Margaret Oakes
Income Fund, The Museum Society Auxiliary, Mr. and Mrs. John N. Rosekrans, Jr., Walter H. and
Phyllis J. Shorenstein Foundation Fund, Mrs. Paul L. Wattis, Bobbie and Mike Wilsey, Mr. and
Mrs. Steven MacGregor Read, Mr. and Mrs. Gorham B. Knowles, Mrs. Edward T. Harrison, Mrs.
Nan Tucker McEvoy, Harry and Ellen Parker in honor of Steven Nash, Katharine Doyle Spann,
Mr. and Mrs. William E. Steen, Mr. and Mrs. Leonard E. Kingsley, George Hopper Fitch, Princess
Ranieri di San Faustino, and Mr. and Mrs. Richard Madden, *cat.no.88*

By contrast, Jess's wistful fantasies, while deriving from childhood memories, magic, and literary associations, have a foothold in natural observation. Some of his earliest paintings depict landscape motifs with a romantic painterliness suggestive of Albert Pinkham Ryder, and Jess has spoken of the importance to his art of the spiritual quality of San Francisco light.[46] Further, he stated that "I see landscape, particularly in [my] early work, as a matrix for the imagination,"[47] referring to the flights of mysticism and free association on a landscape theme seen, for example, in *If All the World Were Paper and All the Water Sink*, 1962 (fig.21).

Fantasy mixed with humor figures importantly in the paintings and drawings of William T. Wiley and the ceramic sculpture of Robert Arneson and Richard Shaw, all of whom began to rise to prominence at this time but whose work will be dealt with in a later chapter. Similar traits mark the large and colorful canvases of Peter Saul, where the visionary collides with acerbic social commentary. Saul's *Government of California* from 1969 (fig.22), for example, projects a Boschian vision of the bay bridges entangled with symbols of government, society, and the economy, all presided over by specters

of then governor Ronald Reagan and the saintly "poor and strong." Socio political landscape is served up with a brashness of pop-art drawing and color.

Against the extreme personalization and humor of such excursions into the absurd, the nature abstractions of David Simpson and Sam Richardson appear particularly cerebral. Simpson's *Storm, Stars, and Stripes*, 1960 (fig.23), not unlike Thiebaud's landscapes of 1967-69, nods toward formal trends in East Coast art, in his case the staining techniques of Mark Rothko and Helen Frankenthaler as well as the banded patterns of Kenneth Noland. Simpson's use of such devices, however, is unique in the suggestion of billowy skies over water and the distinctive light of the Pacific.

Similarly, an elegant clarity of light and form characterizes the sculptures of Sam Richardson. Constructed flawlessly out of lacquered fiberglass, Richardson's tabletop landscapes, such as *The Fog Hangs over Six Miles of That Guy's Valley*, 1969 (fig.24), bring high-tech finish to fragments of western topography. The language may be purposefully abstract, but the smooth and undulating forms are unmistakably Californian.

Almost a textbook illustration of the range of

fig.22 Peter Saul, *The Government of California*, 1969
Oil on canvas, 68 x 96 in.
Courtesy Frumkin/Adams Gallery, New York, *cat.no.141*

landscape modes operating at the time, Richardson's sleek visions contrast diametrically with the raw, earthy, slablike constructions in clay that Stephen De Staebler produced in the late '60s and early '70s (fig.25). These organic, ground-hugging sculptures suggest parched mountain foothills and seem almost to be extruded from the tectonic forces of the earth itself. Interestingly, their closest aesthetic equivalents during this period may be the encrusted surfaces of Jay DeFeo's geologic paintings mentioned earlier.

Facing Eden

From the heated improvisations on natural themes by abstract expressionists in the late '40s and early '50s, to the thoughtful explorations of landscape basic to Bay Area figuration, to the profusion of new stylistic approaches experienced during the '60s, the phenomenology of landscape art in the Bay Area over this short twenty-year span was remarkably diverse. Artists working in the region found the call of the landscape muse difficult to resist. In a statement indicating the faith that he and other artists of his generation placed in nature as inspiration, Richard Diebenkorn in 1989 responded to a question about the direction of his work following his move back to Northern California: "The landscape will sometime lead me to something. It usually has."[48]

By the end of the period under consideration, however, certain basic artistic assumptions had changed, partly as a result of broad political and social transitions. Questions of abstraction versus representation, for example, which provided such a lightning rod for debate and divided loyalties, were no longer an issue. The two approaches became coequal options within a broad array of artistic strategies, more or less devoid of the old doctrinal conflicts. It could also be said that the meaning of landscape lost some of its inviolability. A common denominator linking artists during the early years of the period, regardless of individual approach, was the tendency to identify emotionally with nature in a way that can best be termed romantic. Far removed from the social and political anxiety felt so strongly in East Coast urban centers during the cold-war era, artists such as Park, Diebenkorn, and Bischoff found in the purity of nature a centering influence that affected both art and general attitudes of life.

The tradition of lyrical landscape painting that these artists inherited and dramatically expanded survives today. Its preeminence, however, was shouldered aside long ago by newer agendas. In step with what has been described as a societal coming-of-age during the '60s, and perhaps beginning to reflect the pressures on nature represented by pollution, overdevelopment, and misguided public policy, different attitudes surfaced in landscape art. Irony and myth-deflating humor began to exist side by side with cool formal manipulation.

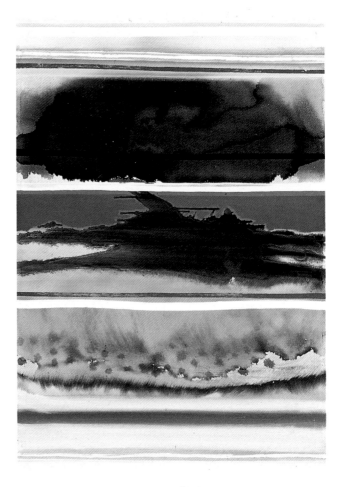

fig.23 David Simpson, *Storm, Stars, and Stripes*, 1960
Oil on canvas, 64 x 45 in.
Collection City and County of San Francisco, San Francisco International Airport, purchased through the Joint Committee of the San Francisco Art Commission and the San Francisco Airports Commission, *cat.no.148*

fig.24 Sam Richardson, *The Fog Hangs over Six Miles
of That Guy's Valley*, 1969
Polyurethane foam, resin, acrylic, and lacquer on wood base,
6¾ x 71 x 6¾ in.; base: 3¾ x 71 x 7 in.
Collection Anderson Gallery, Buffalo, *cat.no.135*

For some artists, the physical fact of landscape could
not be separated from its political associations. Others
found in landscape a source of renewed spirituality,
readily skipping beyond its real-time and real-space
dimensions into their own imagined realities. For each
of these emerging perspectives, stylistic languages
evolved that, for the most part, followed their own
courses without dependence on developments elsewhere, lending credence to the notion of an *école du
pacifique*.

This expanding multiplicity in landscape art has continued until today, affecting not only metaphorical
interpretation but also new ways in which the art is
made. It has not, however, overshadowed the rich
achievement of landscape artists of the '50s and '60s,
which still has the power to quicken our sense of the
magic and meaning of the land itself.

fig.25 Stephen De Staebler, *X with Orange Scar*, 1973
Fired clay, 13 x 92 x 110 in.
Collection of the artist, courtesy Campbell-Thiebaud Gallery,
San Francisco, *cat.no.36*

Notes

1. Quoted in an interview with J. Benjamin Townsend; see *Gallery Notes* (Buffalo, N.Y.: Albright-Knox Art Gallery) 24, no. 2 (Summer 1961): 11.

2. Mary Fuller McChesney's pioneering study of abstract expressionism in San Francisco, *A Period of Exploration: San Francisco, 1945-1950* (Oakland, Calif.: The Oakland Museum, 1973), remains an essential source. The manuscript for this publication, containing additional text, is in the private collection of Mary Fuller McChesney. These sources have recently been supplemented by Susan Landauer's important research, published in part in the exhibition catalogue *The San Francisco School of Abstract Expressionism*, intro. Dore Ashton (Berkeley and Los Angeles: Laguna Art Museum and University of California Press, forthcoming).

3. Quoted by Gerald Nordland in *Edward Corbett*, exh. cat. (College Park, Md.: University of Maryland Art Gallery, 1979), 38, from an interview of Corbett by Mary Fuller McChesney in her *Period of Exploration*, 55.

4. James Schevill, "Richard Diebenkorn," *Frontier* 8, no. 3 (January 1957): 22.

5. McChesney, *Period of Exploration*, 78.

6. McChesney, *Period of Exploration*, 78; illustrated, 41. Calcagno noted to McChesney, 58: "All my roots are there. All my painting comes out of that area, that identification with nature."

7. McChesney, *Period of Exploration*, 55. Frank Lobdell, who still owns this painting, pointed out to the author the motifs of basket and grass and the overall theme of a picnic (interview, May 1993).

8. McChesney, *Period of Exploration*, 62.

9. The Oakland Museum; published in Susan Landauer, *Edward Corbett: A Retrospective*, exh. cat. (Richmond, Calif.: Richmond Art Center, 1990), 42.

10. Recorded by Mary Fuller McChesney as a quote from the painter John Hultberg; manuscript of *Period of Exploration*.

11. Susan Landauer, *Paper Trails: San Francisco Abstract Expressionist Prints, Drawings, and Watercolors*, exh. cat. (Santa Cruz, Calif.: The Art Museum of Santa Cruz County, 1993), fig. 1.

12. Constance Lewallen, "Richard Diebenkorn (1922-1993)," *Overview* (Spring 1993): 1.

13. "The Phillips Collection – Diebenkorn, Woelffer, Mullican: A Discussion," *Artforum* 1, no. 10 (April 1963): 27. See also Schevill, "Diebenkorn," 22, who quotes Diebenkorn: "For years I didn't have the color blue on my palette because it reminded me too much of the spatial qualities in conventional landscapes."

14. Fred Martin, "The Birth of the Thing, or, Some Recent Developments in the Art of the San Francisco Bay Area," manuscript, Fred Martin papers, Archives of American Art, Smithsonian Institution, microfilm roll no. 1129, frame 455.

15. Maurice Tuchman, "Richard Diebenkorn: The Early Years," *Art Journal* 36, no. 3 (Spring 1977): 219.

16. Quoted in Schevill, "Diebenkorn," 22.

17. For several reproductions of abstract landscapes by William Morehouse, see "Reviews and Previews," *ARTNews* 60, no. 2 (April 1961): 18, and *William Morehouse*, exh. brochure, July-August 1960, California Palace of the Legion of Honor, San Francisco. Snelgrove's work generally tends toward the representational side of the abstract/figurative equation. See, for example, his *Land's End* in *A Sense of Place: The Artist and the American Land*, exh. cat. (Joslyn, Neb.: Joslyn Art Museum, 1979), 2, no. 214. An early work in this vein by Paul Wonner entitled *Landscape* (late 1950s) is in the collection of the San Francisco Museum of Modern Art, *San Francisco Museum of Modern Art: The Painting and Sculpture Collection* (New York: Hudson Hills Press, 1985), 392. Wonner indicated to the author (interview, August 1993) that this work is actually based loosely on a view of the drive-in movie theater and screen in El Cerrito, California. See also *Paul Wonner*, exh. brochure, December 1956-January 1957, California School of Fine Arts, San Francisco.

18. Illustrated in Caroline A. Jones, *Bay Area Figurative Art, 1950-1965* (Berkeley: University of California Press, 1990), figs. 2.1 and 2.2.

19. Illustrated in Jones, *Bay Area Figurative Art*, fig. 2.10, and *Elmer Bischoff: Paintings from the Figurative Period, 1954-70*, exh. cat. (San Francisco: John Berggruen Gallery, March-April 1990), 13.

20. Private collections; kindly brought to the author's attention by Nancy Boas.

21. Bill Berkson, "David Park: Facing Eden," *Art in America* 75, no. 10 (October 1987): 199.

22. For examples of formulations of figures in landscape such as these, see the *Red Bather*, in *David Park*, exh. cat. (New York: Whitney Museum of American Art, 1988), 92, and *Nudes by a River*, in Jones, *Bay Area Figurative Art*, fig. 2.13.

23. Dore Ashton, "Art: Elmer Bischoff's Paintings at the Staempfli," *New York Times*, 8 January 1960. A similar critical assessment is echoed in Gay Morris, "Report from San Francisco: Figures by the Bay," *Art in America* 78, no. 11 (November 1990): 92 and 97 (e.g., in discussing Bay Area figuration in general, she contends: "The figure, stripped of its expressive power and made subservient to the manipulation of pigment, became little more than one arbitrary element among many in the painting"). Hilton Kramer had written in 1960 about a show containing works by Diebenkorn, Park, and Bischoff: "The figure here is a shape, without either a psychological or a plastic content. It lacks necessity." In "Month in Review," *Arts* 34, no. 4 (January 1960): 45.

24. Quoted in *Contemporary American Painting*, exh. cat. (Urbana: University of Illinois, 1952), 220.

25. Interviewed by Paul Karlstrom, 1 September 1977, Archives of American Art, Smithsonian Institution, transcript, 46.

26. Bischoff is quoted in Thomas Albright, "Elmer Bischoff: Bay Area Figurative," *Currânt* 1, no. 5 (December 1975-January 1976): 40. Diebenkorn noted, "At one time the common device of using the super-emotional to get 'in gear' with a painting used to serve me for access to painting, too, but I mistrust that now." In Paul Mills, *Contemporary Bay Area Figurative Painting*, exh. cat. (Oakland, Calif.: The Oakland Museum, 1957), 12.

27. Illustrated in Albright, "Bischoff," 41.

28. For example, Bischoff, himself, in discussing his painting entitled *A Woman Bathing*, noted: "The human figure linked with nature, as is the case here, might suggest to some viewers an earlier day of happy accord before the Fall. And I wouldn't object to such a reading." In Suzaan Boettger, "Energy and Light," *California Monthly* 95, no. 5 (May 1985): 16.

29. In a lecture Bischoff delivered on 27 October 1988 at Humboldt State University in Arcata, Calif., he noted: "Some people work beautifully from observation. My wife is a case in point. She can go out and sit in front of a complex scene in nature that would completely overwhelm me [and] would be completely frustrating for me until I took everything back in the studio and reworked it a million times." Recorded on videotape in collection of Adelie Landis Bischoff.

30. Bischoff indicated that his figurative and landscape painting "certainly was not interested in being regional, it was not interested in portraying California for Californians. I think I did want to take on some of the universality that was felt to be the realm of the abstract expressionists' work." Karlstrom, interview, 50.

31. Mills, *Contemporary Bay Area*, 12.

32. E.g., *Chabot Valley*, 1955 (oil on canvas, 19½ x 18¾ in.), illustrated in Gerald Nordland, *Richard Diebenkorn* (New York:

Rizzoli, 1987), 87.

33. Nordland, *Diebenkorn*, 115.

34. From a questionnaire completed by Diebenkorn on 3 April 1973 in preparation for a book; quoted by Nordland, *Diebenkorn*, 88.

35. These two paintings are illustrated in Nordland, *Diebernkorn*, 113 and 138, respectively.

36. Weeks's most concerted period of landscape painting began about 1961-62, but he had done a substantial amount of work in this genre in earlier years. Since he destroyed many paintings from the 1950s, it is difficult to judge the overall role of landscape in his art. He had served, however, as an instructor in landscape painting in 1948 at Marian Hartwell's art school in San Francisco.

37. See Bonny B. Saulnier, *James Weeks*, exh. cat. (Waltham, Mass.: Rose Art Museum, 1978), 15-16, and also for a representative sampling of illustrations of Weeks's landscapes.

38. E.g., Jones, *Bay Area Figurative Art*, fig.4.7. According to Wonner (conversation with the author, August 1993), this is not a beach scene as implied in the title Jones gives, *Untitled (Two Men at the Shore)*. See also *Paul Wonner: Abstract Realist*, exh. cat. (San Francisco: San Francisco Museum of Modern Art, 1981), cat. no. 2.

39. E.g., *Mirror, Skull, Chair*, ca. 1960-62, illustrated in Jones, *Bay Area Figurative Art*, fig. 4.10 (where the prefix "California Land-scape," given to the title, again, according to the artist, is mistaken).

40. This painting is related stylistically and thematically to several others Brown made in the 1960s. Although painted in Los Angeles, it draws heavily upon the artist's memories of life in Davis with Paul Wonner, outings they made to the American River, and swimming in granite pools in the Gold Country. It is a "dream land-scape," the artist has said, unspecific in location but based on his "river experiences" (conversation with the author, July 1994).

41. He said of the importance to him of the Bay Area environment: "I think that I have always felt so conscious of the physical environment, of drawing on that, of being kind of wedded to it, I guess, in a way, that when I've been elsewhere, I've felt a bit like a fish out of water." Karlstrom, interview, 63.

42. E.g., *Hillside*, 1963 (oil on canvas, 16 x 11 in.) in *Wayne Thiebaud Survey, 1947-1976*, exh. cat. (Phoenix, Ariz.: Phoenix Art Museum, 1976), cat. no.35.

43. For similar works, see Karen Tsujimoto, *Wayne Thiebaud*, exh. cat. (San Francisco: San Francisco Museum of Modern Art, 1985), pls. 61- 62.

44. E.g., *The Rock*, 1971, in Thomas Albright, *Art in the San Francisco Bay Area, 1945-1980* (Berkeley: University of California Press, 1985), fig.163.

45. See, for example, his later painting, *Return to the Infinite*, 1977-78, in Albright, *Art in the San Francisco Bay Area*, fig.162.

46. "Well, light evokes a spiritual feeling often . . . much of my light is atmospheric and I suppose quite specific to San Francisco and very conducive to my imagination." Quoted by Michael Auping in *Jess: A Grand Collage, 1951-1993*, exh.cat. (Buffalo, N. Y.: Albright-Knox Art Gallery, 1993), 23.

47. Auping, *Jess*, 23.

48. Julian Machin, "Richard Diebenkorn: A Rare Interview," *San Francisco Chronicle*, 17 November 1992.

Andy Goldsworthy, *Red Earth Splash,*
San Francisco Bay, California, 1994
Unique Cibachrome, 27½ x 26½ in.
Courtesy Haines Gallery, San Francisco, *cat.no.64*

Metaphor, Matter, Canvas, Stage: Conceptual Art 1968 to 1995

Constance Lewallen

The turbulent social and political climate of the 1960s contributed to a new attitude toward the art establishment and the making of art itself. In a spirit of free experimentation artists explored new materials – light, sound, and language – and forms, such as earthworks, body art, performance, site-specific installation, and video, which allowed them to break free of the confines of the commercial gallery and museum structure. Many of these forms eventually came under the rubric *conceptual art*. This, broadly defined, is art in which the idea rather than the object takes precedence. One might not expect a revival of interest in landscape to accompany conceptual art, but, in fact, many conceptual artists turned to the land. Some, seeking a personal, transformative experience, eschewed traditional, representational modes of the past and engaged directly with the land; they made the land- or cityscape the site as well as the subject of their art. Others approached nature from diverse points of view, including the phenomenological, political, cultural, and historical. Today, it can be argued, the most pressing issue artists address in landscape art is the condition of the planet. Having witnessed the disastrous results of decades of environmental disregard, many artists are active in educating the public to the urgent need to care for the ecosphere, either by providing metaphors for thinking about the land or by stimulating practical, remedial solutions to specific environmental problems.

For some artists who came of age in the late '60s, the landscape presented itself as a vast canvas to mark or as material to shape. They went into remote, uninhabited areas, mostly in the West, and used indigenous materials to create massive sculptural works. This approach, known as earth or land art, was spearheaded by Robert Smithson and several artists – Michael Heizer, Walter De Maria, and Dennis Oppenheim – who were raised and educated in the Bay Area.[1] Oppenheim made one of his first earthworks, *Branded Mountain,* in 1969 on a hillside in the East Bay city of San Pablo (fig.1). The artist burned a thirty-five-foot X within a circle into the grass, symbolically claiming ownership of the site by branding it. Few spectators saw the actual earthworks but rather learned of them through secondary material such as drawings, maps, and photographs. Such works redefined the status of the art work as experience and place instead of discrete, salable object.

Not long after the first major earthworks were built, Christo and Jeanne-Claude created *Running Fence, Sonoma and Marin Counties, California,* 1972-76 (fig.2), north of San Francisco. Christo, a Bulgarian-born artist, was already known for spectacular temporary projects such as *Wrapped Coast, Little Bay, One Million Square Feet, Sydney, Australia,* 1969, and *Wrapped Monuments, Milano: Monument to Vittorio Emanuele, Piazza Duomo; Monument to Leonardo da Vinci, Piazza Scala,* 1970. *Running Fence* was an eighteen-foot-high fence of white nylon fabric that extended twenty-four and one-half miles from Cotati in Sonoma County to the Pacific Ocean at Bodega Bay, snaking through the town of Valley Ford and across hills, valleys, and ranches. Whether viewed from close up as a billowing curtain or from a distance as a silvery, undulating line, *Running Fence* intensified one's experience of the contours of the brown, eucalyptus-studded landscape, its barns and corrals, roads, houses, and wooden and barbed-wire fences. It reflected the changing light and weather conditions, at times breathtakingly. *Running Fence* was only up for two weeks but it took Christo and Jeanne-Claude forty-two months of complex negotiations with the local community groups and governmental bodies to gain permission to construct it. The Christos regard the negotiations involved in their projects as crucial to the work as the aesthetic effect of the final result. In their inclusion of vast numbers of people in the process, both as participants and spectators, the Christos differ from the American earth artists who work in isolation, trading the studio for the remote desert. Like earthworks, the Christos' works can't be sold, although the Christos support their projects exclusively through the sale of related documents and drawings.

A great landscape tradition in British art dates from the closely observed views of John Constable and J.M.W. Turner to the works by present-day conceptual artists who continue to evince reverence for the land. But unlike American earth artists, the English conceptualists touch the land lightly or not at all. Hamish Fulton, who, with Richard Long, led the way in the British conceptual landscape movement, simply walks through the

fig.1 Dennis Oppenheim, *Branded Mountain*, 1969
San Pablo, California
Burnt grass, 35 ft.diam.
Courtesy the artist

fig.2 Christo and Jeanne-Claude, *Running Fence, Sonoma
and Marin Counties, California*, 1972-76
18 ft. x 24½ miles
©Christo, 1976

fig.3 David Nash, *Charred Sphere Pyramid Cube in Redwood Stumps* (detail), 1987
Djerassi Resident Artists Program, Woodside, California

countryside and documents his rambles with photographs and text. Second-generation English conceptual landscape artists David Nash and Andy Goldsworthy have made works on and of the land in the Bay Area. Nash, who resides in Blaenau Ffestiniog, a harsh and remote slate-quarrying town in North Wales, makes sculpture from trees. "I see the uniqueness of each single tree . . . as a great emblem of life," he has said.[2] In 1987 Nash spent several weeks at the Djerassi Foundation, an artists' residency program located south of San Francisco on fourteen hundred acres of rolling hills and woods overlooking the Pacific Ocean. There he created two permanent outdoor sculptures from redwood tree trunks (fig.3). Nash manipulated the tree but allowed it to retain its essential character. In an untitled work he made at Djerassi, he carved three roughly geometric shapes from a fallen redwood tree, blackened them by fire, and then set them at the base of three found, burned-out redwood stumps. He then used the charcoal he made from the burned twigs and roots of the tree to make related drawings. As curator Graham Beal pointed out, "Through selective but incisive use of geometry, Nash collaborates with nature to create simple structures that clearly express his respect for wood and his concern for the earth that yields it."[3]

Goldsworthy follows in the tradition of Long and Nash, who was his mentor. He documented with color photographs a series of his ephemeral collaborations with nature at two private Bay Area sculpture parks, the Oliver Ranch and Runnymede Sculpture Farm, where he worked without tools and with materials at hand. Goldsworthy notes that the color red is found in nature "like a vein" throughout the world. It is the "flow of nature" that red represents that fascinates Goldsworthy and has led him to makes works with red leaves, flowers, and earth in Japan ("the spiritual home of red"),[4] Australia, Scotland (where he makes his home), and now in Northern California. *Red Earth Splash, San Francisco Bay, California*, 1994 (page 114), is one of a series of ephemeral works in which the artist throws a fistful of wet soil into the air over a body of water. *Clay Wrapped Boulder*, 1995, is related to the clay-covered rock sculptures Goldsworthy showed for the first time in 1992 at the Haines Gallery in San Francisco. As the clay dried, it shrunk, creating fissures, and pieces fell to the ground, giving the impression that the rock was bursting out of its crust. Here, as in all of his works, Goldsworthy emphasizes process and change, the "life blood of nature."[5] These works not only evoke the beauty and transience of nature but also remind of its fragility.

fig.4 John Roloff, *Metafossil (Metabolism and Mortality)*
Pinus: ponderosa, radiata, balfouriana, 1992
Steel, refractory cement, species-specific pine boughs
50½ x 156 x 29 in.; 72½ x 78 x 32 in.; 66½ x 127 x 33 in.
A view of the work as first installed at Gallery Paule Anglim,
San Francisco, 1992, *cat.no.140*

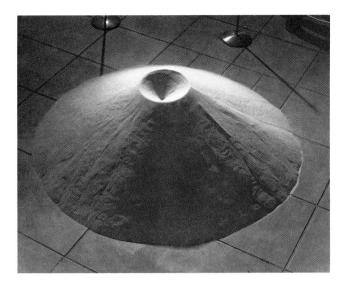

fig.5 Paul Kos, *Sand Piece*, 1971. Site-specific installation at Reese Palley Gallery, San Francisco. A view of one ton of sand before it traveled from the main level of the gallery to the basement through a tiny hole drilled in the floor

fig.6 Paul Kos, *Sand Piece*, 1971. Site-specific installation at Reese Palley Gallery, San Francisco. The resulting mound of sand on the basement floor

Bay Area artist John Roloff also makes sculptures with natural materials that connect them poetically and geologically to particular sites. In *Metafossil (Metabolism and Mortality) Pinus: ponderosa, radiata, balfouriana*, 1992 (fig.4), he covered each of three cement forms, each in the shape of a truncated ship hull, with a single species of pine branches and needles indigenous to the central California region, thus creating a "fossil" of each species. Roloff is associated with the ship motif, which in earlier works acted as "a metaphor for traveling into the distant past, particularly the vast distance of geological time ... [,] a time of primal emotion."[6] The descending ship in *Metafossil* refers both to the human presence in nature and to the process of deposition, i.e., of leaves descending to the ground and then constantly moving farther downward as they are pressed into the earth. The text that accompanies the work is an associative meditation that begins with the scientific species names of the pines, then moves to geography *(Monterey)*, culture *(Ohlone)*, history *(Santa María, Pinta, Niña)*, prehistory *(Mesozoic)*, alchemy *(metallicus)*, poetry *(rilkia)*, and finally to geology and entropy *(fossilis, entropus)*.

The first generation of Bay Area conceptual artists, like their counterparts elsewhere, opposed object making and operated outside the art establishment. This was by both choice and necessity because virtually no institutional support was available for their work. They were certainly aware of earth art and related developments, some of which were taking place in their backyard, but they were not attracted to such large-scale and bold intrusions in and on the land. Bay Area artists, in general, were more at home with private and casual actions and installations than with grand gestures. The Bay Area art scene, relatively small and geographically scattered, has always been characterized by a healthy strain of independence. Critic Barrett Watten put it well when he wrote, "the historical strengths of West Coast Conceptual art [are in its] fusion of philosophical reflection, anarchist wit and romantic nature."[7] Many young conceptual artists, however, clustered around the Museum of Conceptual Art (MOCA) in San Francisco, founded by artist Tom Marioni in 1970 as a "public, social work of art."[8] MOCA, although not a conventional museum, did fulfill museum roles, such as collecting, restoring, exhibiting, and interpreting materials. Its primary function, however, in addition to serving as Marioni's studio, was to provide installation and performance space for local and visiting conceptual artists who, like Marioni, emphasized the process of art making and the fusion of art with the world of everyday experience. Along with MOCA, the city and the surrounding areas became the stages for their activities.

Several of these artists took their inspiration from the land. Paul Kos, a San Francisco Art Institute graduate,

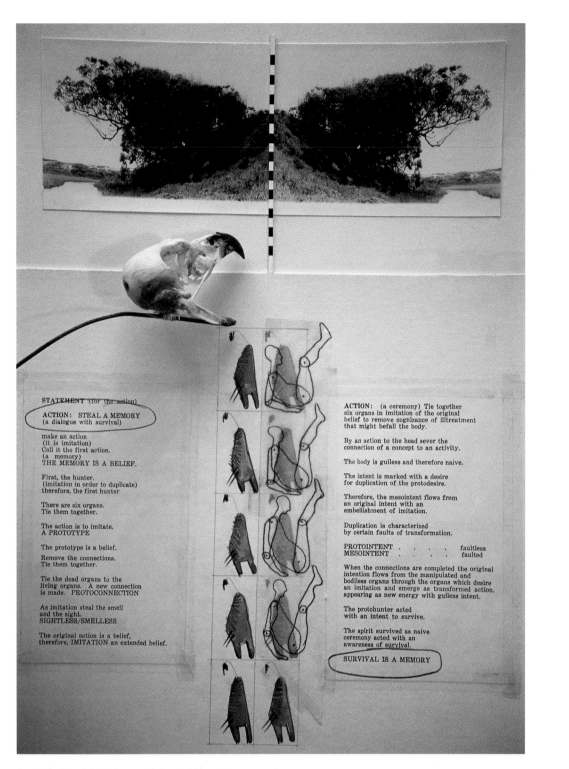

The following text appears within the artwork image:

STATEMENT (for the action)

ACTION: STEAL A MEMORY
(a dialogue with survival)

make an action
(it is imitation)
Call it the first action.
(a memory)
THE MEMORY IS A BELIEF.

First, the hunter.
(imitation in order to duplicate)
therefore, the first hunter

There are six organs.
Tie them together.

The action is to imitate.
A PROTOTYPE

The prototype is a belief.

Remove the connections.
Tie them together.

Tie the dead organs to the
living organs. A new connection
is made. PROTOCONNECTION

As imitation steal the smell
and the sight.
SIGHTLESS/SMELLESS

The original action is a belief,
therefore, IMITATION an extended belief.

ACTION: (a ceremony) Tie together
six organs in imitation of the original
belief to remove cognizance of illtreatment
that might befall the body.

By an action to the head sever the
connection of a concept to an activity.

The body is guiless and therefore naive.

The intent is marked with a desire
for duplication of the protodesire.

Therefore, the mesointent flows from
an original intent with an
embellishment of imitation.

Duplication is characterized
by certain faults of transformation.

PROTOINTENT . . . . . faultless
MESOINTENT . . . . faulted

When the connections are completed the original
intention flows from the manipulated and
bodiless organs through the organs which desire
an imitation and emerge as transformed action,
appearing as new energy with guiless intent.

The protohunter acted
with an intent to survive.

The spirit survived as naive
ceremony acted with an
awareness of survival.

SURVIVAL IS A MEMORY

fig.7 John Woodall, *Dialogue with Survival* (detail), 1974-1976/1995
Mixed media (photographs, text, owl bundle, and skeletal heap),
48 x 36 x 24 in.
Courtesy the artist, *cat.no.172*

fig.8 Mark Thompson, *Immersion*, 1973-76
Stills from 16mm color film, *cat.no.155*

renounced traditional sculpture making in the late '60s. Kos had been making Plexiglas and fiberglass sculptures for patron and collector René di Rosa at di Rosa's Napa Valley vineyard. He credits his experience in the landscape with an epiphanal recognition of the artificiality of what he was doing, the pure folly of wearing a mask and rubber gloves and working with toxic materials in that idyllic landscape. His next two sculptures – colorful towers of sulphur, iodine, and iron salt blocks, using cattle licks purchased from the local feed store – were made for the benefit of the cattle (who eventually licked them away). Kos called the towers *Lot's Wife I* and *II*, 1969, but, unlike that unfortunate biblical woman, he was never tempted to look back to the kind of sculpture he had been doing. Moreover, he realized that his art and his ordinary activities could in fact be coincident and from then on, he said, "wherever I went, whatever I did, whatever interested me, that was where my art was."[9]

During the same period Kos investigated the kinetic properties and beauty of natural phenomena isolated from their normal contexts. These included a series of process sculptures involving the flow of melting ice and site-specific installations such as *Sand Piece*, 1971 (figs.5-6). The latter was a ton of fine white sand on the floor of a San Francisco gallery[10] that, over twelve days, funneled down, hourglass fashion, through a small hole to form a conical mound on the basement floor.

Two other conceptualists, John Woodall and Mark Thompson, sought connections with the animal world. Influenced by German conceptual artist Joseph Beuys, for whom art making was a vehicle for personal and spiritual transcendence, Woodall staged a private "action"[11] in 1976 entitled *Dialogue with Survival* (fig.7). Like Beuys, Woodall admired the Native Americans' harmonious relationship with nature and created situa-

tions in which he believed he could tap into mystical forces. *Dialogue with Survival* was inspired by Native American practices, such as the body-positioning and waiting behavior the California Miwok devised to attract animal prey. At Pescadero Beach, overlooking a salt marsh south of San Francisco, Woodall sat from morning to sundown in a eucalyptus tree where owls nested, waiting for a transformative experience. As he sat, he meditated on animals and humans, on hunter and prey, and on their commonalities and differences. As Woodall later wrote, "The protohunter acted with an intent to survive. The spirit survived as naive ceremony acted with an awareness of survival. Survival is a memory."[12]

Thompson, a student at the University of California, Berkeley, during the early days of MOCA, attended many of MOCA's activities. Thompson had transferred from electrical engineering to the art department where he was influenced by artist and professor Jim Melchert's own experimental work and expansive attitude, and by Berkeley's burgeoning grassroots ecology movement. He was especially drawn to Woodall's work and similarly looked to nature for spiritual growth. From the beginning Thompson has based his work on an ecological model. For over twenty years he has been a beekeeper and, like Kos, conflates his private, personal experiences with his public art making. As Thompson explains:
The honeybee moves lightly in the natural world, drawing from flowers her food. She leaves behind the beginnings of new life in the process of pollination – the seeds for another generation. . . . Similarly, the relationship between the beekeeper and the hive is one of caretaking. The honeybee hive and the beekeeper offer a meaningful, symbiotic guide toward nurturing, interdependence, and balance for the

larger human community. Within the process of caring for honeybees, an essential spiritual relationship is formed with the natural world." [13]

Immersion, 1973-76 (fig.8), was an important early body work for the artist. Thompson did the piece, in private, for film (it took three tries to succeed) on his grandmother's property in Orinda (he has jokingly referred to himself as a "backyard artist").[14] Standing on a wooden tower, he immersed his head in a swarm of bees and remained motionless until, at the end of fifty minutes, all of the bees rested on his head and neck. In the final startling frame of the film, Thompson is covered with a thick helmet of live bees, an unforgettable image suggestive of a hooded hangman, a medieval warrior, and even the transformation from male to female (the hive is almost all female). Thompson shot a segment of the film at two frames a second. When projected at normal speed, the trajectories of the bees appear as linear traces – drawings – of their frenetic movements.

The animal world also played a major part in the work of Bonnie Sherk, who has consistently explored ecological systems as microcosms and laboratories for nurturing interdependent living. Commenting on the alienation of the urban population from nature and demonstrating how to transform and enliven "dead

space," Sherk and Howard Levine installed turf, palm trees, picnic tables, and live cows on elevated freeways and downtown streets of San Francisco, to the bemusement of motorists and pedestrians. The *Portable Park* series was followed in 1971 by *Public Lunch* (fig.9), in which Sherk demonstrated the parallel between human and animal behaviors. Elegantly attired, Sherk ate a catered lunch in an empty cage in the San Francisco Zoo before a large crowd that gathered to watch the lions and tigers in adjacent cages eat their raw meat.

Sherk's interest in animal behavior was intensified after *Public Lunch*. Her subsequent research into animal species and ways they communicate led her to found Crossroads Community/The Farm in 1974 (fig.10). The Farm was one of the country's first alternative art spaces and the only one devoted to the problems of the urban environment. Located on six and three-quarter acres under and adjacent to the intersection of several freeway overpasses in San Francisco, The Farm was the home of domestic animals in The Raw Egg Animal Theater (TREAT) and the site of vegetable and flower gardens. It also included a state preschool and facilities for performance events, dances, and community gatherings. Neighborhood residents as well as the art community were invited to participate in The Farm's interdisciplinary, environmentally oriented activities.

fig.9 Bonnie Sherk, *Public Lunch*, 1971
Performance at the Lion House, the San Francisco Zoo

122

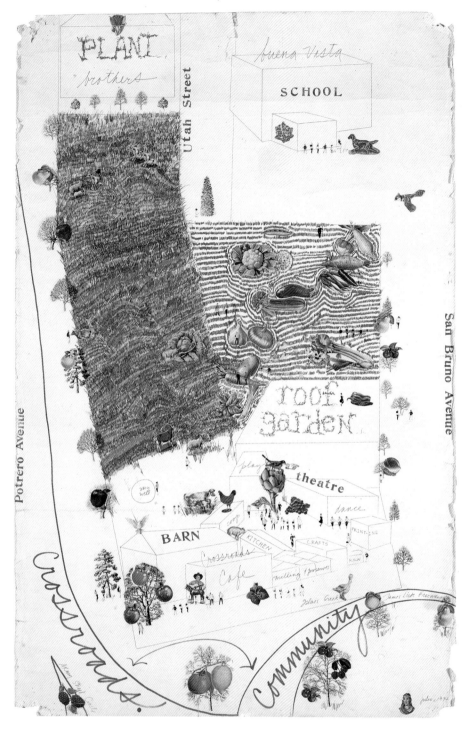

fig.10 Bonnie Sherk
Original Proposal for Crossroads Community (The Farm), 1974
Drawing and collage, 30 x 16 in.
Courtesy the artist, *cat.no.145*

fig.11 Howard Fried, *Long John Servil vs. Long John Silver*, 1972
Gelatin silver print mounted on panel (detail from series)
San Francisco Museum of Modern Art, purchased with the aid
of funds from René di Rosa and the Soap Box Derby Fund, *cat.no.51*

Sherk has expanded ideas first developed in The Farm in her current collaborations with architects, engineers, and others to design large utopian *Life Frames*™ also known as *Living Libraries*® of cultural and ecological diversity. She speaks of these as "public experiential learning laboratories that demonstrate interconnections between systems: biological, cultural, technological."[15] Sherk is a visionary whose work crosses the boundaries between fine art, landscape design, and educational/social/ecological planning. Her ideal future would include a technologically linked network of sustainable, site- and situation-specific communities and environments – branch *Living Libraries*. For Sherk, the term *Living Library* is a metaphor. As she says, *We are all part of A Living Library of diversity – birds, trees, air, people, and all the things we create – art works, computers, buildings, organizations. . . . By being involved in this work we will understand that culture and technology are also a part of nature and our world view and experience will be more whole and complete.*[16]

Howard Fried and Terry Fox were, like Sherk, members of the MOCA inner circle who also chose the city as a site for their activities. Fried, who defined his works of the period as "equivalent structures," created several performances in which he externalized internal conflicts and explored the psychological and physical relationships of people to places. In one action (fig.11), which had the trappings of a French situationist *derive*,[17] Fried, assisted by crutches, wove his way through the gridded streets of San Francisco from sunset to sunrise as the passive yet happy-go-lucky Long John Silver; then, from sunrise to sunset he portrayed the more willful Long John Servil, carrying a fifty-pound sandbag. Fried determined his ricocheting course and the intervals at which he was photographed by a self-generated, complex set of rules cued by architectural features of the city. Silver was less bound by rules – even stopping for beer at one point – while Servil's path was straighter, suggesting his determination to achieve certain goals.

Terry Fox, who moved from Seattle to the Bay Area, traveled and painted in Europe in the late '60s. There he was influenced by Beuys, the theater of Antonin Artaud, and the protoconceptual Fluxus artists, as well as by the May 1968 Paris student riots, an epiphanal event for the young artist. He abandoned painting because "the difference between being involved in direct confrontation and reading about it, say, is . . . the difference between performance and painting to me."[18] Fox put his newfound conviction to work immediately, staging street-theater works in Europe and, soon after, in San Francisco. Fox's theater had no director, no professional actors, no plot, and no script. The stage could be any street corner. In *What Do Blind Men Dream* he arranged for a blind singer-accordionist and her companion, who regularly performed on a downtown San Francisco

fig.12 Mel Henderson, Joe Hawley, and Alf Young, *Oil* (detail), September 1969
Taken at the Richmond Refinery, one of five locations where the artists "wrote"
oil on the San Francisco Bay

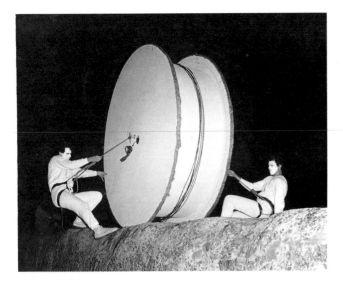

fig.13 Darryl Sapien and Michael Hinton, *Split Man Bisects the Pacific*,
24 September 1974
Performance, Sutro Baths, San Francisco

fig.14 Darryl Sapien, "Murder Scene" from *Crime in the Streets*, 1978
Performance, Adler Alley, San Francisco

street, to appear at the corner of Union and Buchanan
streets from 5:30 P.M. to dusk on a day in April 1969,
announcing the event with posters and postcards.

If Fox was creating small one-act plays, Mel Henderson was staging outdoor theatrical extravaganzas that
usually involved great numbers of participants. Henderson, a sculptor and teacher at San Francisco State University (Bonnie Sherk was one of his students), was
deeply affected by the Vietnam War protests and the
Berkeley Free Speech Movement. He adopted similar
strategies to make political statements in his own work.
His first public event, a collaboration with Joe Hawley
and Alf Young, occurred the evening of 3 June 1969 in
San Francisco. Twenty searchlights were placed the
length of Market Street from the Ferry Building to the
top of Twin Peaks, creating a swath of light that cut
diagonally across the city. Next Henderson and his collaborators warned of the danger of oil spills by writing
"Oil" with urine and marker dye in five different locations in the San Francisco Bay, starting at the Richmond
oil refinery (fig.12). Their more celebratory *Yellow Cabs*
(page xxi) further exemplified the spirit of the times. On
19 November 1969, they asked more than one hundred
friends to take taxis to the same busy San Francisco intersection at Seventeenth, Castro, and Market streets;
from a helicopter and plane they filmed the ensuing
chaos. In addition to causing disruption, the event illustrated the power of each individual. Between 1972 and
1974 Henderson and his collaborators organized several
events in response to the 1971 Attica, New York, prison
riot. Adopting a high-profile style and scale in performance pieces that employed the cityscape as his canvas,
Henderson garnered wide media coverage, enlarging
the public for his work.

Throughout the 1970s urban performance flourished
in San Francisco. Richard Kamler employed (and con-
tinues to engage in) strategies similar to those of Henderson (with whom he has collaborated from time to
time) in installation/events that highlight environmental and social issues, often in relation to the prison system. Linda Montano, Paul Cotton, Lynn Hershman,
and the collaborative group T. R. Uthco (Doug Hall,
Jody Proctor, and Diane Andrews Hall) assumed
fictional personae in urban performances. Darryl
Sapien in the middle and late '70s produced highly theatrical performances such as *Split Man Bisects the Pacific*
(fig.13). The night of 24 September 1974, at the ruins
of the old Sutro Baths where San Francico meets the
Pacific Ocean, Sapien and Michael Hinton rolled an
enormous wood wheel, 8 feet in diameter, along a narrow 150-foot-long-sea wall to an island and back to
shore. The artists balanced the wheel by holding on
to ropes connecting them to either side. Unable to see
over the top of the wheel, they shouted instructions to
each other above the sounds of the surf. Only through

fig.15 Helen Mayer Harrison and Newton Harrison,
*Meditations on the Condition of the Sacramento River,
the Delta, and the Bays of San Francisco* (detail), 1977.
Exhibition held at the San Francisco Art Institute,
sponsored by the Floating Museum, San Francisco

intense concentration and cooperation could they accomplish such a difficult and dangerous feat. In his 1978 *Crime in the Streets* (fig.14), Sapien and his troupe reenacted several murders in North Beach's Adler (now Kerouac) Alley. As a crowd formed, the performers addressed other contemporary urban ills such as police brutality and homelessness. The performance ended on a hopeful note, the resurrected "victims" forming a human bridge across the alley.

In the following decade Survival Research Laboratories (SRL), a still-active group founded by Mark Pauline, also enacted performances that addressed the issue of violence but, reflecting a decidedly nonidealistic postmodern sensibility, offered no such happy endings. SRL builds anthropomorphic machines, often incorporating animal carcasses, and pits the machines against each other in radio- or computer-controlled performances. Many of their performances take place at night in urban vacant lots. Ear shattering and explosive, more cathartic than theatrical, SRL's nihilistic events heighten awareness of the condition of the modern world.

San Francisco street performance was characterized by enormous vitality and variety, ranging from the personal and ritualistic to the political. With the exception of SRL, however, it had more or less run its course by the end of the 1970s. Subsequently, performances were more likely to take place in alternative spaces than in the streets.

Most recent landscape and city-related conceptual work looks for solutions to specific environmental problems. Where early conceptual artists rejected the production-for-sale of elitist objects, second-generation conceptualists took things a step further, expanding the role of art not only into the arena of daily life, but into the political realm as well. In retrospect, we see that Bonnie Sherk pioneered in the activist ecological art movement, along with the San Diego-based collaborative team Helen Mayer Harrison and Newton Harrison. Like Sherk, the Harrisons began by making portable environments, such as *Portable Fish Farm*, 1971, in which they raised shrimp, crabs, and algae in order to demonstrate inexpensive and ecologically sound methods of food production. Since 1977 the Harrisons have widened their concerns, tackling the worldwide problems of large river systems and basins. Two of their water projects relate to the Bay Area: *Meditations on the Condition of the Sacramento River, the Delta, and the Bays of San Francisco*, 1977 (fig.15), and *The Guadalupe Meander: A Refugia for San Jose*, 1983. The Sacramento River work was sponsored by The Floating Museum, a nonprofit organization founded by artist Lynn Hershman, which arranged for the presentation of artwork in appropriate locations outside of established institutions. *Meditations on the Condition of the Sacramento River* was the Harrisons' first bioregional work and typified in

fig.16 Ray Beldner, *Lake Dolores*, from the *Dry Lake Series*, 1994
Wood, dirt, burlap, and steel, 32 x 43 x 3 in.
Courtesy Haines Gallery, San Francisco, and the artist, *cat.no.10*

fig.17 Brian Tripp, *In Memory of Mount Diablo: TU-YOYSH-TAK (TY-YOY-SHIP), Mountain to Mountain, When Straight Line Straightened out Circle* (detail), 1992
Mixed media/assemblage, 120 x 42¼ x 29½ in.
Collection of Robert Benson and Becky Evans, *cat.no.156*

its textural components the work that followed. Its "eighth meditation," for example, read:

IF
The present system of land division and subdivision is
an expression of the paradigm "subdue and have dominion over"
AND
The enactment of that paradigm practiced as exploitation
and consumption independent of long range consequences
is progressively destroying the ecological systems that
comprise the watershed
AND
We depend on both the paradigm and the watershed for our survival
THEN
Contradiction becomes explicit between the socio-
economic practice (divide exploit consume) and
biological imperative
(survival of the species) and the physical laws of the
conservation of energy (transformation of energy from
one form to another incurs a net loss)
THUS
Either we abandon the paradigm or we shall be forced to
abandon the watershed

The error admitted and public interest redefined

The Bay Area water supply has stimulated other local projects, such as *Aqua Pura*, 1992, a permanent educational installation for the San Francisco Water Department by Tim Collins and Reiko Goto, as well as temporary installations by Seattle artist Buster Simpson and Bay Area artist John Wilson White. Simpson's witty, ingenious *Cistern Drums* of 1993 at the Capp Street Project was a prototype for the purification and reuse of rainwater that could be adopted by individuals in the drought-prone Bay Area. White's *San Francisco Water Project*, 1992, an ambitious installation of more than two thousand 35-mm slides, text, and a functioning drinking fountain, traced the city's domestic water distribution system and, as one writer put it, "makes us think before we drink."[19] Ray Beldner's wall reliefs depict the result of uncontrolled water consumption and misuse of natural resources. *Lake Dolores,* 1994 (fig.16), is a miniature replica of a lost San Francisco lake that once drained into Mission Creek. Beldner formed the contour of the lake with steel stripping and then filled the interior with mud taken from the site. He then allowed the mud to dry and fissure just as it has in the lake bed itself.

In 1990 Beldner designed a *faux* nature walk, complete with park-service-like exhibits, which covered nearly eighty acres at Millerton Point in Tomales Bay State Park. At the trailhead visitors picked up a map and brochure admonishing them to stay on the trail

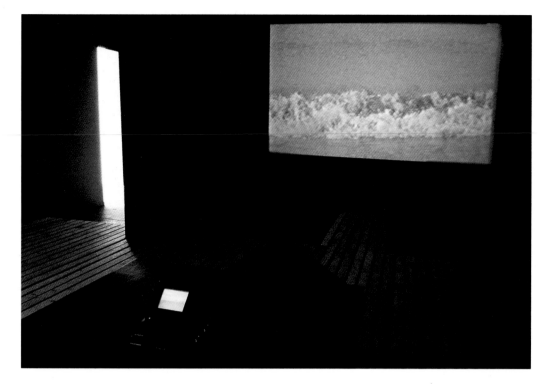

fig.18 Lewis deSoto, *Háypatak, Witness, Kansatsusha*, 1990/95
A view of the original video installation held at the San Francisco Art
Commission Gallery, October through November 1990
Courtesy the artist; Christopher Grimes Gallery, Santa Monica;
and Haines Gallery, San Francisco, *cat.no.35*

fig.19 Douglas Hollis, *A Sound Garden*, 1983
Composed of 23-ft. high "wind-organ" towers at the National
Oceanic and Atmospheric Administration in Seattle, Washington

as well as to abide by a list of other rules. Beneath the humor of the exhibits – a dry birdbath filled with rocks accompanied by synthesized birdcalls, a vista point with the view blocked by two large metal plates – was a serious commentary on nature's role today as a commodity and how our experience of nature is mediated and controlled.

No group has suffered more as a result of land development policies than Native Americans. Native versus non-Native American attitudes toward the land are the subject of Brian Tripp's sculpture, *In Memory of Mount Diablo: TU-YOYSH-TAK (TY-YOY-SHIP), Mountain to Mountain, When Straight Line Straightened out Circle*, 1992 (fig.17), and Lewis deSoto's video installation, *Háypatak, Witness, Kansatsusha*, 1990/95 (fig.18). Tripp succinctly contrasts religious and economic views of the value of the land. His sculpture is composed of a simulated Native American ceremonial fire pit circled by feathers and decorated with a nestlike hoop of painted sticks over which is suspended a plumb bob. The plumb bob hangs from a string threaded over a pulley. The other end of the string holds a merchant's moneybag filled with pennies. Mount Diablo, a powerful Ohlone sacred site, was the peak from which the great 1850s California Land Survey began. Not only was the traditional Native American reliance on circles for many ceremonies at odds with the white man's gridded divisions,[20] but the very concept of individual land ownership and transfer was unknown in the Native American culture. The Mount Diablo survey literally laid the groundwork for the subsequent rampant development that forced Native Americans off their land.

DeSoto's installation, *Háypatak, Witness, Kansatsusha*, titled with the Lake Miwok, English, and Japanese words for "witness," contrasts three cultural modes of consciousness in the context of landscape. Viewers entering deSoto's darkened room confront a wall-sized video projection of the shore at Drake's Bay near San Francisco, where Sir Francis Drake landed in 1579. This date marks the beginning of the cultural clash between English-speaking peoples and the area's indigenous inhabitants. Jerky, chaotic, slowed-down views pan the bay accompanied by electronically altered sounds of the ocean, symbolizing Drake's colonial view of the land as alien and frightening, something to be conquered (manifested by the assignment of men's names to places). The colonial attitude of land domination is borne out by the occasional overlays of barely legible textual fragments from Drake's journal, beginning with "Ever since almighty God commanded Adam to subdue the earth. . . ." Close-up shots of flora and the water's edge, which bring the viewer into the landscape, represent the Native American's affinity with the natural world. Acknowledging the arrival of Buddhism on the West Coast with large groups of Asian immigrants

during the nineteenth and twentieth centuries, deSoto suggests the Asian view of nature in the third segment of the tape in which gently moving clouds symbolize thoughts passing through the mind in a meditative state. The gentle ringing of a Tibetan bell is heard in the background.

As one walks along a strip of the slatted wood flooring extending like a jetty toward the video projection, one's shadow becomes part of the image – "Thus spectatorship becomes a mode of participation instead of the detached state that is asserted by most Western image-making traditions."[21] A tiny video monitor on a pedestal in the middle of the room portrays the back of the artist as he looks out at the water. Texts by Julian Lang, Native American artist, writer, and historian, and religious scholar Patrick Mahaffey accompany the installation.

In deSoto's hands, video installation is a powerful medium that expands time and space so that viewers participate in a world of the artist's devising. DeSoto exploits the interactive characteristics of the form "to exchange given perceptions about reality and relate to other possibilities of human cognition."[22]

Several artists respond to the Bay Area's distinctive geography, geology, and climate. Bill Fontana is among the small group of artists whose work is entirely defined by sonic installations. Fontana's sound sculptures are sophisticated investigations into the way we perceive sounds. His site-specific installations relocate ambient sounds from the urban or natural environment to urban public spaces, thereby bringing new awareness of the aural landscape. In 1981 he created a live acoustic portrait of San Francisco Bay using its distinctive foghorns on the Golden Gate Bridge as a point of reference. Fontana installed microphones around the Bay that simultaneously transmitted to loudspeakers mounted on a pier at Fort Mason. As each of the eight microphone locations picked up the sounds of the foghorns from its own unique perspective, listeners at the pier heard a collage of sounds, including the ambient sounds of the harbor. Sound delays created by the varying distances of the microphones from the bridge added to what Fontana called a cubist sound map. For the fiftieth anniversary of the Golden Gate Bridge in 1987 he created a duet of sounds between the bridge and the Farallon Islands National Wildlife Refuge, transmitting sounds from each to a speaker mounted on the San Francisco Museum of Modern Art.

The seismic conditions of the Bay Area inspired Terry Fox's 1987 Capp Street Project installation, *Instrument to Be Played by the Movement of the Earth*. Each of the constructions that composed the installation – a tower of glasses and glass plates, a lead weight suspended against a thin glass disk – would have produced sound in the event of a tremor. Douglas Hollis, Peter Richards, and Ned Kahn also use scientific principles in the creation

fig.20 Peter Richards and George Gonzalez, *Wave Organ*, 1986
San Francisco Marina Yacht Harbor, related to *cat.no.134*

fig.21 Tim Collins, *Offshore Residence*, 6 October 1988 to 15 March 1989
Wood with stainless steel sheeting, 12 x 12 x 16 ft. View of installation
thirty feet offshore from the Embarcadero, San Francisco

of works. Pushing the boundaries of aesthetic experience, their works heighten perceptual awareness of natural phenomena, particularly water, wind, and fog, all elements in ample supply in the Bay Area. In the '70s Hollis became associated with acoustic structures such as wind harps and organs that are activated by and change with the movement of air. The grove of tall, slender wind organs Hollis made especially for the 1995 exhibition *Facing Eden: 100 Years of Landscape Art in the Bay Area,* formed a canopy of sound spanning the sidewalk in front of the M.H. de Young Memorial Museum in San Francisco. Atop the sixteen-foot-high masts are aluminum wind-organ pipes of varying lengths that turn air currents into sound, like those of the artist's *Sound Garden,* 1983 (fig.19), at the National Oceanic and Atmospheric Administration in Seattle. The tone and intensity of the sound reflects the differing lengths of the pipes and the velocity of the wind. Patricia Fuller described *Sound Garden* as "a place where the physical experiences of sound and space seem to merge . . . [;] soft breezes play sound like long breaths, whereas strong winds produced a sound like boat whistles in the fog."[23] *Zephyr,* Hollis's sound grove, provokes sensory awareness of an aspect of the landscape normally taken for granted.

Peter Richards, who directs the lively artist-in-residence program at the Exploratorium, San Francisco's innovative, hands-on "museum of science, art, and human perception,"[24] also makes environmentally sensitive works. His 1986 *Wave Organ* (with George Gonzalez) is a wave-activated sound sculpture permanently sited at San Francisco's Marina Yacht Harbor (fig.20). How people use the instrument and what sort of music it makes depend on "the interrelationships between weather, tide cycles, moon phases, and seasonal changes."[25] Ned Kahn, also associated with the Exploratorium, makes sculptures and installations using such phenomena as wind and fog.

The environmentally responsive nature of their work led to many public commissions for Fontana, Hollis, Richards, and Kahn. Over the past two decades, public art changed radically in form and intent as it embraced and expanded conceptual art's insistence on site-specificity. *Site-specific* has grown to mean not only sensitivity to the physical characteristics of a particular place, but also to its cultural, political, social, and environmental conditions.

This enlightened approach to art making was fostered by the Headlands Center for the Arts under the leadership of Jennifer Dowley, former executive director. Local and international artists come to the Headlands, located just across the Golden Gate Bridge from San Francisco in the Marin Headlands coastal wilderness, to live and work in the former military barracks that house the center. These artists do not leave behind permanent works. Rather, they use the center as a laboratory for realizing environmentally sensitive and collaborative temporary projects such as Gyongy Laky's three large tape grids on the land that brought attention to its undulating topography, 1984; Veronique Guillaud's performance-procession to the sea, 1991; Mark Thompson and dancer Joanna Haigood's performance, *The Keeping of Bees is Like the Directing of Sunshine,* 1988; Ann Chamberlain's mirroring of the surrounding landscape in *You Are Here,* 1990; and several butterfly habitat pieces by Reiko Goto that culminated in *Cho-en,* her permanent butterfly garden in San Francisco's Yerba Buena Gardens, 1993.

For the past decade public art has been an increasingly present fact of life in the Bay Area. Public projects have included Candlestick Point Park, conceived and guided by artist and San Francisco State University professor Leonard Hunter, which included sculptures by David Ireland, John Roloff, and others; Capp Street Project's off-site series, notably Tim Collins's light-reflective *Offshore Residence* that for several months in 1988 and 1989 glistened in the bay off the Embarcadero (fig.21), and William Maxwell's water-pattern sculpture, *Pandora,* 1988-89, in San Francisco's Palace of Fine Arts lagoon. Public Art Works of Marin, Oakland's Public Art Program, and the San Francisco Art Commission have also sponsored many temporary and permanent works in the area, including Hung Liu's *Map No. 33,* 1991-92, for San Francisco's Moscone Convention Center. *Map No. 33* refers to the historical landscape, incorporating a drawing of the first map of the city of 1839 when it was called Yerba Buena, along with a sampling of objects such as ale bottles, spoons, and cups that belonged to several generations of San Franciscans of varied ethnic backgrounds, unearthed during the construction of the convention center. Liu, herself an immigrant from mainland China, also included as part of the work depictions of Native American artifacts found at the site.

Similarly, David Ireland and Lowell Darling have delved into the history of the Bay Area. Ireland conducted a domestic restoration project that began with his 1975 purchase and subsequent renovation of a typical Victorian worker's house of 1886 in San Francisco's Mission district. Although the artist did not at the start view the project as an artwork, he began to see that what he was doing – making decisions, choosing processes, and working with materials – involved the same kinds of choices and actions that had gone into his painting (and, for that matter, the carpentry he did for a living). Ireland literally peeled away the layers of history of his house as he removed wallpaper, refinished floors, and scraped paint from the walls, preserving under a polyurethane finish every crack and mark, paring down the surfaces of his house to their original

fig.22 In the *Eva Withrow Project*, 1995, the artist Lowell Darling leads an
"art historical" investigation of Withrow and this rediscovered painting,
the focus of the multi-media performance and video installation for *cat.no.29*

fig.23 Mary Lucier, *Asylum (A Romance)*, 1986
Mixed-media installation with video, single-frame
detail from videotape

finishes.[26] Tony Labat, then a student at the San Francisco Art Institute, went to the house almost daily during the renovation and created several video works that show Ireland working on the house, inside and out.

Ireland bought the house from its third owner, a Swiss accordion maker named Greub (traces of his business sign remain painted on the front window). Mr. Greub saved everything: every broom he had ever used was stored in a closet, every rubber band from the daily newspaper was stashed in a drawer. Ireland recycled the objects he found as well as the materials he removed, re-forming them into sculptures. In what could be called a reverse landscape piece, Ireland covered one of his parlor windows with copper sheeting after having described the view on an audiotape. The cassette now sits on a table in front of the window as a substitute for the real thing – a wry denial of traditional landscape painting as a window on the world.

Although it was in deplorable condition, the painting Lowell Darling found and purchased for sixty dollars at the Alameda Flea Market in 1992 aroused his curiosity. The painting portrays an interior with a large, curved window that looks out to the San Francisco Bay, Alcatraz Island, and the hills of Marin County. The tops of some of the fanciful temporary structures that were built for the Panama Pacific International Exposition of 1915 are seen above the trees. The pentimento of a seated woman, made more apparent by recent cleaning of the painting, adds mystery to the scene. The painting is signed "Withrow" and, with some research, Darling learned that Evelyn (Eva) Almond Withrow (1858-1928) was a noted San Francisco artist who is represented in the collection of the de Young Museum by a portrait, *Miss Keith Wakeman*, and who also participated in exhibitions at the museum in 1915 and 1916 (when it was known as the Memorial Museum). Darling became obsessed with Withrow ("It feels like romance," he confessed in a letter). She had painted over sixty portraits of the local gentry and European nobility, as well as many landscapes, and for several years lived in Europe where she "fraternized with the highest exponents of art in Paris and London."[27] Why had this prominent woman, "an artist of international repute," according to her obituary in the *San Francisco Examiner* of 17 June 1928, fallen into complete obscurity? Through his documentary research Darling weaves Withrow's story with many colorful figures and occurrences in San Francisco history, forming a fascinating and amusing story of his rediscovery of Withrow. The painting itself, a historical "recovery"(fig.22); a videotape relating Darling's investigative adventure; and from time to time Darling in person in the gallery, continuing his research, constituted the installation for the exhibition *Facing Eden*.

When portable, affordable video equipment became available in the late '60s, many artists turned their cameras toward the streets and the landscape as a way of reinvigorating the art of representation in a medium analogous to but more flexible than film. In Tom Marioni's two videotapes, *Studio 1979* and *San Francisco*, 1984, he portrays San Francisco as a romantic city obsessed with its own past and on the cutting edge of cultural if not artistic innovation. In *Studio 1979* the artist looks out of his studio window in a building now adjacent to the new San Francisco Museum of Modern Art. He thinks of the window as his "easel," of the traffic as his "river." *San Francisco*, a nostalgia piece, begins with a drive down Highway 280 and includes an earlier video clip of an evening at Breen's, the defunct newspapermen's bar where for many years Marioni held gatherings every Wednesday, a continuing life/artwork he calls *Cafe Society*.

Chip Lord is also drawn to the light, space, and relative ease of life in San Francisco, factors that prevented him from abandoning it for the more professionally, advantageous New York. In his video *Bi-Coastal*, 1981, shot in the crisp style of a television commercial, Lord alternately stands before San Francisco's emblematic Transamerica Pyramid and Coit Tower and New York's World Trade Center towers as he describes his ambivalence.

New York artist Mary Lucier recorded her impressions of the Bay Area in her 1986 videotape *Asylum (A Romance)* (fig.23).[28] Lucier shifts between industrial sites – smokestacks and oil refineries in the East Bay, giant pistons in a factory – and morbid bucolic images, such as the Mission Dolores Cemetery and cows peacefully grazing in front of nuclear power stacks. A beautiful but menacing image of a nuclear reactor set against a dark sky closes the video. As critic Eleanor Heartney wrote: Asylum (A Romance), *as its name suggests, acknowledges modern man's longing to escape from the complexities of contemporary life. At the same time it reminds us, as conservatory ruins and the continuous images on the video make clear, that the escape route back to nature has, for all practical purposes, become closed. The machine has overtaken the garden and left only a trail of picturesque debris in its wake.*[29]

The nature/culture dichotomy is also addressed by Paula Levine in her charming video, *Coyote Cow*, 1994, in which cows learn not to respond to a "moo"-sound toy. Joanne Kelly suggests that there exists a special, spiritual kinship between women and nature in her video *Hear Us Speak*, 1987. Her collage of words (from a text by Susan Griffin), percussive music, and blurred fragments of fields, flowers, sky, and trees abstracted through imaginative camera work (the artist ran, spun, and threw the camera) creates a dizzying sensory fusion.

Doug Hall's video work, *Prelude to the Tempest*, taped in the Marin Headlands in 1985, brings us full circle. Watching the opening frames of ominous, darkening clouds moving across the sky and hearing the low,

rumbling sounds of the wind, we could be looking at
a temporal version of an American nineteenth-century
painting in which the powerful forces of nature are
meant to instill in the viewer a sense of awe and wonder.
Next, with growing feelings of tension, we watch for
several minutes as the artist stands precariously at the
edge of a riverbank while balancing a large rock in his
hand until, no longer able to sustain its weight, he drops
it in the river. A close shot of Hall's head, lit with garish
green and red, shows his mouth open in a silent scream.
We then realize that Hall's images are indeed metaphors
for power, but a power laced with postmodern anxiety.
Furthermore, Hall reminds us that this sylvan wilderness is only minutes away from factories, trains, and
speeding cars – modern symbols of power. As in traditional landscape painting, Hall uses nature as a metaphor for the human condition, but the human condition
has changed irrevocably, along with the landscape and
our relationship to it.

Notes

1. Oppenheim attended the California College of Arts and Crafts and Stanford University (MFA), Heizer, the San Francisco Art Institute, and De Maria, the University of California, Berkeley (MA).

2. John Beardsley, *Earthworks and Beyond* (New York: Abbeville, 1989), 162.

3. Graham Beal, "Respecting the Wood," *A Quiet Revolution: British Sculpture Since 1965*, exh. cat. (Chicago: Museum of Contemporary Art; San Francisco: San Francisco Museum of Modern Art; New York: Thames and Hudson, 1988), 138.

4. Andy Goldsworthy, lecture presented at the City Arts and Lectures series, Herbst Auditorium, San Francisco, 3 May 1994.

5. Goldsworthy, City Arts lecture.

6. John Roloff, in Constance Lewallen, *John Roloff: Matrix/Berkeley 110*, exh. brochure (Berkeley, Calif.: University Art Museum, 1987).

7. Barrett Watten, "Science Fair," *Artweek* (17 February 1994): 11.

8. Tom Marioni, in Suzanne Foley, *Space, Time, Sound: Conceptual Art in the Bay Area: The 70s*, exh. cat. (San Francisco: San Francisco Museum of Modern Art, 1979), 54.

9. Paul Kos, in Roger Downey, "Paul Kos's *Chartres Bleu:* An Aspiration Toward Height", *Object Poems*, exh. cat. (Seattle, Wash.: Henry Art Gallery), 1987. This attitude was gaining currency. German conceptual artist Joseph Beuys, for example, was preaching that everyone is an artist; by logical extension, everything one does is art.

10. Reese Palley Gallery was a commercial gallery that for a short time, under the directorship of Carol Lindsley, invited young conceptual artists to create temporary installations as a part of its program.

11. Action is a term derived from the German *aktion*, which Woodall and many other conceptualists preferred to *performance*, because of the latter's theatrical connotation.

12. John Woodall, *Recipe* (Willets, Calif.: Tuumba Press, May 1977).

13. Mark Thompson, "Fixing the Earth," *Artweek* 24, no. 18 (23 September 1993): back cover.

14. Mark Thompson, conversation with the author, 22 May 1994.

15. Bonnie Sherk, "Fixing the Earth," *Artweek* 24, no.18 (23 September 1993): 15.

16. Bonnie Sherk, conversation with author, 27 June 1994.

17. Situationism (*Internationale situationniste*) was primarily a literary movement with ties to the several artist groups centered in France during the 1950s and 1960s. The objective of the situationists was to alleviate the alienation and boredom found in late-capitalist society by constructing situations that would integrate art into everyday urban life. One of their strategies was the *derive*, or playful passage through the city streets, turning them into an arena for art and politics. They published *The Naked City,* a map of Paris that divided the city into *psychogeographical zones.* Users of the map were to follow a direction of their choosing in response to the terrain in a kind of performance. In so doing, they would retrieve a social and direct experience of space that had been lost in contemporary life in which representation had replaced reality.

18. Terry Fox, in Constance Lewallen, *Terry Fox: Articulations,* exh. cat. (Philadelphia: Moore College of Art and Design, 1992), 8.

19. Steven Jenkins, "Going with the Flow," *Artweek* 25, no. 1 (7 January 1993).

20. "You have noticed that everything an Indian does is in a circle, and that is because the power of the world always works in a circle, and everything tries to be round. The sky is round, and I have heard that the earth is round like a ball, and so are all the stars. . . . Our tepees were round like the nests of birds, and these were always set in a circle, the nation's hoop, a nest of many nests, where the Great Spirit meant for us to hatch our children. But the Wasichus have put us in these square boxes. Our power is gone and we are dying, for the power is not in us any more." Black Elk, a member of the Oglala Sioux, in Michael Freeman, "Ethnic Differences in the Ways That We Perceive and Use Space," *AIA Journal* (February 1977). Cited in Anita Abramovitz, *People and Spaces* (New York: Viking, 1979), 9-10.

21. Rebecca Solnit, "Living Places," *Artspace* (January-April 1992): 40.

22. Lewis deSoto, "Háypatak, Witness, Kansatsusha," installation brochure (San Francisco Arts Commission Gallery, October-November 1990).

23. Patricia Fuller, *Five Artists at NOAA* (Seattle: The Real Comet Press, 1985), 36.

24. Peter Richards, "Fixing the Earth," *Artweek* 24, no. 18 (23 September 1993): back cover.

25. Peter Richards, biographical information provided to author, ca. February 1994.

26. Ireland performed a similar deconstruction in his restoration of two meeting rooms at the Headlands Center for the Arts.

27. San Francisco *Call,* 8 January 1905.

28. This videotape was originally included in an installation that Lucier created for the Capp Street Project in San Francisco.

29. Eleanor Heartney, *Noah's Raven: A Video Installation by Mary Lucier,* exh. cat. (Ohio: Toledo Museum of Art, 1993), 15-16.

Wayne Thiebaud, *Urban Freeways*, 1979
Oil on canvas, 44³/₈ x 36¹/₈ in.
Collection of Paul LeBaron Thiebaud, *cat. no. 153*

Changes like the Weather:
Painting and Sculpture since 1970

Bill Berkson

The activities of artists along the Pacific Rim, of which the San Francisco Bay Area forms a part, mimic atmospheric convergences that produce barely perceptible ground swells or ripples. At a significant remove from more pressured art centers, this climate traditionally fosters the accomplishment of a thing a day, one closely watched idea per month. In the same way, the drift of Bay Area art over the past half century, and most noticeably since the 1960s, has been subject to characteristically independent senses of timing and necessity. The local, geologically youthful, temblor-prone terrain seems to demand representation in an equally erratic range of artistic manners. If accountable to a mainstream timeline, the art history of this region can be said to have skipped or even leapfrogged whole decades. Thus, for the most part, San Francisco avoided '60s minimalism and proceeded directly to postminimal and conceptual art in some of their most idiosyncratic manifestations. As David Ireland put it, "Minimal art was just too spare and intellectual for most people here. . . . The geometry was born out of New York, big-building grid life. Our grids are sloppier than theirs. The West Coast version was shaggier, more rustic."[1]

Well before the dawn of the "pluralist" or "postmovement" '70s, the Bay Area had become firmly identified with displays of hybrid and otherwise uncategorizable genres. By 1977 Carter Ratcliff could observe that "the provincial/cosmopolitan dichotomy no longer describes [San Francisco's] cultural relationship to New York. Instead, well-known artists of the Bay Area have transformed the familiar dichotomy into an aspect of style. This injects irony into local traditions."[2] It was ironic self-consciousness such as this, mixed with defiance of New York's continuing negative response to an alien ethos, that produced Robert Arneson's iconic *California Artist*, 1982 (fig.1), a ceramic likeness of the artist himself as exotic specimen clad in an open denim jacket and sunglasses, empty-headed in a landscape strewn with beer bottles, cigarette butts, and marijuana leaves.

No single artist has come to personify the issues of contemporary San Francisco Bay Area art and its relation to the land so much as William T. Wiley. Typically conflating the personal and the environmental, whether keyed to a specific place (as in the *The Hayward Murals*,

done in 1979 for the Hayward Centennial Hall) or more broadly allegorical, Wiley's vision has a consistently hybrid feel about it. As John Perreault says,
Wiley's West is everybody's – a national fantasy derived from cowboy movies and comic books. He lives in Marin County, not in Tucson or Tombstone. Garages and backyards are as much a part of his fictionalized landscape as the California Gold Rush or the Pacific Frontier.[3]
For Wiley, the fabled California sublime of wide-open, overarching space has been superceded by a dazzling midday plenum where "anything you look at carefully is very complex. There's no surface that isn't just crawling with information.[4]

Both the inner and outer reaches of Wiley's exhaustive informational approach are evident in the watercolors he has made since the '60s. Describing local color and the elusive shimmer of contours glimpsed in the coastal light, these compact works appear at once hallucinated and phenomenally precise, each thing set in plain view but difficult to pick out from the all-enveloping luminosity. The setting of *Lame and Blind in Eden,* 1969 (fig.2), a clearing in the woods, is imaginary, but its landscape coordinates, including the sandy cliffs in the distance, clearly mirror those of coastal Marin. The title and plethora of detail – surveyor's gear aligned along a path between a water trough and a grove of trees, and on the trough itself a drooping life preserver flanked by a hatchet and a test tube – make explicit the way, in Wiley's words, "we tend to put man-made objects in front of nature, ignoring the environment."[5] A complicated assemblage leans beyond a felled tree, and, tucked off toward the left-hand edge, stacked folders bear a pink label stamped "AEC" (for the Atomic Energy Commission, recalling the plutonium-processing plant in Hanford, Washington, near Richland, where Wiley grew up). "Measuring, dividing up, polluting"– such, Wiley tells us, are the ways of being "lame and blind" in providential nature.[6]

Over the past decade or so, since the artist developed a passion for salmon fishing in the ocean waters around the Farallon Islands, many of his territorial chartings have taken on a nautical tinge. An early, cautionary tribute to the Farallones themselves, the mixed-media construction *Nomad Is an Island,* 1981, points up the scandal

fig.1 Robert Arneson, *California Artist*, 1982
Stoneware with glazes, 68¼ x 27½ x 20¼ in.
Collection of San Francisco of Museum of Modern Art,
gift of the Modern Art Council

of the United States government dumping barrels of radioactive waste near the islands during the early 1950s. In a more celebratory mood, the huge, composite aquatic figure spanning most of *Leviathan I*, 1988 (fig.3), throws off iridescent curlicues in its wake, while higher keyed primary colors register simultaneous plays of daylight on the waves. Navigating the picture's surface amid jumbled glyphs and doodles, the eye finds significant markers: a ship's black bow, a storm-twisted anchor shank, a greenish Point Bonita, and, on the far left, the brilliant red of the channel buoy known as "the Light Bucket," tossing thirteen miles out from the Golden Gate Bridge.

The word *bridge* has a special inflection in Wiley's lexicon: its many meanings include a guitar part, a construction spanning the distance between two or more points of land, the artist's works as an extension of self toward other, and, as Wiley added recently, "the bridge between me and my ancestors."[7] *To the Bridge*, 1987, is a mural-sized picture packed with just about every known Wileyan symbol. Celebrating the fiftieth anniversary of the completion of the Golden Gate Bridge, which happened to coincide with the artist's own fiftieth birthday, Wiley wrote across the middle of the canvas: "To the bridge and our 50th. Thanks for the many crossings and fun."

Though nowhere so specific in reference as Wiley's imagery, Robert Hudson's sculptures and paintings appear just as inextricably spun from a sensibility at home in the drifts, incongruities, and poignancies of vision peculiar to this region. The large assemblage *Running through the Woods*, made in the artist's Sausalito studio in 1975 (fig.4), invokes landscape via an agglomerate of symbols – tethered to a paint-splattered scaffolding, a stuffed deer with a globe skewered between its antlers is decked with sundry talismanic trappings – and amounts to what Graham Beal has called "an essay in conflicting natural and geometric forms."[8] It is also an exercise in sympathetic magic, based on an account of a Native American ceremony involving the dressing of a dead deer in beadwork and other ornaments. Acquired from an antique shop in Mill Valley, the deer is framed within a literal "woods" (or thicket) of artistic forms and devices. A pencil grazes the right hind leg, eliciting a red plastic spurt. Stopped and watchful, is the deer, so "trapped" by human artifice, a stand-in for the artist himself?

Aside from the literal conversion of landscape into sculpture, as in earthworks, or the dialectics of site-specific and site-generated art in their recent efflorescences, freestanding "landscape sculpture" has emerged most tellingly as a genre within the context of the polychrome ceramic sculpture innovations of the past four decades. Inherently, landscape is a pictorial mode, and clay, with its long tradition of decorative modeling and

fig.2 William T. Wiley, *Lame and Blind in Eden*, 1969
Watercolor and ink on paper, 30 x 21¹⁵/₁₆ in.
The Harry W. and Mary Margaret Anderson Collection, *cat.no.169*

glazing motifs, allows a greater range of pictorial play than other sculptural materials. (In any case, no matter how cosmetically preemptive the glaze, clay seemingly can't avoid referring to itself in its primordial guise.) Among the California artists of the '60s and '70s who invented a new landscape vocabulary in clay, Robert Arneson (1930-1992) was preeminent.

In 1962 Arneson arrived in Davis to teach ceramics at the local University of California campus. For the next thirteen years he and his family occupied a boxy tract house at the corner of Alice and L streets, 1303 Alice, also known as "the Alice-Street house," or plain "Alice," as Arneson himself eventually preferred. The house soon achieved the status of a principal model for Arneson's increasingly large, colorful ceramic sculptures; beginning with *Box House Landscape* and *Big Alice Street*, both from 1966, and continuing through the almost eight-foot-wide mass of *Alice House Wall*, 1967, the series reached its grand finale in 1974 with *The Palace at 9 A.M.* (fig.5).

Partly inspired by the sculptor's having seen Giacometti's architectural dreamscape, *The Palace at 4 A.M.*

at the Museum of Modern Art, during a fellowship year in New York in 1968, Arneson's "palace" sits imperturbably upon a sloping pedestal, its lateral spread of carefully proportioned, variegated slabs marking off the sculpture's nearly ten-foot length. The foreshortened details fall roughly into line to satisfy the requirements of single-point perspective from just one angle (that of the "near" corner with the street name on a stubby post). By 1970 Arneson had come to think of the house as a kind of all-purpose muse: "a monument, a sculpture, a wall, a trophy, a jar and souvenir plate. It is a slab-floor, one-story, three-bedroom, two-bath, two-car-garage, California-style house. It is for sale."⁹ Indeed, the detailing of house and surroundings in *The Palace* became something of a family project, with each of Arneson's four sons adding a touch to the tableau. A tiny handprint makes a flourish above one of the aluminum windows; on the grass behind the hackberry tree, an older boy stretches out. The pink-painted stucco house's accoutrements are fondly particularized: blue trim and gray asphalt shingles guide the eye along chimney, vents, and T V antenna (the only non-ceramic element– it's epoxy on steel), and on to a backboard and hoop above the garage wherein is housed the family car, a 1972 M G convertible, beside two garbage cans.

Even before attending Robert Hudson's classes at the San Francisco Art Institute and Arneson's at Davis (where he received his M F A in 1968), Richard Shaw had begun to superimpose landscape imagery onto a series of earthenware "couch" sculptures in which this eponymous home furnishing, rendered impeccably in the round, served as support for a (usually) flat depiction in acrylic paints of the world outdoors. In 1967 Shaw joined Hudson and Cornelia Schulz at White Gate Ranch along a slope of Mount Tamalpais above Stinson Beach. The two-piece *Couch and Chair with Landscape and Cows*, 1966-67 (fig.6), shows a quasi panoramic view uphill from the back of Shaw's house. Extending to the ridgeline, the view is capped on the backrest of each piece of furniture with pale sky blue, and the mountain's early spring greenery is interrupted only by dusty outcroppings of serpentine and three big brown-and-white cows. For *Couch with Sinking Ship*, made four years later in 1971, Shaw swiveled his gaze 180 degrees, scrutinizing the view in the opposite direction from his studio out to sea at sundown. In the resultant seascape Shaw interpolated the sculptural relief of a derelict ocean liner half-sunk in the middle distance. This steamship motif, connected to his childhood feeling for the ill-fated SS *Titanic* ("ever since I read [Walter Lord's] *A Night to Remember* in Remedial Reading class"), has persisted in many variations throughout Shaw's career. (Nor, in this instance, is it particularly farfetched, given the long history of marine wreckage along nearby Duxbury Reef.) Interestingly, the cloud of smoke from

fig.3 William T. Wiley, *Leviathan I*, 1988
Pencil and acrylic on canvas, 75 x 140 in.
Mr. and Mrs. James R. Patton, Jr., *cat.no.170*

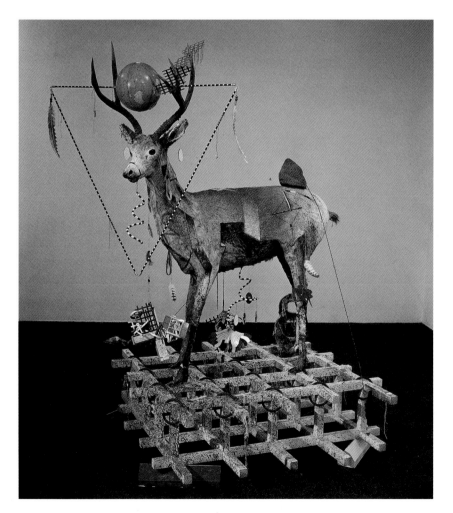

fig.4 Robert Hudson, *Running through the Woods*, 1975
Stuffed deer and mixed media, 77 x 62 x 50¾ in.
Mary and David Robinson, *cat.no.85*

fig.5 Robert Arneson, *The Palace at 9 A.M.*, 1974
Terracotta and glazed ceramic, 118 x 84 x 24 in.
Courtesy Frumkin/Adams Gallery, New York, *cat.no.4*

the funnels that blots the horizon line settles into a fair approximation, though not one intended by Shaw himself, of the Farallones some twenty-four miles offshore.

If Shaw, Hudson, and Arneson are eclectic songster-fabricators of the homely and convivial, the British-born sculptor Dennis Leon must seem a purist by comparison. His site-specific installations, bronzes, and charred and/or stained plywood constructions are regularly geared to the elemental. (He also does plein-air pastel renderings of the coastal terrain.) Within a decade after moving to the Bay Area in 1972, he began to take landforms and the manifold timelines they imply as the prime subject matter of his work. Leon's "faux-geologic objects"[10] can suggest both natural rock formations and the rudely carved remnants of ancient ritual sites. *Loma Prieta*, 1989 (fig.7), is formed of layered plywood sheets of which the outward facets have been smoothed, hacked at, and blackened by paint or burned with a welding torch. From almost every angle the work's rough-hewn geometry appears to soften, permitting a paradoxical image of calm. Fittingly, one of Leon's own bywords for his work is "reverberation." As he recalls,
Loma Prieta *was started in my Oakland studio about two weeks before the big earthquake of October 17, 1989. Since the sculpture was about how some rocks are formed by earthquake action I respectfully named it after the earthquake's epicenter.*[11]

Another important set of sculptural responses to the local environment, both artificial and natural, are the works made by the English sculptor Tony Cragg on two separate visits to San Francisco, the first for a Matrix exhibition at the University Art Museum, Berkeley, in 1986 and the second for a residency over six months in 1988 at the Headlands Center for the Arts in Marin County. Two sculptures Cragg assembled especially for his Matrix show refer to both the region's topology and the material life of its urban overlays. *Pegs: Three Stages* incorporates circular elements (cookie tins, tires, gears, and pulleys) found in local salvage yards to form three tapering vertical stacks. The stacks recall geologic strata while their tapering forms suggest church spires. Likewise, *Isoprene Landscape*'s (fig.8) three-tiered, white-painted Masonite structure partially supported by a moss-covered truck tire alludes to the way the freeways and thoroughfares around the bay follow, alter, or cope with the contours of the land. As Constance Lewallen writes, "The natural and the man-made coexist in. . . Cragg's sculptures, as they do in the world."[12] Working with young artist-assistants at the Headlands, Cragg carved a five-part group – two mortars, a pestle, and two landscapes (fig.9) – from eucalyptus trunks. Where the two landscapes closely followed the topography at hand, Cragg saw the mortar-and-pestle motif as analogous to the human management of the Headlands, which is, as parkland, "so well stamped."[13]

fig.6 Richard Shaw, *Couch and Chair with Landscape and Cows*, 1966-67
Earthenware, acrylic paint, wood – couch: 10 x 18¾ x 9 in.; chair: 9¼ x 9⅝ x 9¼ in.
Collection American Craft Museum, New York, gift of the Johnson Wax Company,
from OBJECTS: USA, 1977; donated to the American Craft Museum by the American
Craft Council, 1990, *cat.no.142*

fig.7 Dennis Leon, *Loma Prieta*, 1989
Plywood, 44 x 137 x 65 in.
Courtesy Haines Gallery, San Francisco, and the artist

fig.8 Tony Cragg, *Isoprene Landscape*, 1986
Rubber with Masonite and steel, 28½ x 48 x 63 in.
Courtesy Marian Goodman Gallery, New York

fig.9 Tony Cragg, *Two Mortars and a Landscape* (detail), 1986-89
Headlands Center for the Arts, Sausalito (Marin County)

The past two decades have seen an extraordinary attentiveness by painters of various persuasions (including divergent degrees of concern for verisimilitude) to Bay Area material life, both in and out of the cities. Coincidentally or not, contemporary painting has tracked the radical transformations since the '50s of the San Francisco skyline, as well as the changes in rural areas where open spaces have been by turns impinged upon by heavy development or designated as recreational or agricultural preserves.

The autobiographical paintings of Joan Brown (1938-1990) from the late '60s claim San Francisco as a correlative to the artist's identity. The titles of Brown's "situation" pictures – *Running in MacArthur Park, At the Beach,* and so on – reflect a new candor as to how specific each work, and the place depicted in it, could be to her everyday life. Brown seems always to have conceived of herself in relation to where she was, whether in her apartment or studio, posed against the backdrop of her hometown, or traveling. The *Alcatraz Swim* cycle of 1974-76 records Brown's vicissitudes throughout repeated attempts, as a member of the San Francisco Dolphin Club, to complete the course from Alcatraz Island to Aquatic Park. (She successfully swam the distance in 1976, in fifty-eight minutes flat.) As Sanford Schwartz noted when the cycle was first shown in New York:

The Alcatraz Swim is not only for real, it's a race [Brown] had participated in. Since she has become such a devoted amateur, she has painted her swim coach, herself in an indoor pool, people swimming, things seen from a swimmer's point of view. In these new paintings, her life as an artist and native San Franciscan hovers over her in the form of paintings on the wall.[14]

The striking subject of *Mary Julia y Manuel,* 1976 (fig.10) – dark-haired Mary Julia Raahauge (now Klimenko), a young poet who was then modeling for a drawing group that included, beside Brown herself, Brown's ex-husband Manuel Neri and Robert Colescott – poses dramatically on a deep red stage in a high-necked, long-sleeved Chinese silk dress. Silhouetted behind her in the distance, Alcatraz, the Bay Bridge, Angel Island, and the downtown San Francisco skyline loom over the moonlit blue eddies of the bay. (The picture served as a kind of *portrait à clef*: both the inscription and the girl's gesture toward it allude to Goya's 1797 portrait of the Duchess of Alba in a similar spirit of romantic disclosure.)

Brown's skyline is an emblem of her Ideal City, familiar to natives and visitors alike. A comparable image, though one proposing a view further downscale in the civic scheme, is Robert Colescott's *Christina's Day Off,* 1983 (fig.11). Colescott situates his heroine, like Brown's, full-length against an urban backdrop. The imaginary housemaid strikes a classic pose at the city dump on the outskirts of Colescott's native Oakland. As Lowery

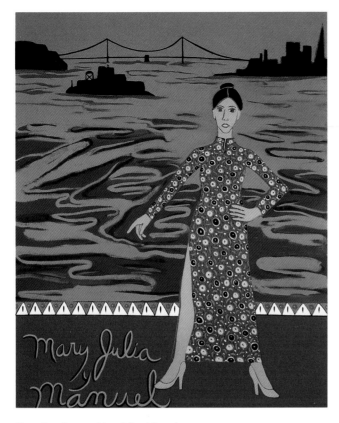

fig.10 Joan Brown, *Mary Julia y Manuel*, 1976
Enamel on canvas, 96 x 75 in.
Courtesy Frumkin/Adams Gallery, New York, *cat.no.18*

S. Sims observed:

In this work we see a characterization of a black woman as complex and clearly defined as any of Colescott's personages. . . . She stands in her Sunday finery in front of a heap of consumer goods that represents both her wishes and desires and her daily drudgery. The American dream seems to be accessible – an entire pie forms a halo for Christina – but the heap also includes symbols of dangers and fears and broken promises. Near the top of the mound is a dove, its breast pierced by an arrow, along with a hammer and sickle and a gun – Colescott's allusions to the global dimensions of the problem of poverty.[15]

Both Richard Estes and Robert Bechtle are photorealists known for evenly focused depictions of city streets populated sparsely or not at all. Originally from Illinois, Estes early on made New York the prime subject of his art, although over the past ten years or so he has diversified. Bechtle, on the other hand, is a San Francisco native who paints his home turf with a deep sense of its familiarity. Since the late '60s Bechtle's eye has been drawn to the bland look of neighborhoods (including his own, on Potrero Hill) mostly well within San Francisco or Oakland city limits, yet often featuring sunlit rows of charming, pastel-colored houses bordered by shrubbery and stretches of empty, immaculate sidewalk. Where Bechtle's earlier images normally zero in on one house at a time, his pictures since the early '80s have pulled back for wider prospects of single streets and intersections, affording uncanny effects of light as well as ever more complicated ways of dividing the canvas.

Regarding the luminist aspect of Bechtle's recent work, Richard Kalina comments:

Bechtle's paintings are not surrealistic, and yet they have a powerful psychological edge. . . . I believe that this is an effect of the light: the objects in the paintings are rendered photographically, but the ambient light is not. . . . The light appears to be seen light.[16]

As Kalina further points out, *Oakland Intersection – 59th St. and Stanford,* 1990 (fig.12), "has two streets and two vanishing points, but the perspectival recession is countered, and the plane of the picture reasserted, by the way the streets converge in the foreground . . . rather than in the background as one would expect."[17] How this works, and how the scene fits together, yoked by its meager trapezoid of grass, has largely to do with Bechtle's newly refined touch, which optimizes nuance even as it keeps to its regimen of clearly reported fact.

Since the early '80s Estes, too, has broadened his pictorial horizons in a series of cityscapes derived partially from multiple wide-angle photographs. In *View from Twin Peaks,* 1990 (fig.13), Estes coolly records the scenic overlook from one of San Francisco's loftiest vantage points. The crisp, multidirectional view affords a panoramic sweep from the foggy bay shore southward, across Hunter's Point and the fabulous distant

fig.11 Robert Colescott, *Christina's Day Off*, 1983
Acrylic on canvas, 84 x 72 in.
The Saint Louis Art Museum, gift of Brooke and Carolyn
Alexander, New York, *cat.no.24*

fig.12 Robert Bechtle, *Oakland Intersection - 59th St. and Stanford*, 1990
Oil on canvas, 40 x 58 in.
Alex Weber, *cat.no.9*

whiteness of downtown, to the greener outer reaches of the Golden Gate. In the foreground, shadows gather about the observation area, where a tourist couple sits for a snapshot by the wall and T-shirt vendors wait. A side glance catches the fender of a dark sedan parked near the frame edge and the license plate reading "ESTES 90."

Oddities of human intervention with the terrain are spread for all to see in Estes's picture. Similar spatial ambiguities and disorienting shifts of scale, vast and dizzying enough to make the proportions of a Bierstadt look picayune by comparison, obtain in the cityscapes Wayne Thiebaud has been painting since the early '70s, when the Sacramento-based artist acquired a second home on Potrero Hill. The city Thiebaud depicts is a composite, modified San Francisco worked up from sketches combined of many different views. Thiebaud is interested in the way the city displays itself, how it is, as he says, "psychologically positioned. I'm a little troubled by how it can appear a little too toylike. But I'm fascinated by the dematerialization of the city, its ethereal character, the various ways of access and sense of elevation."[18] Access and elevation – each thing seen as transitory and pitched to some degree off the ground – are

themes clearly stated in *Urban Freeways* 1979 (page 138), with its monumental arabesques of fast roads whipping past tall buildings and tree-lined, empty lots. In other pictures, Thiebaud will routinely pitch a set of high-rise slabs alongside an unnegotiably steep thoroughfare that may cut, in an illogical but no less accurate montage effect, to bare, rolling hills and waterways. The white side of the building occupying the right foreground of *Day City (Bright City)*, 1982 (fig.14), presents both a megalithic barrier and an abstract blank. Around it gathers, as seen from midair, the recognizable, actual city, a multiplicity of flats and tilts compounded by recent sprouts of concrete, glass, and steel.

Before he committed to becoming a painter in the late '60s, Gordon Cook (1927-1985) had already produced a remarkable set of etchings on site at the San Francisco Headlands (fig.15). Even so, Cook became known mainly as a still-life painter. Between 1980 and 1982 he made a number of paintings and prints focused on the natural gas storage tank at Point Richmond across the bay from his Union Street apartment (figs.16-17). (A fixture of the area since its installation in 1949, the tank was dismantled in 1989 after completion of a condominium development close by.)

148

fig.13 Richard Estes, *View from Twin Peaks*, 1990
Oil on canvas, 36 x 72 in.
Collection of Terry and Eva Herndon, *cat.no.47*

The large cylinder, nestled against the hillsides of Brick-
yard Cove, provided Cook with a motif comparable
to Monet's haystacks. In turn, the tender regard Cook
gave to this unassuming industrial structure graces each
image of it with a monumentality and fervor unparalleled elsewhere in his work. Kenneth Baker has said
that the series is as much about local weather and light
as about the object itself:

*Viewed from the city side of the Bay, the tank is a landmark
that functions like a sundial.... The more often you consult
them, the more the tank's changing aspects, like those of the
Bay, take on resonances that make you more aware of your
own moods. On a hazy day, the tank withdraws until it has
no more presence than a mirage. Under a deck of fog, it can
turn both spectral and leaden. When the fog descends the
tank vanishes from sight and, unlike the landscape, almost
from memory. But when the air is clear, it takes on more
volume and definition than its setting ... a mooring for the
eye in the ocean of open space.*[19]

For Wayne Thiebaud, a vantage point from well
above ground level is an imaginative device to allow
viewer participation in the spatial ambiguities he is
fond of creating (and another way of portraying the
city as an admixture of the plausible and unreal); for

fig.14 Wayne Thiebaud, *Day City (Bright City)*, 1982
Oil on canvas, 48 x 36 in.
Collection of Thomas W. Weisel, *cat.no.154*

fig.15 Gordon Cook, *Headland II*, 1961/85
Etching, 19 x 16½ in.
Limestone Press, Hank Hine

Yvonne Jacquette, however, the airborne overview is first of all literal, and the contemplative distance implied for the viewer is literal, as well. A New York-based realist, Jacquette has developed most of her paintings since the mid-'70s from quick pastel sketches and snapshots of land- and cityscapes seen from high up, aloft in either small planes or the upper floors of skyscrapers. *Telegraph Hill II*, 1984 (fig.18), shows a prospect looking northeast from above the edge of the San Francisco financial district. Like Estes, Jacquette includes more to see from edge to edge than the eye could normally hold. Within her "night burn" textures, tiny details (the traffic flow up Kearny Street and down Montgomery, miniature neons of Chinatown and North Beach) are played against big masses (the Transamerica Pyramid and next to it, dark girders of a building-in-progress). Recalling how her New Yorker's sense of light and proportion was affected by San Francisco's more modest scale, she later said, "You see the light floating up from the street onto the edges of the buildings more precisely."[20]

That it is possible for an abstract painting to resonate with the hues and syncopations associated with city street life is borne out afresh by Mike Henderson's *North Beach*, 1989 (fig.19). San Francisco's North Beach – the corner of Francisco and Powell streets, to be exact – was the locale of the artist's studio for more than a decade until the studio and the large number of paintings it contained were damaged by fire in 1985. Henderson's pictographic spirals and dabs of bright red, pink, yellow, blue, and green – an unusually effulgent palette for this painter, who has lately kept to the dark end of the spectrum – commemorate his passionate attachment to the place. "That painting," Henderson recalls, "was a way of dealing with the fire. It's really like pulling a skin off something and seeing it."[21] In 1986 Henderson moved to Oakland, a city whose sense of urgency has impressed itself upon his work of the past few years. As with North Beach, Henderson's recent paintings are "interpretations . . . of sounds, images, and motions . . . the glint of sunlight off windshields; sirens; heat absorbed and later radiated from concrete; the barking of dogs; sounds of BART trains, traffic, and shattering glass."[22]

"Sense of place" may be all the more fraught in a multicultural context where displacement and hybrid self-images have become the norms. As a Chicana artist from Kingsville, Texas, Carmen Lomas Garza has concentrated mainly on her childhood memories of close-knit communal and family life in a rural South Texas town. Since coming to live in San Francisco in 1976, however, Garza has sometimes taken up aspects of the local scene in her work, most extensively in the eight narrative panels composing *History of California Water*, 1984, commissioned by the San Francisco Water Department and the San Francisco Art Commission.

fig.16 Gordon Cook, *Point Richmond*, ca. 1981
Oil on canvas, 23⅞ x 26 in.
Liadain O'Donovan Cook, *cat.no.26*

fig.17 Gordon Cook, *Point Richmond*, ca. 1981
Oil on canvas, 14¾ x 16 in.
Sukey Lilienthal, *cat. no.25*

fig.18 Yvonne Jacquette, *Telegraph Hill II*, 1984
Oil on canvas, 77¾ x 105 in.
Anonymous loan, *cat.no.87*

fig.19 Mike Henderson, *North Beach*, 1989
Oil on canvas, 72 x 60 in.
Collection of The Oakland Museum of California,
gift of the Collectors Gallery, and The Art Guild, *cat.no.80*

fig.20 Carmen Lomas Garza, *Felino's Breakdancers*, 1988
Gouache on paper, 20¼ x 25¼ in.
Collection of The Oakland Museum of California,
gift of The Art Guild, *cat.no.55*

fig.21 Martin Wong, *DC-3*, 1992
Acrylic on linen, 72 x 36¼ in.
Courtesy P. P. O. W., Inc., New York

fig.22 Willard Dixon, *Bolinas Lagoon Hillside*, 1991
Oil on canvas, 36 x 60 in.
Courtesy Contemporary Realist Gallery, San Francisco, *cat.no.43*

Currently installed in a corridor at the Water Department's suburban facility in Millbrae, the panels show, in Garza's minutely detailed, "dollhouse" manner, phases of Californians' usage and management of available water from precolonial times to the present. Unique among Garza's works thus far in grasping the contemporary look of her adopted city is the brilliant gouache *Felino's Breakdancers*, 1988 (fig.20). Based on her memory of watching, while stuck in a traffic jam, a group of Mission District breakdancers and passersby gathered on the sidewalk outside Felino's, a vintage clothing store then on lower Twenty-fourth Street, the depiction is exquisite in every particular: the sheets of tan, corrugated cardboard with which the dancers cushion their omnidirectional, acrobatic moves; the "stage lighting" provided by Felino's display windows; and the window displays themselves, featuring some of the garb that served as outlandish Chicano/Chicana fashions of the time.

"Everything I paint is within four blocks of where I live and the people are the people I know and see all the time." By these self-proclaimed standards, Martin Wong is a social realist of a rare order. Raised in San

Francisco's Chinatown, Wong now lives on New York's Lower East Side. Exemplifying a progress that is the reverse of Garza's, his *Chinatown USA* series represents a circling back to childhood haunts. Drawing on his own archive of postcards and other memorabilia, Wong creates a multicanvas panorama of (in Holland Cotter's phrase) "Chinatown as a state of mind," the historical locus of Wong's youth and ancestry.[23] In *DC-3*, 1992 (fig.21), with its planeload of smiling passengers banking over Jackson Street, Wong provides his own overview of the neighborhood and its landmark structures. As Elizabeth Hess reported, "The artist's specialty is brick and mortar, and the innumerable buildings are carefully detailed. Many are covered with Chinese signs; the artist's mother, who still lives in San Francisco, did the research for all the Chinese writing in this piece, among others."[24]

One of the few locally based painters to persist in a realist manner at once precise and grand, Willard Dixon has been painting the countryside around Marin and Sonoma counties since the early '70s. Dixon's paintings combine detailed photographic information transferred to canvas from slides with "a landscape vocabulary. . .

fig.23 Christopher Brown, *The River, Evening*, 1984-85
Oil on canvas, 96 x 360 in. (5 panels, each 96 x 72 in.)
Panels 1 - 2: Private collection, *cat.no.16a*

learned at the feet of local hills."[25] *Bolinas Lagoon Hillside,*
1991 (fig.22), shows the lower slopes of Mount Tamalpais and the adjoining estuary long cherished for its
splendor and its efficacy as a breeding site for herons,
egrets, and other bird species. The view is specific: late
afternoon, coastal fog moving in from the west, pink
light cast on the dry mountain grasses under a summer
sky. Dixon, who lived in Bolinas from 1969 to 1974,
has commented,
I know the light, the skies, the hills, grasses, trees, and cows of
Northern California so well, they are what I now think of as
skies, hills, etc. They are my skies and hills, like my face is my
own. We can't see our own faces directly. So the sense of place
in my paintings is best perceived by others.[26]

Of the Bay Area artists who came into major prominence during the early '80s, only Christopher Brown
can be said to have confronted the possibilities of
landscape painting in any sustained way, and even in
Brown's case the confrontation turned out to be brief.
Subtitled *A Cycle of Landscape Paintings*, Brown's *The*
Painted Room – a hundred-foot-long, wraparound set
of two large, multipanel pictures separated by another
couple of smaller canvases – reads as an investigation
of, and veers away from, the naturalistic representation
of figures in landscape. In the process the sequence as a

whole arrived at what Brown called "an emotional realism, not an illusionism, that is true to my feelings about
landscape rather than what landscape looks like."[27]
One of the outsized sections begun in Berkeley during
late summer 1984 and finished in New York the following year, *The River, Evening* (fig.23) was loosely based on
a dream as well as on sketches of actual trees and water
remembered from Lake Anza in Oakland's Tilden Park.
Both the imagery (two figures, male and female, beside
a river at dusk) and the palette have ties to the Bay Area
figurative tradition – to David Park's "bathers" and
Elmer Bischoff's shimmering hues in particular.

For the conceptualist Diane Andrews Hall, landscape
painting is one sign system among others, although it
is one for which she has a decidedly sympathetic bent.
Hall's paintings normally contain freeze-frame images
of sea or sky set either within or beside hard-edged rec-
tangles of abstract color. Although her views are based
on observations and photographs of actual sites (the
ocean at Baker's Beach in San Francisco, for one), they
are put methodically through an abstract distancing
process so that whatever raptures they might occasion
in the viewer are held in check. The diptych *Tule Fog*,
1989 (fig.24), refers directly to Hall's encounter with a
tree obscured by fog during an early morning walk on

Panels 3 - 4: Alex and Eleanor Najjar, *cat.no.16b*

Panel 5: Tom and Barbara Peckenpaugh, *cat.no.16c*

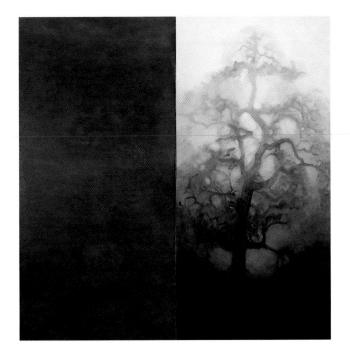

fig.24 Diane Andrews Hall, *Tule Fog*, 1989
Oil on canvas, 100 x 100 in.
Courtesy Haines Gallery, San Francisco, *cat.no.77*

Thanksgiving Day. Hall sought to crystallize the threatening aspect of the low-visibility conditions by abutting to the natural image a monochrome panel of similarly impenetrable inky blue. Thus, as Hall says, "The painting is more than one place."[28]

Although appearing as rigorously nonreferential as can be, John Meyer's primarily white panel paintings are often direct responses to the light and atmosphere around Meyer's studio across the Great Highway from Ocean Beach in San Francisco. For Meyer such temporal nuances constitute parts of his immediate process if not in fact the subject matter of the pictures themselves, which after all have their own agendas of luminosity. Whether in the studio, where a skylight administers regular doses of hazy daylight, or outside, on a nearby cliff or on beaches at Point Reyes and the Marin Headlands, Meyer sometimes works on a panel affixed firmly to an easel with guy wires; painting wet into wet, with his back to the sun, and sun bouncing off the panel, he watches the changes of ambient light as it interacts with his markings and scrapings away of oil paint. The result, as in *Untitled*, 1991, is a kind of palimpsest of passing sensation transmuted into clear pictorial fact: a square white expanse with thin edges of black underpainting showing at the sides. It may well be that, as Jamie Brunson has written of Meyer's paintings, "the object *is* the subject," but ultimately its beauty derives from its powers of suggestion.[29] "I think I see beauty in almost everything around me in the sense of its uniqueness and the magic and mystery of the fact that the whole thing is here."[30]

Extending the tradition of "urban archaeology" begun by such older Bay Area conceptualists as David Ireland, Sono Osato's sculptural installation *Oakland Drawers*, 1993 (in The Oakland Museum Sculpture Court at City Center), amounted to a narrative, via gatherings of assorted types of debris, of that city's multilayered history. During 1986-89 Osato held a studio residency at the Headlands Center for the Arts. Like Tony Cragg and many other artists who have spent time there, she became aware of the ways her work changed in relation to the landscape. Osato speaks of *Portrait of the Headlands*, 1988 (fig.25), as *me internalizing the pulse of the place, which is one of the reasons the layers are so dense, and also why the painting changes color during the day with the changes of light. The painting was inspired by the cliffs. The landscape itself became a mentor to me.*[31]

Taking asphalt mixed with oil paint, beeswax, and sand, Osato creates an equivalent topography in which, for example, the red and purple glimmers of the "portrait" become "metaphors for the dark layers of time."[32]

"Landscape painting seems to serve contemporary artists primarily as a vehicle for allegory and nostalgia."[33] This remark by the New York critic Eleanor Heartney pinpoints how, over the past decade or so, landscape imagery has been returned to its origins in the symbolic order. Whether from irony, nostalgic yearnings, or outright alarm over the consequences of abuse to the natural world, many younger artists such as the Bay Area painters Michael Gregory, Chester Arnold, and Leslie Lerner have taken to the *paysage moralisé* with a vengeance, putting new, often bleakly conceived, twists on "visionary" practice. A plausible antecedent of such modes can be found in Harry Fritzius's (1932-1989) *Untitled (Golden Gate Park Twilight)*, 1986. Unusual for this painter of predominantly metaphysical renderings of the human figure – and unusual, too, in its being a single, stretched canvas rather than a patchwork of canvases that Fritzius would tear up and glue together – the image is simple and poignant. Clumps of trees and their shadows are set darkly under an enormous cloud against the radiant backlighting of a sunset diffused through fog. The scene is one that Fritzius might have observed often on his accustomed dusk-time strolls of the few blocks to the park from his home on Nineteenth Avenue in San Francisco. Recalling moods comparable to Ryder and Inness, or closer to home, the California tonalist Gottardo Piazzoni, a latter-day symbolist enchantment seems the order of the day.

Landscape as an allegorical "elsewhere," at the outer limits of contemporary experience, is writ large across the pictures Michael Gregory painted for about six years beginning in 1987. Built up with varnished tar and chiaroscuro glazes over plywood panels prepared with gessoed cotton fabric – an antiquarian technique

fig.25 Sono Osato, *Portrait of the Headlands*, 1988
Oil, asphalt, sand, and beeswax on canvas, 64 x 76 in.
Courtesy Terrain Gallery, San Francisco, and the artist, *cat.no.122*

fig.26 Michael Gregory, *As if Twelve Princes Sat before a King*, 1988
Oil and tar on board, 40 x 84 in.
Collection of Dr. A. D. Rosenberg, *cat.no.68*

fig.27 Frank Tuttle, *What Wild Indian?*, 1992
Oil on wood, 18 x 20 in.
Collection of Ian and Patricia McGreal, *cat.no.158*

that lends a further déjà-vu eeriness to the work – Gregory's irradiated pastoral zones are dense and clotted. Some of them evoke the flat, amorphous terrain of the Sacramento delta, through which Gregory used to travel by motorbike; others, including *As if Twelve Princes Sat before a King,* 1988 (fig.26) (the title phrase comes from Wallace Stevens's poem "Credences of Summer"), recall the San Francisco Bay as seen from tidal mud flats. Under exploded cumulus the bay looks molten. In the distance, a stark horizontal ridge dotted with industrial structures is, as Gregory says, "where we live."[34] This dislocated romantic vision bears up-to-the-minute evangelical trumpetings of wild longing and endless deferral.

In Frank Tuttle's assemblage paintings, intimations of enchantment against the odds are imbued with both the force of long traditional practice and a sense of emergency. As a Yuki/Wailaki and Concow Maidu artist, Tuttle is concerned with creating "images that reflect personal and communal strength and connectedness with the earth."[35] His mixed-media painting-construction *What Wild Indian?*, 1992 (fig.27), refers to Ishi, the name given to the last surviving member of the Yahi group. After being "discovered" in 1911, Ishi became an object of study for Albert L. Kroeber and other anthropologists and linguists at the University of California,

Berkeley. *Ishi in Two Worlds* by Kroeber's widow, Theodora, was published in 1961 with the subtitle *A Biography of the Last Wild Indian in North America.*[36]

Banded by a kind of trellis (or stockade) of copper wires, the tableau depicts on interlocking panels Tuttle's renditions of two prior images: the late, prominent Concow painter Frank Day's *Ishi at Iamin Mool*, showing Day's recollection from age eight of seeing the Yahi on a high ridge near the Feather River one early morning in 1911, and the official photograph taken some two weeks later after the "wild indian" appeared at a slaughterhouse in Oroville, thence to begin his new life. The upper panel shows Ishi in a meadow between two oak trees, his aspect that of a bushy-haired, angelic healer holding a rope suspended from the sky's zenith. In the panel below, bordered by red vertical marks (through which we see the bearded and bonneted figures of non-native pioneer folk), Ishi's transformative powers are indicated by the wild rosebush blooming from the palm of one hand and the flaming embers held in the other.

Tuttle's iconic Yahi floats between earth and sky and, as the artist says, "above the wonderful, golden hills of California."[37] Such reminders of "connectedness" appear with decreasing frequency in contemporary art, but in the San Francisco Bay region evidence of at least some human attunement to the natural scheme persists.

Notes

1. Bill Berkson, "David Ireland's Accommodations," *Art in America* (September 1989): 183.

2. Carter Ratcliff, "Report from San Francisco," *Art in America* (May-June 1977): 56.

3. John Perreault, "Wiley Territory" in Graham W. J. Beal and Perreault, *Wiley Territory*, exh. cat. (Minneapolis: Walker Art Center, 1979), 13.

4. "Conversation between Robert Hudson and William Wiley," *Robert Hudson: Sculpture /William T. Wiley: Painting*, exh. cat. (Waltham, Mass.: Brandeis University, 1991), 25.

5. Conversation with the author, June 1994.

6. Conversation with the author, June 1994.

7. Conversation with the author, June 1994.

8. Graham W. J. Beal, "Welded Irony," *Robert Hudson: A Survey* (San Francisco: San Francisco Museum of Modern Art, 1985), 14.

9. Lee Nordness, *Objects: USA* (New York: The Viking Press, 1970), 96.

10. Kenneth Baker, "Wood Sculptures as Faux Geology," *San Francisco Chronicle*, 7 February 1990.

11. Dennis Leon, artist's statement, *A Natural Order*, exh. cat. (Westchester, N.Y.: The Hudson River Museum, 1990), 33.

12. Constance Lewallen, *Tony Cragg*, exh. brochure, University Art Museum, Berkeley, Calif., 1986, 2.

13. Constance Lewallen, interview with the artist, "Tony Cragg," *View* (San Francisco: Crown Point Press, 1988), 5.

14. Sanford Schwartz, *The Art Presence* (New York: Horizon Press, 1982), 104.

15. Lowery S. Sims, "Robert Colescott, 1975-1986," *Robert Colescott: A Retrospective, 1975-1986* (San Jose: San Jose Museum of Art, 1987), 7.

16. Richard Kalina, "Painting Snapshots or the Cursory Spectacle," *Art in America* (June 1993): 118.

17. Kalima, "Painting Snapshots," 95.

18. Conversation with the author, December 1993.

19. Kenneth Baker, "Foreword," *Gordon Cook: A Retrospective*, exh. cat. (Oakland and San Francisco: The Oakland Museum and Chronicle Books, 1987), viii.

20. Yvonne Jacquette, lecture, San Francisco Art Institute, 1985.

21. Conversation with the author, June 1994.

22. Todd W. Hosfelt, gallery statement (from conversation with artist), Haines Gallery, San Francisco, 1993.

23. Holland Cotter, "Martin Wong," *New York Times*, 29 January 1993.

24. Elizabeth Hess, "Wong Benevolent Association," *Village Voice*, 26 January 1993, 82.

25. Willard Dixon in Alan Gussow, *The Artist As Native: Reinventing Regionalism* (New York: Chameleon Books, Inc., 1993), 94.

26. Gussow, *Artist*, 94.

27. Christopher Brown in Thomas H. Garver, "Painted Walls — The Painting Room," *Christopher Brown: The Painted Room / A Cycle of Landscape Paintings* (Madison, Wisc.: The Madison Art Center, 1985), n.p.

28. Conversation with the author, June 1994.

29. Jamie Brunson, "John Meyer: The Direct Experience," *Artspace* 15, no.2 (January-February, 1991): 33.

30. Brunson, "John Meyer," 34.

31. Conversation with the author, June 1994.

32. Conversation with the author, June 1994.

33. Eleanor Heartney, "Paul Resika at Salander-O'Reilly," *Art in America* (June 1993): 98.

34. Bill Berkson, "Five Bay Area Artists," *Art International* (Autumn 1989): 50.

35. Frank Tuttle, quote in press release, Meridian Gallery, May-June 1993.

36. Berkeley and Los Angeles: University of California Press, 1961.

37. Conversation with the author, July 1994.

Jo Babcock, *The Cypress, 880 Freeway*, 1989
Color coupler/paper negative, 40 x 71 in.
Courtesy the artist, *cat.no.6*

Seeking Place: Photographic Reflections on the Landscape of the Bay Area

Ellen Manchester

Landscape photography in California has most often been defined by images of spectacular mountains of the high Sierra, rocky cliffs of the coast, or sensuous dunes and arid canyons of the desert. The city of San Francisco and the surrounding region only occasionally have been the subjects of extensive landscape photography. Aside from the compelling documents of San Francisco's catastrophic earthquake and fire of 1906, photographs of the actual landscape and environment of the Bay Area – of the history of the relationship between human culture and nature – have rarely been considered, assembled, or studied as a group.

By its very nature, the gathering of this work implies a shift in several directions in our thinking about the landscape. First, it recognizes new and complex definitions of landscape that consider the total physical environment within which we live, whether it is inner city, urban, suburban, rural, or wilderness. Second, it traces the ways cultural attitudes toward land and landscape of the Bay Area are reflected through the media of the visual arts. And finally, it acknowledges that photographs and paintings are not discrete objects separated from the geographic environment and sociopolitical milieu from which they were made, and that despite their apparent objectivity, they reflect, confirm, or anticipate strongly held social values. As the writer and poet Gretel Ehrlich proposes:

Landscape does not exist without an observer, without a human presence. The land exists, but the "scape" is a projection of human consciousness, an image received. It is a frame we put around a single view and the ways in which we see and describe this spectacle represent our "frame of mind," what we know and what we seek to know.[1]

Until recently, landscape and nature have often been perceived as "out there" and as "the other" – either as a force to be conquered and controlled, or as unspoiled wilderness to be appreciated and revered. This attitude, which we inherited and embraced from the nineteenth century, has allowed us as a society to objectify and therefore exploit without conscience the natural world. It is this historical separation of "nature" from "culture" that has led us in part to the many social and ecological crises we face on the planet today. Ehrlich asks:

[D]id the idea of landscape-as-garden arise from a fear of nature or from a love of wild things? Either way, in the wrong hands this "civilizing" process in effect blinded us. It reduced the wildness, diversity, and transience of nature to a formula that said: this is a flower and this is a weed; this is sublime and this is ugly. As conquerors and as gardeners we came to a landscape with serious intentions: not simply to know, but to change; not just to visit, but to possess. . . .We imposed on what we found; we could not cherish without embellishing or altering what was simply there.[2]

The growing environmental awareness that emerged in the 1950s and '60s, as well as satellite views of Earth from space, have contributed to our modern-day recognition that the planet is finite, that our resources are limited, and that all actions – human, cultural, political, and ecological – are interconnected. We can no longer regard nature and the environment as rarefied commodities that we "do" on weekends, but rather as integral parts of our daily lives, as a reflection of our noblest ideas, darkest desires, and ordinary vernacular expressions. The landscape, whether it be inner city or high Sierra, becomes the place where we put our ideas – where our culture's history and expectations are realized.

The development of photography conveniently parallels the development of San Francisco as a modern city and offers scholars and historians a unique opportunity to trace its physical and cultural growth through the lens of the seemingly objective camera. In the nineteenth century, when photography was still in its infancy, photographs were often regarded as absolute descriptions of the reality of an object, place, or event. It is commonly believed that early viewers of photographs could not significantly distinguish the experience of the photograph from the experience of its subject. The photograph defined reality with a convincingly mechanical precision. Today, we are well aware of the danger of assuming the "documentary" nature of any photograph, and know we must consider every image within the context of its time and as a reflection of an individual artist's ideas and cultural impulses.

This book traces the development of landscape photography in the Bay Area, from the commercial documents of the late nineteenth century that promoted a vision of prosperity through the control of nature, to

fig.1 Eadweard Muybridge, *Panorama of San Francisco from the California Street Hill*, 1878
Albumen silver prints from wet-plate collodion glass negatives,
mounted on paper, 1 of 13 plates, 20½ x 16 in. each
Department of Special Collections,
Stanford University Library, *cat.no.115*

images that use nature as a backdrop for the explorations of pictorial, aesthetic, or psychological ideas, and to the work of contemporary artists that investigates the relationship of human actions and political policies to the natural and cultural landscape. A brief look at the early years of the medium provides a background that is helpful in understanding the evolution of landscape photography in the Bay Area in the twentieth century.

By the early nineteenth century artists and scholars in England and the rest of Europe were tinkering with methods of capturing images from nature on light-sensitive materials, and in the summer of 1839 the French public was given the "magic formula" for the new daguerreotype process. As early as the fall of that year the process was brought to the United States, and within a year daguerrean studios were well established in New York, Boston, Baltimore, and Washington. Americans embraced the new technology with an enthusiasm unparalleled in Europe. Perhaps the country's fascination with the machine, the rise of the industrial era, and honest "Yankee ingenuity" helped American artisans to master the time-consuming and arduous technique.

Because the process required complicated equipment and work with highly toxic chemicals many early photographic explorations concentrated on studio portraiture where the conditions could be carefully controlled by the artist. The demand for quick, inexpensive portraits of loved ones, however, was soon matched by the demand for picturesque images of the nation's countryside. With few national monuments and architectural achievements to its name, the nation sought its identity through photographs of the wonders of the landscape from the White Mountains of New Hampshire and Niagara's majestic falls to the sublime beauty of the Rockies and the Sierra Nevada. Architecture and street scenes of the United States' burgeoning urban culture also drew photographers' attention, and rapidly proved to be popular commodities.[3]

However, by the 1850s and '60s San Francisco was on a course of rapid development, fueled by the explosion of mining, railroads, shipping and agriculture. Daguerrean "practitioners" or "operators," as well as glass-plate artists of the '60s and '70s, recognized the historical importance and commercial value of city views – sweeping vistas or panoramas from the top of prominent hills or buildings. The completion of the transcontinental railroad in 1869 and the move of the Central Pacific Railroad offices to San Francisco in 1873 solidified San Francisco's position as the center of wealth and power for the West. With the railroad industry came the building of enormous mansions for their owners Mark Hopkins, Charles Crocker, and Leland Stanford on the California Street hill. It was from Hopkins's residence that photographer Eadweard Muybridge completed his ambitious panoramas of San Francisco

in 1877 and again in 1878. Working with glass plate negatives as large as 16 x 20 inches, Muybridge produced a comprehensive portrait of the proud city that was widely marketed and appreciated (fig.1). Muybridge's description of this work provides insight into his motivations and considerations for making the image:

I have the pleasure of informing you that I have just published a photographic Panorama of San Francisco, *the points of view being from the tower of the new residence of Mark Hopkins, Esq., about 400 feet above the waters of the Bay.*

The day selected for its execution was remarkable for the clearness of the atmosphere; all the public buildings, hotels and banks, all the wharves, with very few exceptions, and nearly all the stores and private residences within a radius of six miles being clearly distinguishable, the whole forming a complete Panorama of the entire city, its picturesque suburbs and surrounding ranges of hills.

It is nearly eight feet long, mounted on cloth, folded into eleven sections and bound in a cloth cover nine inches wide by twelve inches high, accompanied with a key and index of 220 references.[4]

These grand views, as well as those of earlier artists such as George Robinson Fardon, Isaiah West Taber, and Carleton Eugene Watkins, provided visual proof of San Francisco's powerful role in the industrial age – the city had triumphantly conquered the unruly and difficult nature of its geography and weather, overcoming its steep hills, sandy dunes, marshy wetlands, foggy skies, earthquakes, and fire. The public's fascination with the still-new medium of photography and its ability to record the patterns of environmental change and cultural activity is reflected in the sale of these photographs with extensive documentation and keys to prominent buildings and landmarks throughout the city.[5] Like the satellite images of today, these photographs reaffirmed existence by locating the viewer in a specific time and geographic context. Unlike today, however, these images promoted a vision of nature as something to be overcome, a commodity to be bought, sold, and controlled. It is not surprising that during this same period, the 1860s through the '90s, artists such as Muybridge, Watkins, Timothy O'Sullivan, William Henry Jackson, and A. J. Russell were also going to great effort to make large-scale "views." This time the views were of the wild, untamed landscapes of the American West. The images, which were often produced on commission for the government or railroad companies, served to further promote landscape and nature as a commodity – a view to be owned or a resource to be exploited through mining, water management, agriculture, or urban development. Furthermore, images of the sublime and monumental in nature often brought comfort and solace to a society that was feeling the increased pressures of urban life.[6]

fig.2 Willard Worden, *Presidio and Angel Island, San Francisco Bay*, ca. 1910
Gelatin silver print, 4 x 8 in.
Collection of The Oakland Museum of California,
gift of Dr. Robert Shimshak, *cat.no.174*

With the city comprehensively documented in the late years of the nineteenth century, artists began to turn their attention to what they considered more artistic and aesthetic pursuits. The rise of pictorialism in the late '90s came about partially as a reaction against the mechanical/scientific nature of photography in the nineteenth century and partially, as Sarah Greenough states in *The Art of Fixing a Shadow*,
from a crisis of faith experienced by all the arts in the late 1880s and 1890s. Pictorialism, like symbolist art and literature, was a direct result of a waning belief in the power of science, positivism, and empiricism, and a disenchantment with the dominant materialist ethos of the nineteenth century. . . . Artists of the 1880s and 1890s came to believe that their work, through the expression of subjective and abstract states of being, could reveal a higher and more universal reality than that which could be discovered by any scientific method of investigation.[7]

Pictorialism attempted to bring photography into the world of "high art" by mimicking the world of painting with smaller format cameras, soft-focus images, and intimate and delicate prints. Many artists printed their photographs on hand-prepared papers that had been brushed with non-silver photographic

materials such as gum bichromate or platinum. Often their prints were heavily reworked on the surface, or the brush strokes were consciously evident. In marked contrast to the earlier panoramas of Muybridge, Watkins, or Fardon, Willard Worden's views of Seal Rock and the Presidio and Angel Island (fig.2), taken from the edges of the city looking out, focus more on the beauty of the natural environment surrounding the bay and less on the glorification of the modern city. Worden, like many of the pictorialists, saw the natural world as a convenient and appropriate vehicle for the expression of personal and aesthetic ideas about composition and style. Also, he and other pictorialists in the area may have been influenced by the activities of John Muir and the Sierra Club, founded in San Francisco in 1892. It is interesting to note that under Muir's direction from 1892 to his death in 1914 the club focused its efforts on the protection and conservation of the Sierra Nevada, and specifically, Yosemite, primarily for scenic, aesthetic, and personal reasons – much the way the pictorialists viewed nature and landscape.[8] Little attention was paid to the scientific, biological, and ecological need for the conservation of nature. Worden's images, which generally are dated ca.1902-10, were probably made before

fig.3 J. D. Givens, *Jones and Pine*, 1906
Gelatin silver print, 6 x 16 in.
Courtesy Stephen Wirtz Gallery, San Francisco, *cat.no.61*

April 1906 when the devastating earthquake and fire leveled the city, turning everyone's attention to the smoldering ruins and the task of rebuilding.

No other event in the history of the city has produced such an extensive body of photographs as the San Francisco earthquake and fire of 1906. Recognizing the commercial value of earthquake views, photographers scurried frantically to produce broad panoramas of the leveled, burning city as well as haunting images of the shells of buildings and people's brave efforts at getting on with their lives. J. D. Givens's devastating panorama of the city reduced to smoke and rubble (fig.3) provides a dramatic contrast to Muybridge's earlier panorama, which is so full of the future. Givens had an eye for the unusual and surreal. His compelling images of street scenes after the quake result from his ability to juxtapose strong compositional elements with the ironies of street life in a time of disaster (page 186). These haunting images recall photographs made of shelled cities in the South after the Civil War, and reflect a pervasive nineteenth-century fascination with death and destruction. In addition, as these startling images became known on the East Coast through newspaper reproductions, journals, and the sales of stereo views

and prints, the public's perception of California as an exotic landscape was further reinforced.

Less than three weeks after the earthquake, in marked contrast to the violence and destruction surrounding her, amateur hobbyist Christine Pomeroy turned her camera to the sea, photographing the ships and sailboats in the bay in a delicate and ethereal style. For the next three years, her photographs with their snapshot quality, fresh vision, and strong pictorial aesthetic direct the viewer away from the past and toward the future (fig.4). Her images, made with a small, hand-held camera, also show the influence of the "snapshot" aesthetic that became popular at the turn of the century after the introduction of Eastman's Kodak camera and roll film in 1888. Because of the new cameras and inexpensive processing, photography was now accessible to the lay public. For the first time individuals could make their own photographic responses to the world, unconstrained by the limitations of high art and complicated equipment. The public compulsively documented its environment and every excursion, whether it was to the backyard, city park, or distant wonders of Yellowstone, Yosemite, or the Grand Canyon. These vernacular images reflect the public's fascination with exploring

fig.4 Christine Pomeroy, *USS Honolulu, May 6, 1908*, 1908
Gelatin silver print, 2 x 7 in.
Courtesy Stephen Wirtz Gallery, San Francisco, *cat.no.129*

fig.5 Anne Brigman, *Tranquility*, 1929
Gelatin silver print, 6⅝ x 9¾ in.
San Francisco Museum of Modern Art,
gift of Robert Durden, *cat.no.15*

fig.6 Johan Hagemeyer, *Castles of Today (San Francisco)*, 1922
Gelatin silver print, 8 x 10 in.
Collection, Center for Creative Photography,
The University of Arizona, *cat.no.73*

its personal world, which was further aided by the concurrent development of modern transportation, the railroad, and the establishment of urban and national parks throughout the country.

The work of Anne Brigman fully embraced the pictorialist style that still dominated photographic activity on the West Coast in the early to mid-'20s. Brigman retreated to parks, mountain tops, and other natural environments, often choreographing the nude human figure against the landscape. Her work is strongly symbolic in its attempts to discover a spiritual connection to earth, landscape, nature, and the elements in a postwar society in need of spiritual meaning and direction. Her free spirit and photographic activity certainly anticipated recent performance art and feminist investigations of the forces in nature and rituals in ancient cultures (fig.5).

Emerging from the pictorialist period, Edward Weston, along with Alfred Stieglitz in New York, became a leading proponent of the medium's transition from soft-focus, romantic pictorialism to straight, precisionist photography. Although Weston produced few landscape images in the immediate Bay Area, his influence can be felt in the work of artists such as Johan Hagemeyer, John Paul Edwards, Alma Lavenson, and Ansel Adams. Weston and these other artists began to consider the formal aspects of objective reality and to discover beauty in the natural and manufactured world, rather than in the manipulation of the negative or print. No subject was beyond their inquiry – urban skyscrapers, steel mills, port activity, the human body, and the natural world. The work became straighter, more direct, without cropping or manipulation, and without oppressive allegorical or symbolic meaning, leaving the viewer free to confront the object or the scene itself.

While the photographs of John Paul Edwards and Johan Hagemeyer still bear a resemblance to the pictorial mode, both artists were seeking an objective reality and aesthetic beauty in the formal aspects of the new urban landscape. Hagemeyer, a close associate of Weston, produced an extensive body of work that documented the landscape and industrial buildings of the Bay Area. He often experimented, as in his *Castles of Today (San Francisco)*, 1922 (fig.6), with the artistic device of shooting at extreme angles, or with a telephoto lens to compress objects against the picture plane. The close-up abstractions by these artists were intended to be seen purely as descriptions of the objects themselves, not as symbols or metaphors for larger or more abstract concepts. Alma Lavenson focused her camera on the Port of Oakland and the estuary (fig.7), seeking simple abstractions and beauty in everyday objects of fishing fleets and grain elevators. As photohistorian and curator Susan Ehrens states, Lavenson was drawn to "industrial and architectural themes.

These subjects were traditionally favored by men, and they were often portrayed as symbols of the modern machine age. Alma's interest in machines was strictly formal." Ehrens quotes Lavenson, "I never took them as machinery. I always saw them as a composition of some sort."[10]

Lavenson, Edwards, Adams, and Weston later became part of the Group *f*.64 – an informal association of artists who flatly rejected pictorialism and promoted straight photography. Their efforts were formalized in an exhibition of their photographs at the M. H. de Young Memorial Museum in San Francisco in 1932, and the following year the de Young gave Lavenson a one-person show. Although the artists continued to meet together and maintained many of their associations with each other throughout the years, the group had little official activity and eventually dissolved. Their influence on the medium, however, can still be seen today in the work of many contemporary artists such as Catherine Wagner, Lewis Baltz, and Robert Dawson, who embrace the large-format negative, a straight, unmanipulated printing style, and direct images that are free of romantic or symbolic meaning.

Although she was a close associate of many of the *f*.64 artists, Dorothea Lange was never an official member. Her work, however, was highly respected by the group, and in 1934 one of the members, Willard Van Dyke, gave her an exhibition at his Oakland gallery. It was at this exhibition that agricultural economist Paul Taylor first saw Lange's work. In early 1935 he asked her to accompany him on several of his field visits to provide photographic illustrations for his work on agriculture and the rural poor for the State Emergency Relief Administration. This work eventually led to her being hired by the Farm Security Administration for an ambitious photographic project to document the plight of the rural poor from the backcountry of the southeastern United States to the fields of California's Central Valley. Lange drew from her experience as a portrait photographer in her documentary work for the government and made thousands of images that brought the harsh realities and the poignant ironies of the depression to the public's attention through reproductions in magazines, newspapers, and journals.[11] Her image of a real estate office in Oakland (fig.8), with its handwritten signs filling the frame and the realtor expectantly greeting the housewife, indicates her interest in the rapid transformations our society was experiencing and the effect that the rise of the new urban United States had on the rural poor. With the nude hills in the background waiting to be built upon, Lange's image becomes an ironic picture of expectation and hope for a middle class that would later emerge with strength in the postwar United States. As Sandra Phillips suggests in her recent book and exhibition, *Dorothea Lange: American Photographs,*

fig.7 Alma Lavenson, *Oakland Estuary*, 1926
Gelatin silver print, 10½ x 13⅝ in.
Courtesy Susan Ehrens, *cat.no.98*

fig.8 Dorothea Lange, *Real Estate Office, Oakland, California*, 1936
Modern gelatin silver photographic print from original negative, 8 x 10 in.
Courtesy Ellen Manchester; from the U.S. Farm Security Administration Collection,
Prints and Photographs Division, Library of Congress, Washington, D.C., *cat.no.96*

*Part of what makes Dorothea Lange's work so compelling,
and therefore so appropriate to reconsider, is its vital and
imaginative personal vision. . . . The pictures are saved from
sentimentality by Lange's intelligence and by her realization
of the complexity of events, circumstances, and character.
Although made in the context of social documentation, they
depict an ideal, an America of hard-working, good-spirited,
and fair people, some of whom need a little help. These particular people and circumstances are posed within a large
and coherent world view that valued a certain kind of American culture but also acknowledged its transformation.*[12]

In the early to mid-'30s, in marked contrast to the
work of the Group *f.*64 artists and parallel to the studied
documentary style that emerged during the FSA, the
adoption of the small format and "miniature camera"
(35mm) precipitated the rise of photojournalism and
the illustrated magazine in both Europe and the United
States. In the Bay Area, artists such as John Gutmann
and Peter Stackpole embraced the new medium with
distinctly individual styles and aesthetics. Gutmann,
who was born in Germany and trained as a painter during the Weimar Republic, fled the increasing oppression
of the Third Reich by getting himself hired as a photojournalist after shooting only three rolls of film that he
had store-processed. His eye for the vernacular and for
dynamic juxtapositions and exaggerated perspectives
brought a fresh aesthetic to the teeming social landscapes of Los Angeles and San Francisco in the late '30s.
His photographs speak eloquently and without apology
to the tensions between cultural and ethnic groups, to
the politics of the depression, and to the everyday vitality of urban life. In *Yes, Columbus, Mission District* (fig.9
and back cover) Gutmann's landscape is the city – its
buildings, people, the streets, signs, cars, and graffiti,
unadorned by nature and geography. Ten years later in
A Tree at Hunter's Point, San Francisco, 1948, Gutmann
steps back from the intensity of urban street life and
photographs a stoic tree against the backdrop of workers' housing in the bulldozed landscape at the city's
edge. Both images have a poignancy and style that
reflect Gutmann's European training and his eye for the
vernacular in the American social landscape. As Max
Kozloff comments in his introduction to *The Restless
Decade: John Gutmann's Photographs of the Thirties*,
*It was his good fortune to have gotten under way as an artist
in his homeland but to have come of age, as a photographer,
in his adopted country. What he carried with him and what
he learned were fused vitally into an unexpected pictorial
enterprise. In acting as an instinctual broker between the
visual value systems of the milieu he left and the one he
entered, between two time and space frames, therefore, Gutmann mingled the look of them.*[13]

Until recent years Gutmann's work has been largely
unrecognized in standard histories of photography in
part, perhaps, because his style does not conveniently

fig.9 John Gutmann, *Yes, Columbus, Mission District, San Francisco*, ca. 1938
Gelatin silver print, 8 x 10 in.
Courtesy Fraenkel Gallery, San Francisco, *cat.no.*69

fit the stereotypical, and sometimes romantic, notions
of suffering and despair we so often ascribe to the
depression era.

In 1936 Peter Stackpole, who had been a member
of the Group *f.*64, became one of four original staff
members for the new picture magazine *Life*. During
the depression enormous public works projects such
as the building of the Golden Gate and Bay Bridges were
undertaken and Stackpole documented the construction of both bridges from the dizzying perspective of
an ironworker (fig.10). While clearly in the documentary tradition, his series also reflected the modern fascination in both photography and film for taking the camera to dramatic heights and precarious, disorienting
perches that flattened the picture plane and produced
highly energized abstractions. Alvin Langdon Coburn's
abstract, cubistic *New York from Its Pinnacles*, 1913;
Moholy-Nagy's *From the Radio Tower, Berlin*, 1928; and
Lewis Hine's series of steelworkers on top of the Empire
State Building, 1931, are all possible influences on this
work. The bird's-eye view placed the bridges and the
city in their geographic surroundings, revealed to the
viewer the patterns of human activity on the landscape,
and symbolically helped strengthen a nation's fragile
self-confidence through their sheer size, physicality,
and accomplishment.

Edward Weston's son Brett was also active in the Bay
Area at this period and produced an extensive body of
work documenting San Francisco and the edges of the
city. His *Untitled (View of Hunter's Point)* taken in 1939
demonstrates the influence on his work of the modernist direction of the Group *f.*64, as well as the '30s
fascination for documentation (fig.11).

fig.10 Peter Stackpole
Catwalk and Marin Tower, 1936
Gelatin silver print, 6¼ x 9 ⅜ in.
Collection of The Oakland Museum of California,
The Oakland Museum Founders Fund, *cat.no.150*

fig.11 Brett Weston, *Untitled (View of Hunter's Point)*, 1939
Gelatin silver print, 8 x 10 in.
Collection of Ron and Kathy Perisho, *cat.no.165*

fig.12 Pirkle Jones, *Sunset District and Pacific Ocean, San Francisco,* 1951
Gelatin silver print, 18¼ x 24¼ in.
Courtesy the artist, *cat.no.89*

By the late '40s and early '50s the flowering of photography programs at Bay Area colleges such as the California School of Fine Arts (now the San Francisco Art Institute) brought increased academic inquiry into the nature of the medium, and artists such as Minor White and Pirkle Jones (fig.12) began to explore the more personal and psychological interpretations of photographs. Profoundly influenced by Alfred Stieglitz's equivalents and Edward Weston's commitment to the essence of the object, White pushed the boundaries of the predominant mode of "straight photography" at the time. White, who was brought to the School of Fine Arts by his friend Ansel Adams, undertook an extensive project documenting the urban life of San Francisco. Between 1949 and 1953 he produced more than six thousand negatives for this series, nearly one third of his life's work.[14] Aside from six hundred images that White deposited at the California Historical Society, much of this work went unnoticed until Peter Bunnell's 1989 exhibition and book, *Minor White: The Eye That Shapes.* As Bunnell states,
A fascinating and important aspect of this San Francisco imagery is how it demonstrates White's commitment to photographing, not simply as an activity but as a basis for gaining knowledge and understanding. We know the world – and ourselves – by the use we make of the world. [15]

fig.13 Minor White, *Warehouse Area, San Francisco,* 1949
Gelatin silver print, 8 x 11⅝ in.
The Art Museum, Princeton University,
the Minor White Archive, *cat.no.166*

173

The three photographs, *Daly City Dump, California,
1953; Warehouse Area, San Francisco,* 1949 (fig.13); and
San Francisco, California, 1952, are mysterious, ambiguous, and highly energized depictions of life in a modern
American city grounded by the stuff of urban landscapes
– pavement, sidewalks, warehouses, curbs, and dumps.
While committed to an observed reality, these images
begin to announce White's move toward personal intro-
spection, psychological interpretations, and abstraction
of the photographic image. As White himself explained
in his journal entry "Memorable Fancies, April 2, 1950,"
"Abstraction in photography is to reach towards the
non-objective without ever breaking camera's strongest
point – the magic of its tether to visual reality."[16]

White has profoundly influenced contemporary
photography, not only as a practicing artist, but also
as a dedicated teacher, writer, and editor. His circle of
friends in the Bay Area included Ansel Adams, Edward
Weston, Dorothea Lange, Rose Mandel, and Imogen
Cunningham. Beaumont and Nancy Newhall, the
noted historians and curators, visited often, and in
1952 Adams, Lange, the Newhalls, and White launched
a new photography publication, *Aperture.* White became
the magazine's editor and manager, and through its
high-quality reproductions, critical essays, poetry, and
text he brought a new level of scholarly inquiry and
national recognition to fine-art photography.

Rose Mandel, one of White's students at the School
of Fine Arts, produced some of her strongest work
during the '50s and '60s. Her views of Richmond and
Berkeley from the Marina are evocative images that perhaps reflect her transition from a straight documentary
style to work that is more abstract and psychological
in nature (fig.14).

Ansel Adams was one of the few artists during this
period who was drawn to the large, sweeping vistas of
the natural landscape of the Bay Area. With his grand,
monumental views of *The Golden Gate before the Bridge,
(San Francisco, California),* ca. 1932 (fig.15), and the later
San Francisco from the San Bruno Mountains, California,
ca. 1952 (fig.16), and *Marin Hills, over the Golden Gate from
Lincoln Park, San Francisco,* ca.1950, we see the influence
that nineteenth-century artists such as William Henry
Jackson and Timothy O'Sullivan had on his work. The
large scale of the negative and print, infinite detail, majestic skies, dramatic geography, and the almost physical plunge into perspective from the viewer's position
at the front of the picture plane are all pictorial devices
utilized by nineteenth-century painters and photographers. What is most interesting about this series of
images is that these particular views remain relatively
unchanged today. If one hikes to the original camera
location of any one of these places, the scene appears
similar to what it was forty to sixty years ago except for
the predictable vegetational changes and the growth of

skyscrapers in the distant city. Saved by activists, or
ironically by the presence of the military at the Presidio
and Headlands for so many years, these greenbelts
frame the Bay Area cities with a necklace of parks, trails,
mountain ridges, and wetlands. It is as if Adams had a
premonition that these landscapes might indeed change
dramatically in the years to come. Adams wrote in 1936:
*As I sit writing you I see out of my window the two enormous
towers of the Golden Gate Bridge and I can visualize the still
larger Bay Bridge going up to the east. I am wondering what
these bridges will do to our local civilization. They will open
up a vast territory in which all the miserable fungus of
"development" will flourish. And yet, the bridges are magnificent in themselves; they are potential instruments for
good but they won't be used that way. And the funny thing is
that I don't want to photograph them – I would rather work
on an old fence with moss on it. Do I live in the past – or in
the future?* [17]

By photographing from prominent elevations outside the city, rather than from within the urban core,
Adams continually placed San Francisco within the
spectacular geography of the Bay Area. The monumental scale and dramatic rendering of each of his scenes,
however, tends to further separate human experience
from the landscape. These are not landscapes where
one can feel the texture of the grass, smell the eucalyptus, or observe the smallest stone. Adams's work in
the Bay Area is somewhat of an anomaly for him, as
he was personally most drawn to Yosemite, the high
Sierra Nevada, and the arid landscapes of the Southwest. Except for commissioned work for banks, winer-
ies, and the University of California, Berkeley, Adams
seems to have subscribed to the notion of landscape
being "out there" – places with exotic geography that
are separated from our daily lives by travel and a shift
in perspective. This was a view that was commonly
held by the Sierra Club at the time, and much of the
pioneering work done at the club by executive director
David Brower and trustee Adams perpetuated this idea
of wilderness and nature as the other – as designated
places one travels to in order to experience nature.
Through the exhibition format books in the '50s and
'60s Brower and Adams created in the public deep
appreciation for the beauty of nature and wilderness
though they may, in the long run, have further separated us from a true understanding of landscape and
the ecology of nature.[18]

In seeking a perspective that reflects the patterns
of geography and human activity on the landscape,
William Garnett and Robert Hartman both use aerial
photography; Milton Halberstadt used the pictorial
devise of pushing the horizon to the top of the picture
plane and compressing the space. Halberstadt was
a commercial photographer who had trained at the
Chicago School of Design and assisted Bauhaus artist

fig.14 Rose Mandel, *Berkeley Marina*, ca. 1962
Gelatin silver print, 3¾ x 4¾ in.
Courtesy the artist and Susan Ehrens, *cat.no.103*

fig.15 Ansel Adams, *The Golden Gate before the Bridge (San Francisco, California)*, ca. 1932
Gelatin silver print, 15 ⁵/₁₆ x 19⅛ in.
San Francisco Museum of Modern Art, gift of Alfred Fromm,
Otto Meyer, and Louis Petri, San Francisco, *cat.no.1*

fig.16 Ansel Adams, *San Francisco from the San Bruno Mountains, California*, ca. 1952
Gelatin silver print, 14⅝ x 18 ¾ in.
Collection of The Friends of Photography/Ansel Adams Center
for Photography, San Francisco, *cat.no.3*

fig.17 Milton Halberstadt, *San Francisco from Twin Peaks (Noe Valley)*, 1954
Gelatin silver print, tone-line process, 12½ x 19⅜ in.
Courtesy the artist and Leland Rice, *cat.no.75*

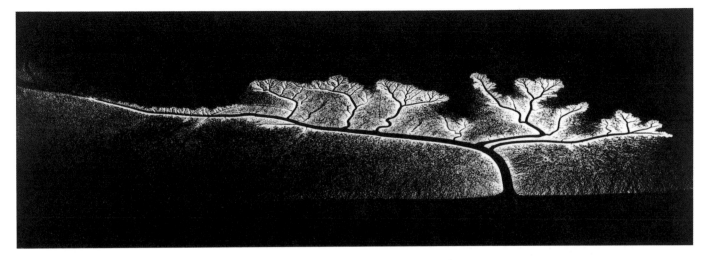

fig.18 William Garnett, *Reflection of the Sun on Dendritic Flow, San Francisco Bay, California*, 1963
Gelatin silver print, 6¾ x 19¾ in.
Courtesy the artist and Vision Gallery, San Francisco, *cat.no.54*

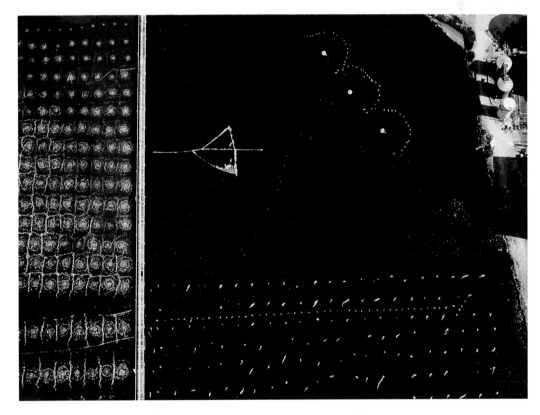

fig.19 Robert Hartman, *Constellations*, 1992
Cibachrome print, 14 x 19½ in.
Triangle Gallery, San Francisco, *cat.no.78*

fig.20 Bill Owens, *In One Day You Have Instant Yard,*
from *Suburbia,* 1972
Gelatin silver print, 7⅞ x 9⅞ in.
Courtesy Bill Owens, *cat.no.123*

Gyorgy Kepes. His graphic, high-contrast prints are a curious combination of Bauhaus style, commercial design, and the influence of Bay Area painters such as Wayne Thiebaud and Richard Diebenkorn (fig.17). William Garnett's earlier work from the '60s seems to focus more on the beauty of the abstractions formed by the physical geography of the bay (fig.18), whereas Hartman's recent work incorporates more of the effects of large-scale human activity on the landscape. The beauty of the modern, abstract designs formed by oil refineries, wastewater treatment plants, and dirt bikes often obscures the reality of the damage these activities have done to our region (fig.19).

Since its earliest days, the Bay Area often has been portrayed through photographs as a region of limitless natural and cultural resources. It was not until the '60s that artists began to seriously question the effects of unchecked urban growth on the landscape of the Bay Area. Bill Owens's *Suburbia* series published in 1972 pointed the way to further investigations of and challenges to the secure, complacent suburban lifestyle (fig.20).[19] With the rise of environmental awareness came the realization that society must begin to take responsibility for the preservation and restoration of cultural and natural landscapes.

The emergence of the environmental movement paralleled a growing interest by photographers in the relationship of landscape photography to cultural geography and landscape history. The writings of preeminent scholar John Brinckerhoff Jackson, published in the late '70s and early '80s, were widely read by photographers who were seeking a broader and more comprehensive

understanding of the landscape they were photographing. Jackson's work looks openly and without political bias at the landscape as a reflection and expression of human and cultural ideas.[20] Artists such as Bill Owens, Catherine Wagner, Lewis Baltz, Jerry Burchard, Hank Wessel, and Robert Dawson began to turn their critical eyes toward an investigation of the social landscape and the relationship of human culture to the land and the environment.[21] Catherine Wagner's images of the Moscone Center's massive construction project that dislocated many lower-income residents (fig.21); Owens's photographs of the exploding suburbs on the countryside; Henry Wessel's ironic and austere portraits of urban trees and homes (fig.22); Jerry Burchard's frantic, highly energized night photographs; and Lewis Baltz's acerbic renderings of neglected landscapes at the fringes of the city challenge us with irony, humor, and sometimes outright despair to consider what our relationships to the urban landscape really mean and how those attitudes will affect the look and health of the Bay Area in years to come.[22]

Lewis Baltz chose the neglected postindustrial area of San Quentin Point to seek a new definition of contemporary landscape (fig.23). At the urban edge, between the horror of one of the nation's most notorious prisons and the insanity of unchecked real estate development in one of the wealthiest counties in the United States, Baltz throws before the viewer in an almost forensic manner the detritus of society – bedsprings, tires, whisky bottles, sheetrock – and tenacious weeds . Through the large scale of the prints and the convention of either placing the horizon at the top of the image or employing a very short focal distance, Baltz pushes the picture plane and the unappealing information in our faces, forcing us to confront not only the evidence but its meaning. Baltz's images encourage questioning why our culture does not consider such landscapes significant or worthy of attention.

In marked contrast to these frightening images, photographers Bob Walker and Robert Buelteman chose to seek out the classic beauty of the greenbelts and undeveloped landscapes of the Bay Area. Both artists have been strongly committed to environmental issues and placed their work in the hands of activist organizations in order to promote conservation and preservation of these last remaining natural areas. Walker (who died tragically at an early age) and Buelteman both adopted a photographic style similar to Ansel Adams in their classic and often romantic descriptions of nature. Both artists saw the pressures of urban development on these landscapes and worked diligently to hold back those intrusions. One needs only to hike the hills of Walker's Dougherty Valley (page xxiii) or drive Highway 280 at any time of day to appreciate what beauty still endures in the Bay Area (fig.24).

fig.21 Catherine Wagner, *George Moscone Site,*
Arch Construction III, San Francisco, CA, 1981
Gelatin silver print, 20 x 24 in.
Courtesy Fraenkel Gallery, San Francisco, *cat.no.161*

fig.22 Henry Wessel, *Point Richmond, CA,* 1985
Gelatin silver print, 24 x 20 in.
Courtesy Fraenkel Gallery, San Francisco, *cat.no.164*

fig.23 Lewis Baltz, *San Quentin Point, #11,* 1982-83
Gelatin silver print, 20 x 24 in.
Courtesy Stephen Wirtz Gallery, San Francisco, *cat.no.7*

179

fig.24 Robert L. Buelteman, Jr., *280 Sunrise*, 1988
Gelatin silver selenide print, 19 x 19 in.
Courtesy the artist and Vision Gallery, San Francisco, *cat.no.20*

fig.25 Lyle Gomes, *Double Arrow, San Francisco Presidio*, 1990
Gelatin silver print, 7 x 19 in.
Courtesy the artist and Vision Gallery, San Francisco, *cat.no.67*

In the work of Jo Babcock, Douglas Muir, and Lyle Gomes we see the full spectrum of what it means to live and work in the landscape of the Bay Area. From Babcock's frightening image of the collapse of the Cypress Freeway to Muir's *Citicorp Atrium, San Francisco* and Gomes's poetic vision of the Presidio we have landscapes full of horror, landscapes of the working world, and landscapes filled with promise for the future (pages 162, xxi, and fig.25).

Departing from traditional landscape photography, Robin Lasser and the collaborative team of Jock Reynolds and Suzanne Hellmuth began to work across disciplines and employed photographs as part of larger conceptual and installation projects. Their work came from a period in the '60s and '70s when artists such as Robert Smithson, Michael Heizer, and Nancy Holt began to question the commodification of art, moving their work into the area of performance art or outside the studio and gallery to produce large-scale, mostly temporary works on the landscape. Lasser uses the abandoned bunkers at Marin Headlands as a stage to produce her own contemporary ritual events that often have surreal and mysterious overtones. Many of her pieces acquire the feel of an archaeological site – of digging and unveiling layers of human history in the landscape (fig.26).[23] Reynolds and Hellmuth's work is the result of several projects that investigated human activity around the bay. In the *Pacific Bay Series* they collaged images that documented the daily lives and activities of fishermen on the bay (fig.27). In these images they brought the landscape of the ocean and the bay back to a human scale by emphasizing the human relationship to the sea and its life-giving elements. In the work of Hellmuth, Reynolds, and Lasser the photograph was de-emphasized as an art object and became more a part of a larger artistic process of inquiry. In the spirit of collaboration the works began to move away from the modernist approach of the single artist producing unique, monumental, and collectible objects to projects where artists worked together as teams reaching into history and the life of a community. Hellmuth and Reynolds have produced many projects that involved research into historical archives, community participation, and interdisciplinary installations. Lasser also worked on many projects that crossed in and out of photography, sculpture, installation, and performance.

In the mid-'80s Robert Dawson collaborated with photographer Stephen Johnson and writer Gerald Haslam on the *Great Central Valley Project* (fig.28). The project, which grew out of Johnson and Dawson's interest in revisiting their birthplace, focused on the agricultural landscape of one of California's most significant and productive regions.[24] The act of making the photographs, and the photographs themselves, became

fig.26 Robin Lasser, *Arson and Graffiti*, 1989
Gelatin silver print, 24 x 20 in.
Collection of Richard Titus, courtesy the artist, *cat.no.97*

part of a personal search by the artists to understand their homeland, as well as part of a larger interdisciplinary inquiry into the nature of the landscape and its meaning to contemporary California. While not overtly political, the book and the project as a whole tend to raise difficult questions about the effects of multinational agribusiness on the landscape and culture of this rural area. Both Johnson and Dawson previously fought to save Mono Lake by making their photographs of the area available to activists and lobbyists and by placing their images in larger group exhibitions and publications in an effort to educate the public about the environmental issues surrounding the lake. Dawson has continued to work on many other interdisciplinary and collaborative projects that deal with landscape and environmental issues in the American West.[25]

As part of a larger interdisciplinary project sponsored by Headlands Center for the Arts, Mark Klett used the Marin Headlands as a landscape to study human history in collaboration with conceptual artists Mike Mandel and Larry Sultan, writer/historian Paul Metcalf, and designer Miles DeCoster. In the publication *The Headlands Guidebook*[26] Klett demonstrates with sensitivity, humor, and new perspectives how landscapes are not anonymous places, but rather specific sites of natural and human histories. Through personal interviews, oral histories, portraiture, and historical research the project views the military's presence as an integral and often positive aspect of the history and preservation of this spectacular landscape.

fig.27 Jock Reynolds and Suzanne Hellmuth, *Low Tide*, from the *Pacific Bay Series*, 1981
Gelatin silver print, 20 x 72 in.
Courtesy Stephen Wirtz Gallery, San Francisco, *cat.no.133*

fig.28 Robert Dawson, *Farm and Windmills, Altamont Pass,
California*, from the *Great Central Valley Project*, 1986
Gelatin silver print, 13¹¹/₁₆ x 18⅛ in.
Courtesy the artist and Vision Gallery, San Francisco, *cat.no.33*

Klett challenges our notions of traditional landscape photography by using the large-format camera in combination with notations handwritten across the bottom of the print in silver ink, much the way one would caption a snapshot in an old family album with black pages. The photographs become a record of Klett's personal journey through the geography and the history of the Headlands as well as an invitation to explore the dramatic terrain (fig.29).

On the surface the work of these contemporary artists is not much different from that of their predecessors one hundred years earlier. However, their context and intent is radically different. These are no longer landscapes of unlimited resources and unrestrained human endeavor, but rather fragile ecological and cultural systems that are intricately connected on every level. The photographs are no longer isolated art objects that merely reflect a personal or aesthetic concern, but vital parts of an interdisciplinary process that inquires into the meaning of the landscapes we ourselves have produced. It is hoped that through these artists' unique and sometimes odd ways of seeing their home, we will experience the walk past the vacant lot to the corner grocery store, the drive across the Bay Bridge, or the hike through the East Bay hills in new and provocative ways. Each artist asks that we regard the landscape not merely as a scene to be viewed but rather as an organic, living, evolving experience where culture, personal history, and nature meet.

fig.29 Mark Klett, *Mounting Block above Fort Barry Rifle Range with Shield for Stray Bullets*, 4 July 1982
Gelatin silver print, 16 x 20 in.
Courtesy Fraenkel Gallery, San Francisco, *cat.no.94*

Notes

1. Gretel Ehrlich, "Surrender to the Landscape," *Harpers* (September 1987): 24-27.

2. Ehrlich, "Surrender," 24-27.

3. For an interesting social history of early photography in America, see Robert Taft, *Photography and the American Scene: A Social History, 1839-1889* (New York: Dover Publications, 1964).

4. David Harris, with Eric Sandweiss, *Eadweard Muybridge and the Photographic Panorama of San Francisco, 1850-1880* (Montreal: Canadian Centre for Architecture, 1993), 37. From a prospectus published by Morse's Gallery, 417 Montgomery Street, San Francisco, September 1877.

5. See Harris and Sandweiss, *Eadweard Muybridge*, for a thorough presentation of landscape photography of early San Francisco.

6. Images of the Rocky Mountains, Yellowstone, the Sierra Nevada, Yosemite, and the canyons of the Colorado River were especially popular and commercially successful on the East Coast from the 1870s through the '90s. Although prints made from glass-plate negatives as large as 20 x 24 inches were widely exhibited and published, it was the stereo view that captured the nation's attention and enjoyed broad commercial success. The stereo was a small card that, when viewed through a special holder, produced a three-dimensional effect. Pictures of sublime wilderness as well as vibrant new cities were immensely popular.

7. Sarah Greenough, "The Curious Contagion of the Camera, 1880-1918" in Sarah Greenough, Joel Snyder, David Travis, and Colin Westerbeck, *On the Art of Fixing a Shadow: One Hundred and Fifty Years of Photography* (Washington, D.C., and Chicago: The National Gallery of Art and The Art Institute of Chicago, 1989), 145.

8. For a history of the Sierra Club, see Michael P. Cohen, *The History of the Sierra Club, 1892-1970* (San Francisco: Sierra Club Books, 1988).

9. For information on Brigman and other California pictorialist photographers see *Pictorialism in California: Photographs 1900-1940*, essays by Michael G. Wilson and Dennis Reed (Malibu and San Marino: The J. Paul Getty Museum and The Henry E. Huntington Library and Art Gallery, 1994).

10. Susan Ehrens, *Alma Lavenson Photographs* (Berkeley: Wildwood Arts, 1990), 6.

11. The Farm Security Administration files are housed in the Library of Congress' Division of Prints and Photographs, and contain more than 150,000 prints made from the more than 272,000 negatives produced under the direction of Roy Stryker.

12. Sandra Phillips, Therese Thau Heyman, and John Szarkowski, *Dorothea Lange: American Photographs* (San Francisco: San Francisco Museum of Modern Art and Chronicle Books, 1994), 10.

13. Max Kozloff, *The Restless Decade: John Gutmann's Photographs of the Thirties* (New York: Harry N. Abrams, Inc., 1984), 9.

14. For further reading on this crucial period in White's career, see Peter Bunnell, *Minor White: The Eye That Shapes* (Princeton: The Art Museum, Princeton University, 1989).

15. Bunnell, *Minor White*, 52.

16. Bunnell, *Minor White*, 26

17. Letter from Adams to Alfred Stieglitz, 15 March 1936, from Mary Street Alinder and Andrea Gray Stillman, *Ansel Adams: Letters and Images, 1916-1984* (Boston: Little, Brown and Company, 1988), 83. Stieglitz was a prominent New York photographer, critic, editor, and gallery owner.

18. See Cohen, Sierra Club, for an account of Adams's long involvement with the Sierra Club and his relationship to David Brower.

19. See Bill Owens, *Suburbia* (San Francisco: Straight Arrow Books, 1972).

20. Publications by and about J. B. Jackson that were an influence on landscape photographers of the 1970s and '80s include John Brinckerhoff Jackson with Ervin H. Zube, ed., *Landscapes: Selected Writings of J.B. Jackson* (Amherst: University of Massachusetts Press, 1970); John Brinckerhoff Jackson with Ervin H. and Margaret J. Zube, eds., *Changing Rural Landscapes* (Amherst: University of Massachusetts Press, 1977); and John Brinckerhoff Jackson, *The Necessity for Ruins* (Amherst: University of Massachusetts Press, 1980).

21. For a discussion of the influence of Ansel Adams on contemporary landscape photographers see *Ansel Adams: New Light. Essays on His Legacy and Legend* (San Francisco: The Friends of Photography, 1993). From lectures and panel discussions held at the Ansel Adams Scholars Conference, The Friends of Photography, July 1992.

22. For a related discussion on the history of landscape photography in the American West see Deborah Bright, "Of Mother Nature and Marlboro Men: An Inquiry into the Cultural Meaning of Landscape Photography," *Exposure* 23, no. 4 (1985): 126-143.

23. For an in-depth history of performance art and site-specific work that deals with landscape, ritual, and myth, see Lucy Lippard, *Overlay: Contemporary Art and the Art of Prehistory* (New York: Pantheon Books, 1983).

24. See Robert Dawson, Gerald Haslam, and Stephen Johnson, *The Great Central Valley: California's Heartland* (Berkeley: University of California Press, 1993).

25. See Robert Dawson, *Photographs* (Tokyo: Gallery Min, 1988). Also, for a discussion of Dawson's involvement in the Water in the West Project see Ellen Manchester, *Arid Waters: Photographs from the Water in the West Project* (Reno: University of Nevada Press, 1992).

26. See Miles DeCoster, Mark Klett, Mike Mandel, Paul Metcalf, and Larry Sultan, *Headlands: The Marin Coast at the Golden Gate* (Albuquerque: University of New Mexico Press, 1989).

Works in the Exhibition

J.D. Givens, *Market and Sutter*, 1906
Gelatin silver print, 6 x 16 in.
Courtesy Stephen Wirtz Gallery, San Francisco, *cat.no.62*

Works of art are first listed alphabetically by artist and then chronologically by date of execution. Dimensions are given in inches and feet. In all measurements, height precedes width, which precedes depth.

Key to Acronyms

CCAC	*California College of Arts and Crafts*
CSAC	*California School of Arts and Crafts*
CSD	*California School of Design*
CSFA	*California School of Fine Arts*
MHIA	*Mark Hopkins Institute of Art*
SFAA	*San Francisco Art Association*
SFAI	*San Francisco Art Institute*
SFIA	*San Francisco Institute of Art*
SFSC	*San Francisco State College*
SFSU	*San Francisco State University*
UC	*University of California*

History of the San Francisco Art Institute

1871 – San Francisco Art Association (SFAA) founded
1874 – SFAA established the California School of Design (CSD)
1893 – Mark Hopkins Institute of Art (MHIA) established by SFAA on Nob Hill
1906 – MHIA razed by fire
1907 – school rebuilt and reopened; name changed to the San Francisco Institute of Art (SFIA)
1916 – CSD name changed to California School of Fine Arts (CSFA)
1926 – new school built on Russian Hill
1961 – CSFA and SFAA join under one name, the San Francisco Art Institute (SFAI)

History of California College of Arts and Crafts

1936 – California School of Arts and Crafts, Berkeley (CSAC), renamed California College of Arts and Crafts, Oakland (CCAC)

Ansel Adams
(San Francisco, Calif. 1902-1984 Carmel, Calif.)
Photographer. Largely self-taught, he began making
photographs during trips to Yosemite Valley, 1916. In
1919 he joined the Sierra Club and became their assistant manager and photographer in 1928. Formed Group
f.64 in 1932 in collaboration with Edward Weston, Imogen Cunningham, Sonya Noskowiak, John Paul
Edwards, Henry Swift, and Willard Van Dyke; group
held its first show at the M.H. de Young Memorial
Museum during the same year. Opened Ansel Adams
Gallery in San Francisco, 1933-34. In 1937 he moved to
Yosemite Valley to operate Best's Studio and in 1940
helped found the department of photography at The
Museum of Modern Art, New York. Founded the first
department of photography at CSFA in 1946.

1. *The Golden Gate before the Bridge (San Francisco,
California)*, ca. 1932
Gelatin silver print, 15⁵/₁₆ x 19⅛ in.
San Francisco Museum of Modern Art, gift of Alfred
Fromm, Otto Meyer, and Louis Petri, San Francisco

2. *Marin Hills, over the Golden Gate from Lincoln Park,
San Francisco*, ca. 1950
Gelatin silver print, 14⅞ x 19⅛ in.
San Francisco Museum of Modern Art, gift of Alfred
Fromm, Otto Meyer, and Louis Petri, San Francisco

3. *San Francisco from the San Bruno Mountains, California*,
ca. 1952
Gelatin silver print, 14⅝ x 18¾ in.
Collection of The Friends of Photography/Ansel Adams
Center for Photography, San Francisco

Robert Arneson
(Benicia, Calif. 1930-1992 Benicia, Calif.)
Sculptor. Attended College of Marin, Kentfield (1948-
51), CCAC (1950-53, BA), and Mills College (1957-58,
MFA). Taught at Santa Rosa Jr. College (1958-59), Mills
College (1960-62), and UC Davis (1962-92). Lived in
Davis from 1962 until 1975 when he moved to Benicia.

4. *The Palace at 9 A.M.*, 1974
Terracotta and glazed ceramic, 118 x 84 x 24 in.
Courtesy Frumkin/Adams Gallery, New York

Arthur Atkins
(Liscard, Chester, England 1873-1899 Piedmont, Calif.)
Painter. Moved to California in 1891. Attended
CSD/MHIA (1895-97). In 1897 he studied in England and
France, returning to San Francisco in 1898. Maintained
studio on Jackson Street that burned during the 1890s,
destroying many paintings.

5. *Piedmont Hills, Summer*, ca. 1896
Oil on paper board, 20 x 25⅞ in.
Ruth Vickery Brydon

Jo (Joseph) Babcock
(b. Saint Louis, Mo. 1954)
Photographer, sculptor. Attended UCLA (1975) and SFAI,
studying with Pirkle Jones (BFA, 1976; MFA, 1979).
Taught at Colgate University (1987), SFAI (1989, 1990),
and Visual Studies Workshop, Rochester, N.Y. (1990).
Worked as exhibit designer for Levi Strauss & Co., San
Francisco, 1989-92. Currently lives and works in San
Francisco.

6. *The Cypress, 880 Freeway*, 1989
Color coupler/paper negative, 40 x 71 in.
Courtesy the artist

Lewis Baltz
(b. Newport Beach, Calif. 1945)
Photographer. Attended SFAI (BFA, 1969) and Claremont Graduate School (MFA, 1971). Taught at Pomona
College, Claremont (1970-72); California Institute of the
Arts, Valencia (1972); UC Davis (1981); UC Riverside
(1990); California Institute of the Arts (1992); Yale University (1992); and École des Beaux-Arts, Paris (1992).
Lives and works in Sausalito.

7. *San Quentin Point, #11*, 1982-83
Gelatin silver print, 20 x 24 in.
Courtesy Stephen Wirtz Gallery, San Francisco

8. *San Quentin Point, #54*, 1982-83
Gelatin silver print, 20 x 24 in.
Courtesy Stephen Wirtz Gallery, San Francisco

Robert Bechtle
(b. San Francisco, Calif. 1932)
Painter. Attended CCAC (1950-54, 1956-58; BA, 1954; MFA, 1958) and UC Berkeley (summers 1960, 1961). Served in U.S. Army, 1954-56. Worked as graphic designer for Kaiser Graphic Arts, 1956-59. Taught at UC Berkeley (1965-66); UC Davis (1966-68); CCAC (1963-65); and SFSU (1968-present). Except for brief time spent in Sacramento, 1966-68, has lived in Bay Area and currently resides in San Francisco.

9. *Oakland Intersection - 59th St. and Stanford*, 1990
Oil on canvas, 40 x 58 in.
Alex Weber

Ray Beldner
(b. San Francisco, Calif. 1961)
Sculptor, installation artist. Attended SFAI (1982-86, BFA) and Mills College (1987-89, MFA). Taught at Mills College (1990), SFAI, and as guest lecturer at educational institutions throughout the Bay Area (1990-present). Lives and works in San Francisco.

10. *Lake Dolores*, from the *Dry Lake Series*, 1994
Wood, dirt, burlap, and steel, 32 x 43 x 3 in.
Courtesy Haines Gallery, San Francisco, and the artist

Elmer Bischoff
(Berkeley, Calif. 1916-1991 Berkeley, Calif.)
Painter. Attended UC Berkeley (1934-39; BA, 1938; MA, 1939). Taught at CSFA/SFAI (1946-52, 1956-63); Yuba College, Marysville (1953-56); and UC Berkeley (1963-85). Lived and worked most of his life in the Bay Area.

11. *Two Figures at the Seashore*, 1957
Oil on canvas, 56 x 56¾ in.
Collection Newport Harbor Art Museum, museum purchase with additional funds provided by the NEA

Ray Boynton
(near Whitten, Iowa 1883-1951 Albuquerque, N. Mex.)
Painter, muralist. Moved to Chicago in 1903 where he attended art school. Moved to Spokane, Wash., ca. 1908-09. Settled in San Francisco in 1915. Taught at CSD/CSFA (1919-23) and UC Berkeley (1923-48). Employed under Civil Works Administration/Public Works of Art Project, 1934, producing mural for Coit Tower. Moved to Albuquerque, N. Mex., in 1948.

12. *The Bay*, 1920
Oil on canvas, 35⅞ x 48 in.
The Fine Arts Museums of San Francisco, gift of Albert Bender

Anne Bremer
(San Francisco, Calif. 1868-1923 San Francisco, Calif.)
Painter. Attended CSD, studying under Arthur Mathews and Emil Carlsen (ca. 1886-89); Art Students' League, New York (ca. 1888-89); and Académie Moderne and La Palette, Paris (1901-02). Returned to San Francisco in 1902. Opened studio and art school in 1903. President of Sketch Club, 1905-07. Except for brief period in France, 1910-12, lived in San Francisco.

13. *Across Carquinez Straits*, ca. 1906
Oil on canvas, 24 x 32 in.
Mills College Art Gallery

14. *An Old-Fashioned Garden*, ca. 1915
Oil on canvas, 20 x 24 in.
Mills College Art Gallery

Anne Brigman
(Honolulu, Hawaii 1869-1950 El Monte, Calif.)
Photographer. Moved to Los Gatos, Calif. in 1885. Self-taught in photography, which she turned to in 1902. Moved to Oakland, 1903, became an associate of the Photo-Secession and began corresponding with Alfred Stieglitz. In 1906 she was elected a fellow of the Photo-Secession. Traveled to New York to meet Stieglitz in 1910. Worked in Oakland until 1929 when she moved to Long Beach area. Returned to the Bay area briefly, 1939-40.

15. *Tranquility*, 1929
Gelatin silver print, 6⅝ x 9¾ in.
San Francisco Museum of Modern Art, gift of Robert Durden

Christopher Brown
(b. Camp Lejeune, N.C. 1951)
Painter. Lived in Ohio, 1954-1964, when he moved to Illinois. Attended University of Illinois, Champaign-Urbana (BA, 1972) and UC Davis (1973-76, MFA). Traveled to Europe after first year at Davis. Awarded Fulbright fellowship for study in Germany, 1978-79. Moved to San Francisco in 1979. Taught briefly at American River College, Sacramento (1976-77) and at UC Berkeley (1981-94). Lives in Berkeley.

16. *The River, Evening*, 1984-85
Oil on canvas, 96 x 360 in. (5 panels, each 96 x 72 in.)
A: Panels 1-2: Private collection
B: Panels 3-4: Alex and Eleanor Najjar
C: Panel 5: Tom and Barbara Peckenpaugh

Joan Brown
(San Francisco, Calif. 1938-1990 Proddatur, India)
Painter, sculptor. Attended CSFA, studying with Elmer
Bischoff and Frank Lobdell (1955-60; BFA, 1959; MFA,
1960). Taught at CSFA (1960); University of Colorado at
Denver (summer 1964); Academy of Art College, San
Francisco (1971-77); and UC Berkeley (1974-90). Married
to artists William Brown, 1955-60; Manuel Neri, 1962-
66; and Gordon Cook, 1969-76. Died in accident while
working on an art commission in India.

17. *Things in a Landscape II*, 1959
Oil on canvas, 73½ x 71½ in.
Private collection, courtesy Campbell-Thiebaud
Gallery, San Francisco

18. *Mary Julia y Manuel*, 1976
Enamel on canvas, 96 x 75 in.
Courtesy Frumkin/Adams Gallery, New York

William Theophilus Brown
(b. Moline, Ill. 1919)
Painter. Attended Yale University (BA, 1937). Studied
with Amédée Ozenfant, Ozenfant School of Fine Arts,
N.Y. (1948) and at Atelier Fernand Léger, Paris (1949).
Began graduate studies at UC Berkeley in 1952 (MA,
1953). Taught at CSFA (1955-57) and UC Davis (1958-59).
Lived and worked in Davis with Paul Wonner (1957-60).
Moved to Southern California in 1961. Returned to
the Bay Area in 1974 and has lived in San Francisco
since 1976.

19. *River Bathers*, 1968/71
Acrylic on canvas, 48 x 72 in.
Collection of Martha and Allen Koplin, Los Angeles

Robert L. Buelteman, Jr.
(b. New York, N.Y. 1954)
Photographer. Family moved to Woodside in 1954.
Attended University of Colorado, Boulder; SFSU; and
UC Berkeley. Currently lives and works in San Francisco.

20. *280 Sunrise*, 1988
Gelatin silver selenide print, 19 x 19 in.
Courtesy the artist and Vision Gallery, San Francisco

Jerry Burchard
(b. Rochester, N.Y. 1931)
Photographer. Employed by Eastman-Kodak,
Rochester, N.Y. (1950-52). Worked as photography mate
for the U.S. Navy; placed with NATO as a staff photographer in Naples, Italy, 1952-56. Attended CSFA (1956-60,
BFA). Lives in San Francisco, teaching at SFAI since 1966.

21. *July 4 77*, 1977
Gelatin silver print with selenium toning, 13 x 19¹/₁₆ in.
San Francisco Museum of Modern Art, gift of Clay
Luraschi

Giuseppe Cadenasso
(Maragolia, Italy 1858-1918 San Francisco, Calif.)
Painter. Came to U.S., settling in Capay in Northern California, ca. 1867. Studied privately with Joseph Harring-
ton and at CSD/MHIA with Arthur Mathews (mid-
1890s). Lived and worked in San Francisco until 1906
when he moved his studio to Oakland. Moved his
studio once again in 1909 to Alameda County. Taught
at Mills College (1902-18).

22. *Alameda Marsh*, ca. 1900
Pastel on paper, 12 x 19 in.
Private collection, San Francisco

Christo
born Christo Javacheff
(b. Gabrovo, Bulgaria 1935)
Environmental and conceptual artist. Attended Fine
Arts Academy, Sofia, Bulgaria (1952-56); Theatre of Emil
Frantisek Burian, Prague, Czechoslovakia, studying
stage design and theatre (1956); and Vienna Fine Arts
Academy (1957). Moved to Geneva, Switzerland, in the
fall of 1957, then to Paris in 1958. Relocated to New York
in 1964, where he lives with Jeanne-Claude, his artistic
collaborator.

23. *Running Fence, Project for Sonoma and Marin Counties,
California*, 1972-76
Charcoal, pastel, and pencil drawing, 42 x 96 in.; topo-
graphical map, 15 x 96 in.; color photograph, 28 x 39¼ in.
San Francisco Museum of Modern Art, gift of the
Modern Art Council

Robert Colescott
(b. Oakland, Calif. 1925)
Painter. Attended UC Berkeley (BA, 1949; MA, 1952)
and Atelier Fernand Léger, Paris (1949-50). Lived in:
Washington and Oregon, 1952-64, 1965-66; Egypt,
serving as artist-in-residence at the American Research
Center, 1964-65, and on the faculty at American University, 1966-67; and France, 1967-69. Settled in California
by 1970, residing in Oakland. Taught at Portland State
University (1957-66); California State College, Stanis-
laus (1970-74); UC Berkeley (1974-79); SFAI (1979-85);
and University of Arizona, Tucson (1983, 1985-present).
Lives and works in Tucson.

24. *Christina's Day Off*, 1983
Acrylic on canvas, 84 x 72 in.
The Saint Louis Art Museum, gift of Brooke and
Carolyn Alexander, New York

Gordon Cook
(Chicago, Ill. 1927-1985 San Francisco, Calif.)
Painter, printmaker. Attended Illinois Wesleyan
University, Bloomington (1945-50, BFA); American
Academy of Art, Chicago (1948-49); School of the Art
Institute of Chicago (1949); and Iowa State University,
Iowa City (1950-51). Lived in San Francisco 1951 to
1969, when he moved to Rio Vista. Returned to San
Francisco in 1971 and remained until his death. Taught
at SFAI (1960-71), Sacramento State College (now Cali-
fornia State University, 1970-71), Academy of Art Col-
lege (1971-73), San Francisco State College (now Califor-
nia State University, 1974-75), UC Davis (1975, 1979),
Mills College (1983), and CCAC (1983).

25. *Point Richmond*, ca. 1981
Oil on canvas, 14¾ x 16 in.
Sukey Lilienthal

26. *Point Richmond*, ca. 1981
Oil on canvas, 23⅞ x 26 in.
Liadain O'Donovan Cook

Ralston Crawford
(St. Catherines, Ontario, Canada 1906-1978
Houston, Tex.)
Painter, printmaker, photographer. Studied Otis Art
Institute, Los Angeles (1927); Pennsylvania Academy
of the Fine Arts (1927-30); The Barnes Foundation,
Marion, Pa. (1927-28); summer classes with Hugh
Breckenridge, The Breckenridge School, Gloucester,
Mass.; Académie Colarossi and Académie Scandanav,
Paris (1932-33); and Teachers College, Columbia Uni-
versity (1933). Settled in New York, 1931-35. Employed
under Civil Works Administration/Public Works of Art
Project, 1934. Moved to Exton, Pa., in 1935, returning to
New York in 1939. Served in U.S. Army, 1932-45. Traveled to California in 1946 on the occasion of his exhibi-
tion at the Santa Barbara Museum of Art, subsequently
shown at the M.H. de Young Memorial Museum.

27. *Fisherman's Wharf, San Francisco*, 1947-1950
Oil on canvas, 30 x 40 in.
Private collection

Rinaldo Cuneo
(San Francisco, Calif. 1877-1939 San Francisco, Calif.)
Painter. Studied at CSD/SFIA with Arthur Mathews,
Gottardo Piazzoni, and Arthur Putnam (1910) and at
Académie Colarossi, Paris (1911). Worked for Crowley
Launch and Tugboat Company, San Francisco, 1916-
after 1924, while actively painting and exhibiting work.
Taught at CSFA (1931 and summers 1936, 1937), assum-
ing Piazzoni's teaching post there in 1939. Employed
under Civil Works Administration/Public Works of Art
Project, 1934, producing mural for Coit Tower. Main-
tained studio in North Beach and regularly exhibited in
the city through the end of his life.

28. *California Landscape*, ca. 1928
Oil on canvas, three-part screen, 66 x 66 in.
Zora and Les Charles

Lowell Darling
(b. Jacksonville, Ill. 1942)
Conceptual artist. Moved to Davis in 1970. Relocated
to Los Angeles in 1972 to teach at Otis Art Institute.
Returned to Bay Area in 1976. Currently lives
in Occidental.

29. *Eva Withrow Project*, 1995
Multi-media performance and video installation
with painting
Courtesy the artist

Arthur B. Davies
(Utica, N.Y. 1862-1928 Florence, Italy)
Painter, printmaker. Studied privately with Dwight
Williams (1877). Moved to Chicago in 1878 where he
studied with J. Roy Robertson at Chicago Academy of
Design until 1879. In 1883 he returned to Chicago from
Colorado and Mexico to study with Charles Corwin at
School of the Art Institute. Moved to New York in 1886,
studying at the Art Students' League and the Gotham
Art Students School. Visited Rocky Mountains and
Pacific Coast, June to September 1905, arriving in San
Francisco in July.

30. *View of San Francisco*, 1905
Oil on wood panel, 5⅛ x 9⅜ in.
Collection of The Oakland Museum of California, gift
of Mr. and Mrs. Robert Leefeldt

31. *Pacific Parnassus, Mount Tamalpais*, ca. 1905
Oil on canvas, 26¼ x 40¼ in.
The Fine Arts Museums of San Francisco, Museum pur-
chase, gift of The Museum Society Auxiliary

32. *Mount Tamalpais*, 1905
Oil on wood, 5¼ x 9⅜ in.
Collection of The Oakland Museum of California, gift
of Concours d'Antiques, and The Art Guild

Robert Dawson
(b. West Sacramento, Calif. 1950)
Photographer. Attended UC Santa Cruz (BA, 1972) and
SFSU (MA, 1979). Taught at Mills College, SFAI, City College of San Francisco (1991-93), and San Jose State University (1993-present). Founder and codirector of Water
in the West Project, a collaboration with other photographers. Currently working on several environmental
photography projects. Lives in San Francisco.

33. *Farm and Windmills, Altamont Pass, California*, from
the *Great Central Valley Project*, 1986
Gelatin silver print, 13¹¹⁄₁₆ x 18⅛ in.
Courtesy the artist and Vision Gallery, San Francisco

Jay DeFeo
(Hanover, N.H. 1929-1989 Oakland, Calif.)
Painter, collagist. Moved to San Francisco in 1931 and
attended high school in San Jose. Attended UC Berkeley
(1946-51; BA, 1950; MA, 1951). Lived in San Francisco on
Fillmore Street in a house that became a center for pro-
gressive artists, writers, and poets, 1956-64. Taught at
SFAI (1962-70), Sonoma State University (1976-80),
CCAC (1978-81), and Mills College (1981-89).

34. *Mountain No. 2*, 1955
Oil on canvas, 46 x 36 in.
The Fine Arts Museums of San Francisco, Museum
purchase, gift of the 20th-Century Art Council

Lewis deSoto
(b. San Bernardino, Calif. 1954)
Conceptual, installation, and video artist. Attended UC
Riverside (1978, BFA) and Claremont Graduate School
(MFA, 1981). Taught at Otis Art Institute, Los Angeles
(1983-85); Cornish College of Arts, Seattle (1985-88);
SFSU (1988); and CCAC, director of graduate studies
(1993-present). Lives in San Francisco.

35. *Háypatak, Witness, Kansatsusha*, 1990/95
Video installation
Courtesy the artist; Christopher Grimes Gallery, Santa
Monica; and Haines Gallery, San Francisco

Stephen De Staebler
(b. St. Louis, Mo. 1933)
Sculptor. Moved to California in 1957. Attended Black
Mountain College, Black Mountain, N.C., studying with
Ben Shahn and Robert Motherwell (summer 1951),
Princeton University (1950-54, BA); and UC Berkeley
(1958-61, MA). Taught at SFSC (1961-62), SFAI (1961-67),
and SFSU (1967-present). Lives in Berkeley.

36. *X with Orange Scar*, 1973
Fired clay, 13 x 92 x 110 in.
Collection of the artist, courtesy Campbell-Thiebaud
Gallery, San Francisco

Richard Diebenkorn
(Portland, Oreg. 1922-1993 Healdsburg, Calif.)
Painter. Attended Stanford University (1940-43; BA, 1949), UC Berkeley (1943), CSFA (1946), and the University of New Mexico (1950-51, MFA). Taught at CSFA (1947-50); University of Illinois at Urbana-Champaign (1952-53); and CCAC (1955-57). Lived in the Bay Area from 1953 to 1966, when he moved to Santa Monica to teach at UCLA (1966-73). Returned to Northern California in 1988.

37. *No. 3*, 1948
Oil on canvas, 27 x 38 in.
San Francisco Museum of Modern Art, gift of
Charles Ross

38. *Berkeley No. 44*, 1955
Oil on canvas, 59 x 64 in.
Private collection

39. *Berkeley No. 53*, 1955
Oil on canvas, 49½ x 47½ in.
Anonymous loan

40. *Seawall*, 1957
Oil on canvas, 20 x 26 in.
Phyllis Diebenkorn

41. *View from the Porch*, 1959
Oil on canvas, 70 x 66 in.
The Harry W. and Mary Margaret Anderson Collection

Maynard Dixon
(Fresno, Calif. 1875-1946 Tucson, Ariz.)
Painter, muralist, illustrator. Came to Bay Area in 1893. Largely self-taught. Briefly attended CSD/MHIA with Arthur Mathews (1893) and studied privately with Raymond Yelland. Worked as commercial illustrator through 1907. Moved to New York, 1907, and worked for *Century* and *Scribner's*. Returned to San Francisco in 1912, dedicating himself to mural and easel painting. Married to photographer Dorothea Lange, 1920-1935, and to painter Edith Hamlin, 1937. With Ray Strong and others, he revived Art Students' League, San Francisco, 1935. Employed as muralist under Works Progress Administration/Federal Art Project, 1936-37, and Treasury Department Section of Painting and Sculpture, 1942. Settled in Tucson, Ariz., 1939.

42. *No Place to Go*, 1935
Oil on canvas, 25⅛ x 30 in.
Museum of Art, Brigham Young University

Willard Dixon
(b. Kansas City, Mo. 1942)
Painter. Came to California in 1953. Attended Art Students' League, N.Y.; Cornell University; Brooklyn Museum School of Art, N.Y.; and SFAI (MFA, 1969). Taught at CSU Hayward (1971-72); CCAC (1973-74, 1976); Academy of Art College, San Francisco (1974-76); SFAI (1975); and SFSU (1989-90). Lives in San Rafael.

43. *Bolinas Lagoon Hillside*, 1991
Oil on canvas, 36 x 60 in.
Courtesy Contemporary Realist Gallery, San Francisco

Charles Stafford Duncan
(Hutchinson, Kans. 1892-1952 New York, N.Y.)
Painter and lithographer. Studied at CSD/SFIA (1910). Won national recognition in prestigious annual exhibitions, including the National Academy of Design (Altman Prize, 1935). Directed McCann Erickson Advertising Agency. Lived in San Francisco and Sausalito.

44. *The Dark Hills of Saratoga*, ca. 1929
Oil on canvas, 19 x 50 in.
Private collection

45. *San Francisco Bay - Alcatraz*, ca. 1935
Oil on Masonite, 38¾ x 50½ in.
Private collection

John Paul Edwards
(Minneapolis, Minn. 1884-1968 Oakland, Calif.)
Photographer. Came to Calif. in 1901, eventually working in Sacramento. Moved to Oakland by 1923. Exhibited widely in pictorialist salons in London, Los Angeles, Pittsburgh, New York, and Toronto. In 1932 he helped found Group *f*.64 and contributed many articles to *Camera Craft* to clarify the group's aims.

46. *Cliff Dwellers, San Francisco*, 1924
Black and white photograph, 9½ x 12¼ in.
Collection of The Oakland Museum of California, gift of Mr. John Paul Edwards

Richard Estes
(b. Kewanee, Ill. 1932)
Painter. Raised in Evanston, Ill. Attended Art Institute of Chicago (1952-56). Worked as commercial artist in publishing and advertising, 1956-66. Moved from Chicago to New York in 1959. Lived in Spain, 1962. Currently lives in New York and Maine.

47. *View from Twin Peaks*, 1990
Oil on canvas, 36 x 72 in.
Collection of Terry and Eva Herndon

Lyonel Feininger
(New York, N.Y. 1871-1956 New York, N.Y.)
Painter, printmaker, illustrator. Studied music in Hamburg, Germany (1887). Studied painting, Kunstgewerbeschule, Hamburg (1887); Berliner Kunstakademie (1888); Collège St. Servais, Liège, Belgium (1890); Académie Colarossi, Paris (1892-93). Settled in Berlin, working as cartoonist and illustrator, 1893-1906. Moved to Paris, 1906-07, and produced cartoons for French publications and for *Chicago Sunday Tribune*. Returned to Berlin, 1908-19, but traveled widely. Taught at the Bauhaus, Weimar (1919-24) and at Dessau (1925-32). With Wassily Kandinsky, Paul Klee, and Alexej von Jawlensky, formed the Blue Four and exhibited regularly with the group, 1925-34. Returned to U.S. to teach summer course at Mills College (1936, 1937). Settled in New York in 1937. Taught summer session at Black Mountain College, N.C., 1945.

48. *Bay*, 1939
Watercolor on paper, 15 x 21 in.
Collection of Marvin and Alice Sinkoff

E. Charlton Fortune
(Sausalito, Calif. 1885-1969 Carmel Valley, Calif.)
Painter, craftsperson. Attended Edinburgh College of Art, Scotland, and St. John's Wood School of Art, London (1904). Returned to San Francisco in 1905 to enter the CSD/MHIA, studying under Arthur Mathews. Studied at the Art Students' League, New York (ca. 1907-10). Went to Europe again to study, 1910-12. In 1912 she returned to U.S., settling in Carmel. Moved to San Francisco in 1913 and opened a studio on Sutter Street. In 1914 she established another studio in Monterey. Lived in Europe from 1921 until 1927 when she returned to Carmel. Founded the Monterey Guild in 1928, dedicated to ecclesiastical art and to decorating Catholic churches across the country.

49. *Panama Pacific International Exposition*, 1915
Oil on canvas, 12 x 16 in.
Collection of Dr. and Mrs. Oscar Lemer

Terry Fox
(b. Seattle, Wash. 1943)
Sculptor, conceptual, video, performance, and installation artist. Largely self-taught. Attended Cornish School of Applied Arts, Seattle (1961) and Accademia di Belle Arti, Rome (1962). Came to San Francisco in 1963. Lived in Paris (1967-68, 1972) and Naples, Italy (1983-84). Returned to San Francisco from 1963-66 and 1968-78. Struck with Hodgkins' disease in 1960, becoming cured by 1972. From 1978 he lived in New York until permanently relocating to Europe in 1980. Currently he resides in Liège, Belgium.

50. *Instrument to be Played by the Movement of the Earth*, 1987
Glass and metal, 72 x 24 in.
Collection of Ann Hatch and William Farley

Howard Fried
(b. Cleveland, Ohio 1946)
Video, conceptual, and performance artist. Attended Syracuse University (1964-67), SFAI (BFA, 1968), and UC Davis (MFA, 1970). Taught at SFAI (1968-85). Resides in Vallejo.

51. *Long John Servil vs. Long John Silver*, 1972
Gelatin silver prints mounted on panels, 49⅝ x 19⅝ in.
San Francisco Museum of Modern Art, purchased with the aid of funds from René di Rosa and the Soap Box Derby Fund

Harry Fritzius
(Blytheville, Ark. 1932-1989 San Francisco, Calif.)
Painter, assemblage artist. Attended Memphis School of Art. Worked in New York City during the 1950s. Abandoned art to head his own public relations agency during the 1960s. Moved to San Francisco during the early 1970s where he resumed painting.

52. *Untitled (Golden Gate Park Twilight)*, 1986
Oil on canvas, 55 x 86 in.
Dr. Phyllis A. Kempner and Dr. David D. Stein

Oliver Gagliani
(b. Placerville, Calif. 1917)
Photographer. Moved to South San Francisco in 1919.
Attended San Francisco State College (1940-42); CSFA,
studying with Ansel Adams and Minor White (1946);
and CCAC (MFA, 1972). Taught at SFSU (1974-76), SFAI
(1975), CCAC (1975), and Stanford University (1975).
Also teaches Virginia City Zone System workshops
(since 1974). Lives in South San Francisco.

53. *Untitled (Surf Sequence)*, 1965
Gelatin silver print, four photographs, 9 x 11½ in. each
Courtesy the artist, collection of Ron and Kathy Perisho

William Garnett
(b. Chicago, Ill. 1916)
Photographer. Moved to Altadena, near Los Angeles in
1920. Attended Art Center School, Los Angeles (1937-
38). Left school to pursue career in commercial photography. Began aerial photography in 1945. Received
pilot's license in 1948. Moved to Napa Valley in 1958,
working as commercial photographer until 1968.
Taught photography at the College of Environmental
Design, UC Berkeley (1968-84). Lives in Napa.

54. *Reflection of the Sun on Dendritic Flow, San Francisco
Bay, California*, 1963
Gelatin silver print, 6¾ x 19¾ in.
Courtesy the artist and Vision Gallery, San Francisco

Carmen Lomas Garza
(b. Kingsville, Tex. 1948)
Painter. Attended Texas Arts & Industry University,
Kingsville (BS, 1972); Juarez-Lincoln/Antioch Graduate
School, Austin (MED, 1973); and SFSU (MA, 1980).
Moved to San Francisco in 1976. Worked as assistant
curator and curator at Galeria de la Raza, San Francisco,
1976-81. Lives and works in San Francisco.

55. *Felino's Breakdancers*, 1988
Gouache on paper, 20¼ x 25¼ in.
Collection of The Oakland Museum of California, gift
of The Art Guild

August François Gay
(Rabou, France 1890-1948 Carmel, Calif.)
Painter, muralist, craftsperson, etcher. Came to
Alameda ca. 1901. Attended CSAC briefly (1918-19) and
CSFA night school (1918-19). Studied privately with
Selden Gile. Moved to Monterey, ca. 1919, where he met
and worked with Clayton S. Price (ca. 1920-28), Armin
Hansen, and other members of the Monterey Group.
Exhibited with Society of Six, 1923-28. By 1928 he
devoted most of time to woodworking and gilding.
From 1934-38 he painted murals for Public Works
of Art Project and Federal Arts Project. Settled in
Carmel, 1941.

56. *Decoration*, ca. 1927
Oil on artist board, 22¼ x 24½ in.
Gay Collins, Santa Barbara

Yun Gee
(Gee Village, Kai Ping County, Canton, China 1906-1963
New York, N.Y.)
Painter. In China he studied with Chinese master Chu
(1918-19). Lived in San Francisco, 1921-27. Attended
CSFA, studying with Otis Oldfield and Gottardo Piaz-
zoni (1924-26). Moved to Paris in 1927, then to New
York in 1930. Painted in Paris, 1936-39; then returned to
New York.

57. *Camping with Otis Oldfield*, 1926
Oil on paperboard, 12 x 17¾ in.
Collection of Helen Gee

Selden Connor Gile
(Stow, Maine 1877-1947 Lucas Valley, Calif.)
Painter. Came to California ca. 1901, working near
Sacramento. Largely self-taught but studied privately
with E. Spencer Macky, Perham Nahl, and others. Lived
in Oakland from 1905-27, employed by Gladding
McBean and Co. Exhibited with Society of Six, 1923-28.
Moved to Tiburon, then to Belvedere in 1927. Traveled
to Southwest in 1926, 1931, and 1934. Served as librarian
in Belvedere, ca. 1938-42.

58. *Untitled (Cows and Pasture)*, ca. 1925
Oil on canvas, 12 x 16 in.
Robert Aichele, Menlo Park

59. *The Soil*, 1927
Oil on canvas, 30⅛ x 36 in.
Private collection, San Francisco

J. D. Givens
(biographical dates unknown)
Photographer.

60. *Broadway and Jones*, 1906
Gelatin silver print, 6 x 16 in.
Courtesy Stephen Wirtz Gallery, San Francisco

61. *Jones and Pine*, 1906
Gelatin silver print, 6 x 16 in.
Courtesy Stephen Wirtz Gallery, San Francisco

62. *Market and Sutter*, 1906
Gelatin silver print, 6 x 16 in.
Courtesy Stephen Wirtz Gallery, San Francisco

63. *Market and Third*, 1906
Gelatin silver print, 6 x 16 in.
Courtesy Stephen Wirtz Gallery, San Francisco

Andy Goldsworthy
(b. Cheshire, England 1956)
Conceptual artist. Attended Bradford Art College, Yorkshire (1974-75) and Preston Polytechnical Institute, Lancashire Annex (1975-78). Lives in Scotland.

64. *Red Earth Splash, San Francisco Bay, California*, 1994
Unique Cibachrome, 27½ x 26½ in.
Courtesy Haines Gallery, San Francisco

65. *Clay Wrapped Boulder*, 1995
Clay and boulder, ca. 24 x 24 x 24 in.
Courtesy Haines Gallery, San Francisco

Joseph Goldyne
(b. Chicago, Ill. 1942)
Painter, printmaker. Attended UC Berkeley (1960-64,
BA), UCSF (1964-68, MD), and Harvard University (1968-
70, MA). Returned to San Francisco in 1970, where he
currently lives and works.

66. *Goya's Bull Coming in over Marin* (version 2), 1973
Etching and monotype, 6 x 9 in.
Courtesy the artist and Richard York Gallery, New York

Lyle Gomes
(b. San Francisco, Calif. 1954)
Photographer. Attended SFSU (BFA, 1978; MA, 1980).
Taught part-time at the College of San Mateo (1980-84),
becoming chairperson of the art department and head
of the photography department in 1984. Lives and
works in South San Francisco.

67. *Double Arrow, San Francisco Presidio*, 1990
Gelatin silver print, 7 x 19 in.
Courtesy the artist and Vision Gallery, San Francisco

Michael Gregory
(b. Los Angeles 1955)
Painter. Attended City College of San Francisco and
SFAI (BFA, 1980). Taught at SFAI (1986, 1988). Currently
resides in Bolinas.

68. *As if Twelve Princes Sat before a King*, 1988
Oil and tar on board, 40 x 84 in.
Collection of Dr. A.D. Rosenberg

John Gutmann
(b. Berlin, Germany 1905)
Photographer, painter. Attended State Academy of Arts
and Crafts, Breslau, studying with Otto Mueller (BA,
1927) and Institute of Higher Education, Berlin (MA,
1928). In 1933 he left Germany for the U.S., settling
immediately in San Francisco. Taught at SFSU (1936-73).
Resides in San Francisco.

69. *Yes, Columbus, Mission District, San Francisco*, ca. 1938
Gelatin silver print, 8 x 10 in.
Courtesy Fraenkel Gallery, San Francisco

70. *A Tree at Hunter's Point, San Francisco*, 1948
Gelatin silver print, 11 x 14 in.
Courtesy Fraenkel Gallery, San Francisco

Edward Hagedorn
(San Francisco, Calif. 1902-1982 Berkeley, Calif.)
Painter, printmaker. Studied briefly at CSFA (1924-25).
Maintained studio in Berkeley through the end of his
life. Exhibited paintings sporadically in one-person and
group shows, and regularly exhibited prints in national
group shows. Employed as watercolor painter and
graphic artist under Works Progress Administration/
Federal Art Project.

71. *Green Mountains, Pale Yellow Bolt*, 1935
Graphite, ink, and watercolor on paper, 19½ x 25½ in.
Courtesy Denenberg Fine Arts, Inc., San Francisco

72. *Blue Mountains, Large 3-Forked Bolt*, 1937
Graphite, ink, and watercolor on paper, 19 13/16 x 26 in.
Courtesy Denenberg Fine Arts, Inc., San Francisco

Johan Hagemeyer
(Amsterdam, Netherlands 1884-1962 Berkeley, Calif.)
Photographer. Emigrated to California. Met Alfred
Stieglitz during a trip to New York and decided to
become a professional photographer. Returned to California, becoming Edward Weston's apprentice and then
assistant in 1917. Maintained successful portrait studios
in the Bay Area and Carmel.

73. *Castles of Today (San Francisco)*, 1922
Gelatin silver print, 8 x 10 in.
Collection, Center for Creative Photography, The Uni-
versity of Arizona

74. *Trees on Telegraph Hill*, 1925
Gelatin silver print, 8 x 10 in.
Collection of the Center for Creative Photography, The
University of Arizona

Milton Halberstadt
(b. Boston, Mass. 1919)
Photographer. Apprenticed as photographer in Boston
area, 1936-39. Worked for Works Progress Administration, 1938-39. Attended School of Design, Chicago (now
the Institute of Design, 1939-41); taught classes with
László Moholy-Nagy and Gyorgy Kepes. Established
Milton Halberstadt Illustration Photography, in San
Francisco, 1945-73, specializing in advertising photography. Taught at Ansel Adams' Yosemite Photography
Workshops for seven years, UC Berkeley (summers 1973-
75), and University of Oregon, Eugene (1979-82). Lives
in San Francisco.

75. *San Francisco from Twin Peaks (Noe Valley)*, 1954
Gelatin silver print, tone-line process, 12½ x 19⅜ in.
Courtesy the artist and Leland Rice

John Haley
(Minneapolis, Minn. 1905-1991 Point Richmond, Calif.)
Painter. Studied Minneapolis School of Art, with
Cameron Booth and Vaclav Vytlacil (1924-27); Hans
Hofmann School of Fine Arts, Capri (summer 1927);
and Hofmann Schule für Moderne Kunst, Munich, as
recipient of the Ethel Morrison Van Derlip scholarship
for study abroad (1927-28). Taught at Minneapolis
School of Art (1928-30) and UC Berkeley (1930-72).

76. *Lawrence House, End of Ocean Avenue, Point
Richmond*, 1936
Watercolor on paper, 15 x 20 in.
Private collection

Diane Andrews Hall
(b. Dallas, Tex. 1945)
Painter, video and performance artist. Began as painter
in late 1960s. Attended Sophie Newcomb College, New
Orleans (BFA, 1967), and the Maryland Institute, Baltimore (MFA, 1969). During the 1970s she began collaborating on video and performance pieces with husband
Doug Hall and the conceptualist group T.R. Uthco.

77. *Tule Fog*, 1989
Oil on canvas, 100 x 100 in.
Courtesy Haines Gallery, San Francisco

Robert Hartman
(b. Sharon, Pa. 1926)
Photographer. Attended Colorado Springs Fine Arts
Center with Vaclav Vytlacil and Emerson Woelffer
(summers 1947-51), University of Arizona (BFA, 1951;
MA, 1952), and Brooklyn Museum Art School (1953-54).
Came to California in 1961. Taught at University of Ari-
zona (1952-53); Texas Technological College, Lubbock
(1955-58); University of Nevada, Reno (1958-61); and UC
Berkeley (1974-91). Resides in Oakland.

78. *Constellations*, 1992
Cibachrome print, 14 x 19½ in.
Courtesy Triangle Gallery, San Francisco

Childe Hassam
(Dorchester, Mass. 1859-1935 Easthampton, N.Y.)
Painter. In 1876 he apprenticed as wood engraver.
Worked in Boston as free-lance illustrator, 1876-78.
Attended Académie Julian, studying with Gustave
Boulanger and Jules Lefebvre (1886). Moved to Paris in
1887. In 1890 returned to U.S., settling in New York.
Lived and worked primarily in New York and New Eng-
land. Made trips to Bay Area in 1908, 1914-15, and 1927.

79. *The Silver Veil and the Golden Gate, Sausalito,
California*, 1914
Oil on canvas, 30 x 32 in.
Valparaiso University Museum of Art,
Sloan Fund purchase

Mike Henderson
born William Howard Henderson
(b. Marshall, Mo. 1943)
Painter, filmmaker. Came to San Francisco in 1965. Attended SFAI (1965-70; BFA, 1969; and MFA, 1970) and Skowhegan School of Painting and Sculpture (summer 1968). Taught at UC Davis (1970-present). Lived in San Francisco through 1986, then moved to Oakland, where he currently resides.

80. *North Beach*, 1989
Oil on canvas, 72 x 60 in.
Collection of The Oakland Museum of California, gift of the Collectors Gallery, and The Art Guild

Hans Hofmann
(Weissenburg, Germany 1880-1966 New York, N.Y.)
Painter. Studied in Munich with impressionist Willie Schwarz. Worked in Paris (1904-14), studying at Académie Colarossi and at École de la Grande Chaumière, where Henri Matisse was a classmate and friend. Established Hofmann Schule für Moderne Kunst, in Munich suburb of Schwabing (1915-30), teaching summer sessions in Bavarian Alps, Capri, and St. Tropèz. Came to U.S. to teach summer classes at University of California (1930-31). Also taught at Chouinard School of Art, Los Angeles (1931); Art Students' League, New York (1932-33); and summer classes at Thurn School, Gloucester, Mass. (1932-33). Settled permanently in U.S. in 1932, becoming legal citizen in 1941. Opened Hans Hofmann School of Fine Art, New York (1933) and Provincetown, Mass. (1934), actively teaching there until 1958.

81. *San Francisco Bay from Richmond*, 1931
India ink on paper, 10½ x 13½ in.
Collection of The Oakland Museum of California, gift of Concours d'Antiques, The Art Guild, and Oakland Museum Association

Douglas Hollis
(b. Ann Arbor, Mich. 1948)
Sculptor, conceptual artist. Attended University of Michigan (BFA, 1970). Moved to Bay Area in 1973. Lived in Berkeley. Currently resides in San Francisco.

82. *Zephyr*, 1995
12 aluminum and steel poles, 20 ft. x 6 ft. x 3 in. (each)
Courtesy the artist

Edward Hopper
(Nyack, N.Y. 1882-1967 New York, N.Y.)
Painter. Studied through Correspondence School of Illustrating, New York (1899-1900); New York School of Art (1900-06), with illustrators Arthur Keller and Frank Vincent DuMond and with painters Robert Henri, William Merritt Chase, and Kenneth Hayes Miller. Began work as commercial illustrator in New York, 1906, and traveled throughout Europe, 1906-07 and 1909. By 1912 he began regular summer painting sojourns in such places as Gloucester, Mass., Ogunquit and Monhegan Island, Maine, and Cape Cod, Mass. Built summer studio in South Truro, Mass., 1934. First visited California on cross-country car trip in 1941, stopping briefly in Bay Area.

83. *House in San Mateo*, 1941
Watercolor on paper, 13¾ x 19¾ in.
Private collection

John Langley Howard
(b. Upper Montclair, N.J. 1902)
Painter. Son of John Galen Howard. Family moved to California in 1902. Attended UC Berkeley (1920-21), California Guild of Arts and Crafts (1922), and Art Students' League, New York (1922-23). Returned to California in 1926, living in Calistoga, San Francisco, Monterey, Menlo Park, and Palo Alto before moving briefly to Santa Fe, N. Mex. Employed under Civil Works Administration/Public Works of Art Project, 1934, producing mural for Coit Tower. Settled in Mill Valley, 1940, and studied ship drafting at Heald College, San Francisco. Taught at CSFA (summer 1950) and Pratt Institute, Brooklyn, N.Y. (1953). Lived in London and Greece, 1965-70. Returned to California in 1970, settling in San Francisco by 1983.

84. *Embarcadero and Clay*, 1935
Oil on canvas, 35⅞ x 43½ in.
Mr. and Mrs. Norman Lacayo

Robert Hudson
(b. Salt Lake City, Utah 1938)
Sculptor. Raised in Richland, Wash. Came to San Francisco in 1957. Attended SFAI (BFA, 1962; MFA, 1963). Taught at SFAI (1964-66), UC Berkeley (1966-73, 1975), Maryland Institute of Art (1974), Kansas City Art Institute (1974), University of Wisconsin (1974), Fresno State University (1974), and SFAI (1976-85). Resides in Cotati.

85. *Running through the Woods*, 1975
Stuffed deer and mixed media, 77 x 62 x 50¾ in.
Mary and David Robinson

John Hultberg
(b. Berkeley, Calif. 1922)
Painter. Attended Fresno State College (1939-43, BA),
CSFA (1947-49), and Art Students' League of New York
(1949-51). Settled in New York, 1949, spending portions
of 1954, 1956, and 1959 in Paris. Taught at the Art Students' League, New York (1961-present). Divides time
between New York and Monehagan Island, Maine.

86. *San Francisco Bay*, 1948-49
Oil on canvas, 47½ x 63¾ in.
The Fine Arts Museums of San Francisco, gift of the
Richard Florsheim Art Fund and the artist

Yvonne Jacquette
(b. Pittsburgh, Pa. 1934)
Painter, printmaker. Attended Rhode Island School of
Design (1952-56) and studied privately with Herman
Cherry and Robert Roche. Taught at Moore College of
Art, Philadelphia (1972); University of Pennsylvania
(1972-76, 1979-84); Nova Scotia College of Art (1974);
Parsons School of Design (1975-78); and Pennsylvania
Academy of the Fine Arts (1991-present). Worked in
San Francisco, 1983. Currently lives in New York.

87. *Telegraph Hill II*, 1984
Oil on canvas, 77¾ x 105 in.
Anonymous loan

Jess
born Burgess Collins
(b. Long Beach, Calif. 1923)
Painter, collagist. Trained and worked as chemist, 1939-
49. Attended Long Beach Junior College (1941); California Institute of Technology, Pasadena (1942-43, 1946-48;
BS, Chemistry, 1948); and CSFA (1949-51). In 1949 he
moved from Richland, Wash., to Berkeley. Moved to
Stinson Beach, Marin County, in 1958 until 1961 when
he settled in San Francisco.

88. *If All the World Were Paper and All the Water Sink*, 1962
Oil on canvas, 38 x 56 in.
The Fine Arts Museums of San Francisco, Museum pur-
chase: Roscoe and Margaret Oakes Income Fund,
The Museum Society Auxiliary, Mr. and Mrs. John N.
Rosekrans, Jr., Walter H. and Phyllis J. Shorenstein
Foundation Fund, Mrs. Paul L. Wattis, Bobbie and
Mike Wilsey, Mr. and Mrs. Steven MacGregor Read,
Mr. and Mrs. Gorham B. Knowles, Mrs. Edward T. Har-
rison, Mrs. Nan Tucker McEvoy, Harry and Ellen Parker
in honor of Steven Nash, Katharine Doyle Spann,

Mr. and Mrs. William E. Steen, Mr. and Mrs. Leonard E.
Kingsley, George Hopper Fitch, Princess Ranieri di San
Faustino, and Mr. and Mrs. Richard Madden

Pirkle Jones
(b. Shreveport, La. 1914)
Photographer. Came to the Bay Area in 1942 as part of
his service with the Army. Attended CSFA, where he met
his wife, photographer Ruth-Marion Baruch (1946-49).
Taught at CSFA (1952-58); Ansel Adams's Workshops,
Yosemite (1966-70); and SFAI (1970-present). Lives in
Mill Valley.

89. *Sunset District and Pacific Ocean, San Francisco*, 1951
Gelatin silver print, 18¼ x 24¼ in.
Courtesy the artist

William Keith
(near Old Meldrum, Aberdeenshire, Scotland 1838-1911
Berkeley, Calif.)
Painter, illustrator. Emigrated to New York in 1850.
Trained as wood engraver. In 1858 briefly came to San
Francisco to work as illustrator for *Harper's Weekly*.
Returned to Scotland and England in 1859. At the end of
1859 he settled in San Francisco and worked in engraving shop of Harrison Eastman. Studied painting with
Samuel Marsden Brookes (1863), abandoning engraving
for painting by 1868. Studied in France, Italy, and Germany, 1870-71. Returned to Boston in 1871 where he
opened a painting studio. In 1872 he moved to San Francisco and befriended naturalist John Muir; with Muir
he began exploring remote areas of California. Traveled
to Europe, studying in Munich, 1883-85. Returned in
1885 to settle in Berkeley. Became director of San Francisco Art Association in 1895. In 1907 he cofounded the
Del Monte Art Gallery, Monterey.

90. *The Glory of the Heavens*, ca. 1891
Oil on canvas, 35¼ x 59¼ in.
The Fine Arts Museums of San Francisco, presented to the City and County of San Francisco
by Gordon Blanding

91. *Looking across the Golden Gate from Mount Tamalpais*,
ca. 1895
Oil on canvas, 40 x 50⅝ in.
Private collection

92. *From Point Richmond Looking toward the
Golden Gate*, 1898
Oil on canvas, 30 x 40 in.
Private collection

Michael Kenna
(b. Widnes, Cheshire, England 1953)
Photographer. Attended Upholland College,
Lancashire, England (1965-72); the Banbury School
of Art, Oxfordshire (1972-73); and London College of
Printing (1976). Moved to the U.S. in 1977 and came to
San Francisco in 1978. Since 1980, he has held workshops and lectures at UC Extension, UC Berkeley, Headlands Center for the Arts, and City College of San Francisco. Currently resides in San Francisco.

93. *Steps, Marin County, California*, 1982
Gelatin silver print, 8¾ x 5½ in.
Courtesy Stephen Wirtz Gallery, San Francisco

Mark Klett
(b. Albany, N.Y. 1952)
Photographer. Attended St. Lawrence University, Canton, N.Y. (BS, Geology, 1974) and State University of
New York at Buffalo, Visual Studies Workshop (MFA,
1977). Chief photographer for the Rephotographic Survey Project, 1977-83. Studio manager and professor at
Print Collaborative Facility, Arizona State University
(1981-present). Worked at the Headlands Center for the
Arts during the late 1980s. Lives in Tempe, Ariz.

94. *Mounting Block above Fort Barry Rifle Range with Shield
for Stray Bullets*, 4 July 1982
Gelatin silver print, 16 x 20 in.
Courtesy Fraenkel Gallery, San Francisco

Paul Kos
(b. Rock Springs, Wyo. 1942)
Sculptor, conceptual and installation artist. Attended
Georgetown University, Washington, D.C., and SFAI
(BFA, 1965; MFA, 1967). Currently teaches at SFAI (since
1978). Resides in Soda Springs.

95. *Lot's Wife*, 1969/1995
Photodocument, 25¼ x 40 in.
Collection of the artist, courtesy Gallery Paule Anglim,
San Francisco

Dorothea Lange
(Hoboken, N.J. 1895-1965 San Francisco, Calif.)
Photographer. Apprenticed in Arnold Genthe's portrait
studio, New York (1912-14). Attended New York Training School for Teachers, 1914-17; studied with Clarence
White, Columbia College, 1917-18. Came to San Francisco in 1918, opening portrait studio that remained in
operation until 1932. In 1929 she was hired by the California State Emergency Relief Administration to photograph migratory workers. Photographed for the U.S.
Resettlement Administration, later the Farm Security
Administration, 1935.

96. *Real Estate Office, Oakland, California*, 1936
Modern gelatin silver photographic print from original
negative, 8 x 10 in.
Courtesy Ellen Manchester; from the U.S. Farm Secu-
rity Administration Collection, Prints and Photographs
Division, Library of Congress, Washington, D.C.

Robin Lasser
(b. Buffalo, N.Y. 1956)
Photographer, multi-media installation artist. Attended
UCLA (BA, 1979) and Mills College (MFA, 1988). Taught
at SFSU (1989-94), CCAC (1990-94), San Jose State
University (1990-present), and SFAI (1992-94).
Lives in Oakland.

97. *Arson and Graffiti*, 1989
Gelatin silver print, 24 x 20 in.
Collection of Richard Titus, courtesy the artist

Alma Lavenson
(San Francisco, Calif. 1897-1989 Piedmont, Calif.)
Photographer. In 1906 moved to Oakland. Attended UC
Berkeley (BA, 1919). Began photographic career around
1923. In 1930 began working with Imogen Cunningham,
Edward Weston, and Consuelo Kanaga. In 1932 joined
Group *f.64*, abandoning earlier pictorialist style.

98. *Oakland Estuary*, 1926
Gelatin silver print, 10½ x 13⅝ in.
Courtesy Susan Ehrens

99. *March of the Poles*, 1930
Gelatin silver print, 9½ x 13⅜ in.
Courtesy Susan Ehrens

Dennis Leon
(b. London, England 1933)
Sculptor, painter. Attended Tyler School of Fine Arts,
Temple University, Philadelphia (BFA, BS in education,
MFA). Taught at Philadelphia College of Art (1960-72);
CCAC (1972-89); and Sheffield Polytechnical Institute,
England (1973, 1975-76). Settled in Oakland by 1972.

100. *Heelstone*, 1990
Plywood, 38 x 40 x 29 in.
Courtesy Haines Gallery, San Francisco, and the artist

Maurice Logan
(San Francisco, Calif. 1886-1977 Orinda, Calif.)
Painter. Lived in Oakland. Attended Partington Art
School, San Francisco (ca. 1902); CSD/SFIA, studying
with Theodore Wores (1907-13); and School of the Art
Institute of Chicago. Worked as freelance commercial
artist in 1915. Moved to Chicago in 1919, employed by
Charles Everett Johnson Co. commercial art agency.
Returned to Bay Area in 1920. Exhibited with Society of
Six, 1923-28. Traveled to Africa and Europe, 1924-25,
then to Southwest with Selden Gile in 1926, 1931, and
1934. Taught at Académie of Advertising Art, now the
Academy of Art College (1933-35) and CSAC/CCAC (1935-
44). By 1935 he founded a commercial art business,
Logan, Staniford and Cox.

101. *Point Richmond*, 1929
Oil on canvas, 15 x 18 in.
Collection of The Oakland Museum of California, gift
of Louis Siegriest

Erle Loran
(b. Minneapolis, Minn. 1905)
Painter. Attended University of Minnesota (1922-23)
and Minneapolis School of Art (1923-26). In 1926 he was
awarded Paris Prize by John Armstrong Chaloner Foundation for three years study in France, settling in Paul
Cézanne's studio at Aix-en-Provence (1926-29). Also
studied briefly with Hans Hofmann, New York, 1960.
Taught at UC Berkeley (1936-72). Lives in Kensington,
Calif.

102. *Victory Shipyards I*, 1945
Watercolor and gouache on paper, 15½ x 22½ in.
Anne Schechter and Reid Buckley

Rose Mandel
(b. Czaniec, Poland 1910)
Photographer. Attended the University of Geneva,
Switzerland (1939), where she studied education and
child psychology with Jean Piaget, and the Jean Jacques
Rousseau Institute. In 1942 she emigrated to the U.S.,
settling in California after traveling to New York.
Attended CSFA, studying with Ansel Adams and Minor
White (1946-48). Worked as photographer for the Art
Department, UC Berkeley, 1948-67. Lives in Berkeley.

103. *Berkeley Marina*, ca. 1962
Gelatin silver print, 3¾ x 4¾ in.
Courtesy the artist and Susan Ehrens

104. *View from Marina to Richmond*, 1965
Gelatin silver print, 3¾ x 4¾ in.
Courtesy the artist and Susan Ehrens

Xavier Martinez
(Guadalajara, Mexico 1869-1943 Carmel, Calif.)
Painter. Received early art training in Guadalajara.
Came to San Francisco in 1893. Attended the CSD/MHIA,
studying with Arthur Mathews (1893-97); École des
Beaux-Arts, Paris, studying in the atelier of Jean-Léon
Gérôme (1897-99); and Académie Carrière (1900-01).
Returned to San Francisco in 1900, establishing a stu-
dio. In 1902, with Gottardo Piazzoni and others, he
formed California Society of Artists in protest to San
Francisco Art Association. Moved studio and home to
Piedmont in 1906. Cofounded the Del Monte Art
Gallery, Monterey, in 1907. Taught at CSAC/CCAC (1908-
42). Moved to Carmel in 1942.

105. *The Road*, ca. 1907
Oil on canvas, 30 x 36⅛ in.
The Fine Arts Museums of San Francisco, Museum pur-
chase, Skae Fund Legacy

106. *The Bay*, 1918
Oil on canvas, 30 x 36 in.
Collection of The Oakland Museum of California, gift
of Dr. William S. Porter

Arthur Mathews
(Markesan, Wis. 1860-1945 San Francisco, Calif.)
Painter, muralist, designer. In 1867 he came to California, settling in Oakland. Served as an architectural draftsman apprentice at father's Oakland office, 1875-79. Employed as designer and lithographer for Britton & Rey, 1881-84. Attended Académie Julian under Gustave Boulanger and Jules Lefebvre, Paris (1885-89). Returned to San Francisco in 1889. Taught at Art Students' League and CSD/MHIA (1889-1906, director from 1890). Married Lucia Kleinhans in 1894. With Lucia, opened Furniture Shop, began publication of monthly magazine *Philopolis*, and established Philopolis Press in 1906.

107. *Discovery of the Bay of San Francisco by Portolá*, 1896
Oil on canvas, 70¼ x 58½ in.
Courtesy Garzoli Gallery, San Rafael

108. *California*, 1905
Oil on canvas, 26 x 23½ in.
Collection of The Oakland Museum of California, gift of The Art Guild

109. *View from Skyline Boulevard, San Francisco*, 1915
Oil on canvas, 30 x 40 in.
Collection of The Oakland Museum of California, gift of Concours d'Antiques and The Art Guild

Lucia Kleinhans Mathews
(San Francisco, Calif. 1870-1955 Los Angeles, Calif.)
Painter, designer. Attended Mills College (1892-93); CSD/MHIA, studying with Arthur Mathews (1893-94); and James McNeill Whistler's Académie Carmine, Paris (1899). Married Arthur Mathews in 1894. Opened Furniture Shop with Arthur in 1906. Aided in reestablishing Sketch Club in 1907; served on board of directors, 1907-08, and as president, 1908-09. Lived and worked in San Francisco until 1951 when she moved to Los Angeles.

110. *Dining Table with Decorated Top*, 1918
Oil and gold leaf on wood, 30 x 61 x 109¼ in.
Collection of The Oakland Museum of California, gift of The Art Guild

John Meyer
(b. Louisville, Ky. 1943)
Painter. Attended University of Louisville, Ky. (1962-63); École de la Musée de Montreal, Canada (1968-70); and École Nationale des Beaux-Arts de Lyon, France (1970-71). Came to California in 1971. Lives and works in San Francisco.

111. *Untitled*, 1991
Oil on panel, 24 x 24 in.
Courtesy Gallery Paule Anglim, San Francisco, and the artist

José Moya del Piño
(Priego, Córdoba, Spain 1891-1969 Ross, Calif.)
Painter, muralist. Studied at Granada School of Arts and Crafts, Spain (1904); Escuela Especial de Pintura y Grabado Escultura, Madrid (1907); Academy, Rome, and Académie Colarossi, Paris, as a recipient of Prix de Rome (1908). Came to U.S. in 1925, settling in San Francisco. Employed under Civil Works Administration/Public Works of Art Project (1934), producing mural for Coit Tower, and by Treasury Department Section of Painting and Sculpture (1936-41). Taught at Art Students' League, San Francisco (1935).

112. *Chinese Mother and Child*, 1933
Oil on canvas, 40 x 30 in.
Mrs. John Dowling Relfe

Douglas Muir
(b. Syracuse, N.Y. 1940)
Photographer. Began photographing in 1953. Moved to San Francisco in 1962. Lives and works in Mill Valley as photographer and steamfitter..

113. *Citicorp Atrium, San Francisco*, 1985
Ektacolor print, 12¾ x 18¾ in.
Douglas Muir

Hermann Dudley Murphy
(Marlboro, Mass. 1867-1945 Lexington, Mass.)
Painter. Attended Boston Museum School, with Joseph DeCamp and Otto Grundman (1886), and Académie Julian, Paris, studying with Jean-Paul Laurens (1891-97). Worked as illustrator for various magazines and newspapers, 1886-92. Returned to U.S. in 1897, settling in Winchester, Mass. Taught at Harvard University School of Architecture (1901-37).

114. *Coyote Point, Salt Flats, California*, ca. 1916-17
Oil on canvas, 17½ x 53¾ in.
Mr. and Mrs. Mason Walsh, Jr.

Eadweard Muybridge
born Edward James Muggeridge
(Kingston-upon-Thames, Surrey, England 1830-1904
Kingston-upon-Thames, Surrey, England)
Photographer. Primarily self-taught. Came to U.S. in
1851. Moved to San Francisco in 1855, where he opened
bookstore. Returned in 1860 to England, taking up photography. Returned to San Francisco in 1867 under the
name Eadweard Muybridge. Worked as a commercial
photographer under the name Helios until 1872.
Remained in California until 1881. Around 1896 he
returned to his native town in England.

115. *Panorama of San Francisco from the California
Street Hill*, 1878
Albumen silver prints from wet-plate collodion
glass negatives, mounted on paper
13 plates, 20½ x 16 in. each
Department of Special Collections, Stanford
University Library

David Nash
(b. Esher, Surrey, England 1945)
Sculptor. Attended Kingston Art School (1963-67) and
Chelsea School of Art (1969-70). Resident sculptor at
Yorkshire Sculpture Park, 1981-82. In 1987 visited and
worked briefly in San Francisco at the Djerassi Founda-
tion. Lives and works in Blaenau Ffestiniog, North
Wales, England, where he moved in 1967.

116. *Charred Sphere Pyramid Cube in Redwood Stumps*, 1995
Pastel and charcoal on paper mounted on canvas,
72 x 106 in.
Courtesy L.A. Louver Gallery, Venice

Irving Norman
(Poland 1910-1989 Half Moon Bay, Calif.)
Painter, draftsman. Came to U.S. in 1923. Settled in San
Francisco by 1940. Self-taught except for brief study at
CSFA (1945) and Art Students' League, New York (1945-
46). Worked as barber in San Francisco for 46 years
while exhibiting in one-person and group shows in
San Francisco and occasionally in New York from
1948 onward.

117. *City Rush*, 1941
Graphite on paper, 30 x 24 in.
Courtesy Jan Holloway Fine Art, San Francisco

Sonya Noskowiak
(Leipzig, Germany 1900-1975 Greenbrae, Calif.)
Photographer. Moved to Sacramento in 1915 from Valparaiso, Chile. In 1929, while working as a receptionist
at Johan Hagemeyer's studio in Los Angeles, he met
Edward Weston and lived with him until 1934. Founding member of Group *f*.64 in 1932. Maintained studio in
San Francisco, 1934-50, working as portrait, commercial, and fashion photographer.

118. *Untitled (View of Ferry Building and Bay Bridge)*, 1940
Gelatin silver print, 8 x 10 in.
Collection of Ron and Kathy Perisho

Chiura Obata
(Okayama-ken, Honshu, Japan 1885-1975
Berkeley, Calif.)
Painter, printmaker. Studied privately with Chikusen
Moniwa, master of sumi painting, Sendai (ca. 1892-99);
Japan Fine Arts Academy, Tokyo; and with Tanryo
Murata, Kogyo Terasaki, and Gah Hashimoto (1899-ca.
1902). Moved to San Francisco in 1903, working as illus-
trator and painting landscapes throughout California.
Taught at UC Berkeley (1932-42, 1945-54); summer ses-
sions in Yosemite (1937-41); and University of New
Mexico (summer 1949). Imprisoned at Tanforan deten-
tion center and at Topaz Relocation Center, Topaz,
Utah, where he directed Topaz Art School (1942-43).
Became U.S. citizen in 1954. Traveled throughout Calif.
lecturing on and demonstrating sumi painting, 1955-70.

119. *View of San Francisco*, 30 April 1942
Sumi on paper, 15 x 20½ in.
Collection of the Obata Family

120. *Rolling Hills*, 1946
Sumi on paper, 15 x 20½ in.
Collection of the Obata Family

Otis Oldfield
(Sacramento, Calif. 1890-1969 San Francisco, Calif.)
Painter. Attended Best's Art School, San Francisco
(1908-10) and Académie Julian, Paris (1911-12). Lived in
Paris, 1910-24, establishing a studio by 1918. Settled in
San Francisco by 1925. Taught at CSFA (1925-42), CCAC
(1945-52), and privately. Employed under Civil Works
Administration/Public Works of Art Project (1934),
producing mural for Coit Tower.

121. *Telegraph Hill*, ca. 1927
Oil on canvas, 40 x 33 in.
The Delman Collection, San Francisco

Sono Osato
(b. Baden Baden, Germany 1960)
Painter. Came to California in 1983. Attended Bemis Art
School, Colorado Springs (1965-75); Arizona State Uni-
versity, Tempe (BFA, 1983); and CCAC (MFA, 1986).
Taught at Kansas City Art Institute (1990); Mills College
(1992); SFAI (1992-93); and CCAC (1994-present).
Resides in Oakland.

122. *Portrait of the Headlands*, 1988
Oil, asphalt, sand, and beeswax on canvas
64 x 76 in.
Courtesy Terrain Gallery, San Francisco, and the artist

Bill Owens
(San Jose, Calif. 1938)
Photographer. Attended Chico State College (BA, 1963)
and SFSU (1966). Worked as photojournalist for *Liver-
more Independent*, 1967-78. Since 1983 has lived in Hayward. Currently works as brewmaster and publishes
American Brewer and *Beer the Magazine*.

123. *In One Day You Have Instant Yard*, from *Suburbia*, 1972
Gelatin silver print, 7⅞ x 9⅞ in.
Courtesy Bill Owens

David Park
(Boston, Mass. 1911-1960 Berkeley, Calif.)
Painter. Moved to Los Angeles in 1928 and then to
Berkeley, 1929-36. Studied at Otis Art Institute, Los
Angeles (1928), and worked in the Bay Area for Works
Progress Administration in the early 1930s. Taught at
the Winsor School near Boston (1936-41), but returned
to the Bay Area after 1941, where he stayed. Taught at
CSFA (1943-52) and UC Berkeley (from 1955).

124. *Riverbank*, 1956
Oil on canvas, 59⅝ x 69¹¹/₁₆ in.
Williams College Museum of Art, bequest of Lawrence
H. Bloedel, Class of 1923, 77.9.75

Charles Rollo Peters
(San Francisco, Calif. 1862-1928 San Francisco, Calif.)
Painter. Attended CSD, studying with Virgil Williams
and Christian A. Jorgensen, and studied privately with
Jules Tavernier. Attended École des Beaux-Arts, Paris,
studying with Jean-Léon Gérôme and Fernand-Anne
Cormon (1886-90), and Académie Julian, studying with
Gustave Boulanger and Jules Lefebvre (1886-90). Exhibited in Paris Salon of 1889, then returned to San Francisco in 1890. Returned to Paris in 1891 until ca. 1895,
when he settled in Monterey. In 1907 he cofounded the
Del Monte Art Gallery, Monterey. Moved to England in
1909. Returned to San Francisco in 1911, remaining until
1920 when he left again for Paris. After falling ill in 1920
he returned to New York and then to San Francisco.

125. *Houseboats and Wharf Nocturne*, ca. 1925
Oil on canvas, 19¼ x 25⅜ in.
G. Breitweiser

Gottardo Piazzoni
(Intragna, Switzerland 1872-1945 Carmel Valley, Calif.)
Painter, muralist. Emigrated to Carmel Valley, ca. 1886.
Attended CSD/MHIA, studying with Raymond Yelland
and Arthur Mathews (1891-93); Académie Julian, Paris
(1895-96); and École des Beaux-Arts, Paris (1896-98). In
1898 he returned to San Francisco, establishing Piazzoni
Atelier d'Art, ca. 1899. Formed California Society of
Artists in 1902 in protest to the San Francisco Art Asso-
ciation. Moved to Belvedere in Marin County, 1915-25.
Made several extended trips to Europe after 1898.
Taught at the CSFA (1918-35).

126. *The Land*, 1915
Oil on canvas, 53 x 124 in.
University Art Museum, University of California,
Berkeley, gift of Helen and Ansley Salz

127. *The Sea*, 1915
Oil on canvas, 53 x 124 in.
University Art Museum, University of California,
Berkeley, gift of Helen and Ansley Salz

Christine Pomeroy
(biographical dates unknown)
Photographer.

128. *Off Yerba Buena, May 6, 1908*, 1908
Gelatin silver print, 2 x 7 in.
Courtesy Stephen Wirtz Gallery, San Francisco

129. *USS Honolulu, May 6, 1908*, 1908
Gelatin silver print, 2 x 7 in.
Courtesy Stephen Wirtz Gallery, San Francisco

Bruce Porter
(San Francisco, Calif. 1865-1953 San Francisco, Calif.)
Painter, muralist, garden designer, stained-glass maker,
architect. Largely self-taught though he traveled to
Europe on at least six occasions, studying in Paris, Lon-
don, and Venice. Served as the secretary of the Guild
for Arts and Crafts, founded in 1894. Originator with
Gelett Burgess of *The Lark*, published 1895-97.

130. *Presidio Cliffs*, 1908
Oil on canvas, 27 x 32 in.
Private collection

Clayton S. Price
(Bedford, Iowa 1874-1950 Portland, Oreg.)
Painter, muralist. Moved to Wyoming in 1886. Attended
St. Louis School of Fine Arts, Missouri (1906). Returned
to Wyoming. Left for Alberta in 1908, then moved late
that year to Calgary to work as an illustrator for *Pacific
Monthly Magazine*. Sometime after 1910 he left for Port-
land to work at magazine's headquarters. Moved to Bay
Area in 1915, where Gottardo Piazzoni was a mentor.
Moved to Monterey ca. 1920-21 where he shared a
house/studio with August Gay and other artists. While
in Monterey, studied with Armin Hansen. Left Monterey in 1928, visited Canada, and then moved back to
Portland by 1929.

131. *Coastline*, ca. 1924
Oil on canvas, 40⅛ x 50 in.
Hirshhorn Museum and Sculpture Garden, Smithson-
ian Institution, gift of Joseph H. Hirshhorn, 1966

Granville Redmond
(Philadelphia, Pa. 1871-1935 Hollywood, Calif.)
Painter. Moved to San Jose in 1874. Attended CSD/MHIA,
with Arthur Mathews (1890-93) and Académie Julian,
Paris (1893). Remained in Paris and St. Symphorien,
France, until 1898 when he moved to Los Angeles and
opened a studio. In 1908 he moved to Parkfield in Mon-
terey County, to San Mateo in 1910, and then to
Belvedere in 1916. Returned to Los Angeles in 1918,
where he remained until his death.

132. *Poppies in Marin County*, n.d.
(also known as *Lupine and Poppies, Marin*)
Oil on canvas, 25¼ x 30¼ in.
Collection of Dr. and Mrs. Oscar Lemer / on loan to
State Capital Restoration Project

Jock Reynolds and Suzanne Hellmuth

Jock Reynolds
(b. New Brunswick, N.J. 1947)
Sculptor, photographer, conceptual, performance and
installation artist. Attended UC Santa Cruz (1965-69, BA)
and UC Davis (1970-72, MFA). Taught at UC Davis (1972-
73) and SFSU (1973-83). Began collaborating with
Suzanne Hellmuth on photographic projects mounted
in installations in late 1970s. Served as executive director, Washington Project for the Arts, Washington, D.C.,
1983-90. Since 1989 he has served as the director of the
Addison Gallery of American Art, Andover, Mass.,
where he currently resides.

Suzanne Hellmuth
(b. New Haven, Conn. 1947)
Photographer, installation, video and performance
artist. Attended University College, Dar Es Salaam, Tan-
zania (1966); Swarthmore College (1964-67); Oberlin
College (1967-68, BA); and SFSU (1970-72, MA). Taught at
SFSU (1977) and SFAI (1978). Lives in Andover, Mass.

133. *Low Tide, from the Pacific Bay Series*, 1981
Gelatin silver print, 20 x 72 in.
Courtesy Stephen Wirtz Gallery, San Francisco

Peter Richards
(b. Pagosa Springs, Colo. 1944)
Sculptor, installation artist. Attended Colorado College, Colorado Springs (BA, 1967) and Rinehurt School of Sculpture, Maryland Institute of Art, Baltimore (MFA, 1969). Came to the Bay Area in 1970. Currently serves as Director of the Arts Program at the Exploratorium, San Francisco.

134. *Wave Organ*, 1981
Pencil on vellum, 30 x 42 in.
Courtesy the artist

Sam Richardson
(b. Oakland, Calif. 1934)
Sculptor. Studied at CCAC (BA, 1956; MFA, 1960). Served as art director at Museum of Contemporary Crafts, New York (1961-63). Has taught at San Jose State University (1963-present). Lives in Oakland.

135. *The Fog Hangs over Six Miles of That Guy's Valley*, 1969
Polyurethane foam, resin, acrylic, and lacquer on wood base, 6¾ x 71 x 6¾ in.; base: 3¾ x 71 x 7 in.
Collection Anderson Gallery, Buffalo

Diego Rivera
(Guanajuato, Mexico 1886-1957 Mexico City)
Painter, muralist. Studied at Academy of San Carlos, Mexico City (1896, 1898-1905), and privately with Victor-Octave Guillonet, Paris (1910). Worked in Paris from 1912 until 1921, returning to Mexico City where he undertook his first mural projects and assumed various art-related government positions. Visited the Soviet Union in celebration of the 10th anniversary of the October Revolution (1927-28). Named director, Academy of San Carlos, 1929, but forced to resign after a few months. First visit to U.S., 1930-31, under commission to paint murals in San Francisco; subsequent mural work in Detroit and New York, including the controversial project for Rockefeller Center (destroyed 1934). Returned to Mexico in 1933, working on mural projects through 1937 and again after 1943. Second visit to San Francisco in 1940 to paint mural for the Art in Action Program of the Golden Gate International Exposition.

136. *Study No.1 for "Still Life and Blossoming Almond Trees" (The Stern Mural)*, 1931
Charcoal on paper, 18⅝ x 23½ in.
Private collection

137. *Study No.2 for "Still Life and Blossoming Almond Trees" (The Stern Mural)*, 1931
Charcoal on paper, 17½ x 23½ in.
Private collection

138. *Study No.3 for "Still Life and Blossoming Almond Trees" (The Stern Mural)*, 1931
Graphite, charcoal, and watercolor on paper, 18⅝ x 23½ in.
Private collection

139. *Still Life and Blossoming Almond Trees (The Stern Mural)*, 1931
Fresco, 62¼ x 105 in.
University of California, Berkeley, gift of Rosalie M. Stern (Mrs. Sigmund Stern)

John Roloff
(b. Portland, Oreg. 1947)
Sculptor, environmental artist. Attended UC Davis (BA, 1970) and Humboldt State University (MA, 1973). Taught at SFAI (1973-74, 1978-present); University of Kentucky (1974-78); Mills College (1980-91); and University of Southern California (1987-88). Lives and works in Oakland.

140. *Metafossil (Metabolism and Mortality) Pinus: ponderosa, radiata, balfouriana*, 1992
Steel, refractory cement, species-specific pine boughs, 50½ x 156 x 29 in.; 72½ x 78 x 32 in.; 66½ x 127 x 33 in.
Courtesy Gallery Paule Anglim, San Francisco

Peter Saul
(b. San Francisco, Calif. 1934)
Painter. Attended Stanford University; CSFA (1950-52); and Washington University in Saint Louis (1952-56, BFA). Lived in Europe, 1956-64, and then in Mill Valley, 1964-74. Resides in Austin, Tex.

141. *The Government of California*, 1969
Oil on canvas, 68 x 96 in.
Courtesy Frumkin/Adams Gallery, New York

Richard Shaw
(b. Hollywood, Calif. 1941)
Sculptor. Attended Orange Coast College, Costa Mesa
(1961-63); State University of New York at Alfred
(1965); SFAI (BFA, 1965); and UC Davis (MFA, 1968).
Taught at SFAI (1965-87); University of Wisconsin,
Madison (summer 1971); and UC Berkeley (1987-present). Resides in Fairfax.

142. *Couch and Chair with Landscape and Cows*, 1966-67
Earthenware, acrylic paint, wood – couch: 10 x 18¾ x 9
in.; chair: 9¼ x 9⅝ x 9¼ in.
Collection American Craft Museum, New York, gift of
the Johnson Wax Company, from OBJECTS: USA, 1977;
donated to the American Craft Museum by the American Craft Council, 1990

Charles Sheeler
(Philadelphia, Penn. 1883-1965 Irvington, N.Y.)
Painter, photographer. Attended Philadelphia Museum
School of Industrial Art (1900-03); Pennsylvania Academy of the Fine Arts, with William Merritt Chase (1903-
06); and private summer classes with Chase. Traveled
to Europe 1905-06 and 1908-09. Moved to Manhattan,
1919, subsequently to South Salem, New York, 1927, to
Ridgefield, Conn., 1932, and finally to Irvington-on-
Hudson, New York, 1942. Visited San Francisco in 1954
and 1956, making photographs of the area on which he
would base future paintings.

143. *Golden Gate*, 1955
Oil on canvas, 25 x 34 in.
The Metropolitan Museum of Art, New York, George A.
Hearn Fund, 1955

Millard Sheets
(Pomona, Calif. 1907-1989 Gualala, Calif.)
Painter. Attended Chouinard School of Art, Los Angeles
(1925-29). Traveled in South America, Central America,
and Europe (1929-30). Returned to Los Angeles in 1930,
becoming leader in California Water Color Society
(named president, 1946-47). Taught at Scripps College
(1932-55; named director of arts, 1936). Worked as
designer for U.S. Army Air Corps (1939-41) and as artist-
correspondent for U.S. War Department (1942-43).
Served as director of Otis Art Institute, Los Angeles
(1953-59). In 1956 he founded an architectural design and
mural firm, Millard Sheets Designs, Inc., Claremont.

144. *Church of Saints Peter and Paul, San Francisco*, 1933
Watercolor on paper, 22 x 13¾ in.
Collection of Mr. and Mrs. Brayton Wilbur, Jr.

Bonnie Sherk
(b. New Bedford, Mass. 1945)
Conceptual artist. Attended Rutgers University (BA,
1967) and SFSU (MA, 1970). Lives in San Francisco.

145. *Original Proposal for Crossroads Community (The
Farm)*, 1974
Drawing and collage, 30 x 16 in.
Courtesy the artist

146. *Agora/Agri/Horti Culture, Proposal for Todos
Santos Plaza, Concord, CA*, in collaboration with
Mark Bunnell, 1987
Hand-colored black lined print, 30½ x 41 in.
Courtesy the artist

Louis Siegriest
(Oakland, Calif. 1899-1989 Berkeley, Calif.)
Painter. Attended CSAC, studying with Perham Nahl
(1914-16); CSFA (1917-18); and Van Sloun School (1917-
1919). Moved to Seattle to work as poster artist in 1921
until 1923 when he returned to Bay Area. Exhibited with
the Society of Six, 1923-28. From 1926 he lived in Dallas,
Chicago, and Milwaukee, where he taught at Layton Art
School (1926-31), returning to Bay Area in 1931. Worked
for Works Progress Administration/Federal Art Project,
1938-39. Moved to Virginia City, Nev., 1945. Returned to
East Bay in 1948 to reside permanently. Taught at the
Art League of California (1948-51). Traveled extensively
in Mexico, 1955-59, 1964, 1966, and 1970. Awarded honorary doctorate of fine arts from CCAC in 1987.

147. *Tiburon Buildings*, ca. 1923
Oil on canvas, 11¼ x 15¾ in.
Private collection

David Simpson
(b. Pasadena, Calif. 1928)
Painter. Studied at Pasadena City College (1942-43),
CSFA (1949-51, 1955-56, BFA), and San Francisco State
College (1956-58, MFA). Taught at UC Berkeley (1965-92).
Lives in Berkeley.

148. *Storm, Stars, and Stripes*, 1960
Oil on canvas, 64 x 45 in.
Collection City and County of San Francisco, San Francisco International Airport, purchased through the
Joint Committee of the San Francisco Art Commission
and the San Francisco Airports Commission

Nell Sinton
(b. San Francisco, Calif. 1910)
Painter. Attended CSFA (1926-28). Worked with Maurice Sterne on Federal Art Project murals in San Francisco (1938-40). Taught at SFAI (1970-71) and Institute for Creative and Artistic Development, Oakland (from 1974). Resides in San Francisco.

149. *Ideas for a Landscape #1*, 1959
Ink and gouache on board, 13¾ x 59¼ in.
Private collection

Peter Stackpole
(b. San Francisco, Calif. 1913)
Photographer. Son of sculptor Ralph Stackpole. Lived in Paris, 1923-24. Worked as apprentice news photographer for Oakland's *Post Enquirer*, 1931. Photographed the construction of the Bay bridges, 1934-36. Became a member of the Group *f*.64 in 1935. Became one of *Life Magazine*'s first four staff photographers, 1936-61, dividing time between New York and Hollywood. After his retirement from *Life* he returned to San Francisco. Resides in Oakland.

150. *Catwalk and Marin Tower*, 1936
Gelatin silver print, 6¼ x 9⅜ in.
Collection of The Oakland Museum of California, The Oakland Museum Founders Fund

Ray Stanford Strong
(b. Corvallis, Oreg. 1905)
Painter, muralist. Studied CSFA (1924) and Art Students' League, New York (1926). Returned to San Francisco in 1933, working on several mural commissions. With Maynard Dixon and others he revived Art Students' League, San Francisco in 1935. Employed under Civil Works Administration/Public Works of Art Project in 1934 and as muralist under Treasury Department Section of Painting and Sculpture in 1938. Taught at College of Marin and Mendocino Arts Center. Appointed artist-in-residence, Museum of Natural History, Santa Barbara (1960-64). Established Santa Barbara Institute of the Arts (1967-75). Lives in Santa Barbara.

151. *Golden Gate Bridge*, 1934
Oil on canvas, 44⅛ x 71¾ in.
National Museum of American Art, Smithsonian Institution, transfer from the U.S. Department of Interior, National Park Service

Wayne Thiebaud
(b. Mesa, Ariz. 1920)
Painter. Moved to Long Beach, Calif., in 1921, then to Huntington Park, 1929-31. Lived in Utah from 1931-33. Attended Frank Wiggins Trade School, Los Angeles (1938), and Long Beach City College (1940-41). Worked as freelance illustrator and cartoonist in Southern California, 1939-49. Attended San Jose State College (1949-50) and California State University, Sacramento (1950-53; BA, 1951; MA, 1953). Taught at Sacramento City College (1951-60) and UC Davis (1960-present). Lives in Sacramento and San Francisco.

152. *Diagonal Ridge*, 1968
Acrylic on canvas, 72 x 72 in.
Private collection, courtesy of the Allan Stone Gallery, New York

153. *Urban Freeways*, 1979
Oil on canvas, 44⅜ x 36⅛ in.
Collection of Paul LeBaron Thiebaud

154. *Day City (Bright City)*, 1982
Oil on canvas, 48 x 36 in.
Collection of Thomas W. Weisel

Mark Thompson
(b. Fort Sill, Okla. 1950)
Installation, conceptual, and performance artist, sculptor. Attended UC Berkeley (BA, 1972; MA, 1973). Taught at SFSU (1988-89, 1991, 1992); Slade School of Fine Art, University College, London (1990); and CCAC (1993-present). Helped to establish the Headlands Center for the Arts, 1985-88, and served as one of the first artists-in-residence. Lives in Oakland.

155. *Immersion*, 1973-76
Color photographs, 36 photographs, 4 x 5½ in. each
Courtesy the artist

Brian Tripp
(b. Eureka, Calif. 1945)
Painter, sculptor, installation artist. Moved to Arcata in 1968. Attended Humboldt State University (1969, 1971). Taught Native American art history course at Humboldt State University (1973-77). Traveled to Davis frequently, 1974-1980, where he met and worked with Native American artists Frank LaPena and George Longfish. Returned to Arcata in 1980, focusing on his art full-time. Organized many significant Native American art exhibitions, 1980-85. Since 1985 he has lived in Eureka. Resumed teaching at Humboldt State University, 1988.

156. *In Memory of Mount Diablo: TU-YOYSH-TAK (TY-YOY-SHIP), Mountain to Mountain, When Straight Line Straightened out Circle*, 1992
Mixed media/assemblage, 120 x 42¼ x 29½ in.
Collection of Robert Benson and Becky Evans

157. *Whose Land Is It?*, 1992
Acrylic on paper, 35 x 23 in.
Courtesy Terrain Gallery, San Francisco

Frank Tuttle
(b. Oroville, Calif. 1957)
Painter. Attended Humboldt State University (1975-81, BA, with emphasis in Native American studies). Currently teaches at Mendocino College (since 1989). Lives and works in Ukiah.

158. *What Wild Indian?*, 1992
Oil on wood, 18 x 20 in.
Collection of Ian and Patricia McGreal

Bernard von Eichman
(San Francisco, Calif. 1899-1970 Santa Rosa, Calif.)
Painter. Attended CSAC (1915); CSFA, studying with Frank Van Sloun (1916); and Van Sloun School, San Francisco (1917). Traveled to China (1921-23). Exhibited with Society of Six, 1923-28. Moved to New York in 1928; worked as window dresser, 1930-40. After abandoning painting, returned to Bay Area in 1942 and worked at shipyards in Sausalito and Vallejo. Later worked as housepainter and renovator, living in Vallejo, 1945, Mill Valley, 1946-ca. 1954, and Monterey, ca. 1954-1968.

159. *The Red House*, ca. 1920
Oil on board, 15½ x 19½ in.
Mr. and Mrs. C. Richard Kramlich

160. *Shopping*, ca. 1928
Oil on board, 16 x 18 in.
Collection of Judy and Sheldon Greene

Catherine Wagner
(b. San Francisco, Calif. 1953)
Photographer. Attended Instituto de Allende, Mexico (1970-71); SFAI (1971); College of Marin (1972-73); and SFSU, studying with Jack Welpott (1974-77; BA, 1975; MA, 1977). Studied with Oliver Gagliani (1975). Taught at College of Marin (1975-77); College of San Mateo (1978); Diablo Valley College, Pleasant Hill (1978); SFSU (1979-85); and Mills College (1979-present). Lived in San Rafael and now in San Francisco.

161. *George Moscone Site, Arch Construction III, San Francisco, CA*, 1981
Gelatin silver print, 20 x 24 in.
Courtesy Fraenkel Gallery, San Francisco

Bob Walker
(Syracuse, N.Y. 1952-1992 San Francisco, Calif.)
Photographer. Worked as freelance photographer specializing in landscape and as a consultant to the East Bay Regional Park District. Worked as volunteer for many preservation campaigns and educated others about the region and the protection of wild areas.

162. *Dougherty Valley*, ca. 1986
Cibachrome print, 16 x 20 in.
The Oakland Museum of California, Natural Sciences Division

James Weeks
(b. Oakland, Calif. 1922)
Painter. Attended CSFA (1940-42, 1946-47, BA); Hartwell School of Design, San Francisco (1946-47); and the Escuela de Pintura y Escultura, Mexico City (1951). Taught at CSFA/SFAI (1948-51, 1958-67); Hartwell School of Design (1948); and CCAC (1959-60). Lived in Bay Area until 1967 when left to teach at UCLA. Moved to Massachusetts in 1970 to teach at Boston University. Lives in Bedford, Mass.

163. *Looking North, Baker Beach*, 1962
Oil on canvas, 48 x 49 in.
Mrs. Pierre Etcheverry

Henry Wessel
(b. Teaneck, N.J. 1942)
Photographer. Attended Pennsylvania State University
(BA, 1966) and State University of New York at Buffalo
(MFA, 1972). Taught at Pennsylvania State University
(1967-69); Center of the Eye, Aspen, Col. (1973); UC
Berkeley (1973); SFAI (1973-present); SFSU (1974); UC
Davis (1977); and CCAC (1977). Lives in Point Richmond.

164. *Point Richmond, CA*, 1985
Gelatin silver print, 24 x 20 in.
Courtesy Fraenkel Gallery, San Francisco

Brett Weston
(Los Angeles, Calif. 1911-1993 Kona, Hawaii)
Photographer. In 1925, with his father, the photographer Edward Weston, he went to Mexico and began
work as photographer. Returned to Glendale, Calif., in
1927. Worked as business partner with his father in
establishing several portrait studios: Glendale, 1928;
San Francisco, 1928; and Carmel, 1929-30. By 1930
moved back to Glendale and established his own portrait studio. In 1935 he opened another studio jointly
with Edward in Santa Monica. Supervised photographic section of the Federal Art Project in Los Angeles, 1935-37. Drafted into U.S. Army in 1943 and sta-
tioned in New York City, where he met Paul Strand.
Settled in Carmel in 1948.

165. *Untitled (View of Hunter's Point)*, 1939
Gelatin silver print, 8 x 10 in.
Collection of Ron and Kathy Perisho

Minor White
(Minneapolis, Minn. 1908-1976 Boston, Mass.)
Photographer. Attended University of Minn. (BA, 1934).
Came to San Francisco, where he lived with Ansel
Adams, in 1946; served as Adams's assistant at CSFA.
Continued teaching there until 1953. Cofounder and
manager of *Aperture* magazine in 1952. Moved to
Rochester, N.Y., in 1953; taught part-time at the
Rochester Institute of Technology (1953-56). Became
visiting professor at Massachusetts Institute of Technol-
ogy (MIT) in 1965 and by 1968 had built their photogra-
phy program. Retired from MIT in 1974.

166. *Warehouse Area, San Francisco*, 1949
Gelatin silver print, 8 x 11⅝ in.
The Art Museum, Princeton University, the Minor
White Archive

167. *San Francisco, California*, 1952
Gelatin silver print, 6 x 8⁷⁄₁₆ in.
The Art Museum, Princeton University, the Minor
White Archive

168. *Daly City Dump, California*, 1953
Gelatin silver print, 7⅛ x 7½ in.
The Art Museum, Princeton University, the Minor
White Archive

William T. Wiley
(b. Bedford, Ind. 1937)
Painter, printmaker, sculptor. Raised in Richland,
Wash. Moved to San Francisco in 1956. Attended SFAI
(1959-62; BFA, 1960; MFA, 1962). Taught at UC Davis
(1962-73); SFAI (1963, 1966-67); University of Nevada,
Reno (1967); Washington State College, Pullman (1967);
UC Berkeley (1967); School of Visual Arts, New York
(1968); and University of Colorado, Boulder (1968).
Lives in Forrest Knolls and maintains a studio in
Woodacre.

169. *Lame and Blind in Eden*, 1969
Watercolor and ink on paper, 30 x 21¹⁵⁄₁₆ in.
The Harry W. and Mary Margaret Anderson Collection

170. *Leviathan I*, 1988
Pencil and acrylic on canvas, 75 x 140 in.
Mr. and Mrs. James R. Patton, Jr.

Paul Wonner
(b. Tucson, Ariz. 1920)
Painter. Came to California in 1937. Studied at CCAC
(1937-41, BA) and Art Students' League, New York
(1947). Lived in New York from 1946 until 1950.
Attended UC Berkeley (1950-55; BA, 1952; MA, 1953; MLS,
1955). Worked at the main library of UC Davis, 1956-60.
Returned briefly to San Francisco in 1960, moving in
1961 to Southern California. Taught at UCLA (1961) and
Otis Art Institute (1965). In 1976 he returned to San
Francisco, where he presently resides.

171. *River Bathers*, 1961
Oil on canvas, 50 x 50 in.
Roselyne and Richard Swig

John Woodall
(b. Lakeland, Fla. 1940)
Conceptual artist, sculptor, video artist. Attended University of Florida (1958-62); Pasadena Art Museum School (summer 1963); Pasadena City College (1963-65); and SFAI (1965-69; BFA, 1968; MFA, 1969). Taught at SFAI (1978, 1983, 1984); University of San Francisco (1985); Hayward State College (1985); John F. Kennedy University, Oakland (1987); Claremont Graduate School, Pomona (1989); College of Marin (1988); SFAI (1989-90); and CCAC (1989-92). Lives in San Francisco.

172. *Dialogue with Survival*, 1974-1976/1995
Mixed media (photographs, text, owl bundle, and skeletal heap), 48 x 36 x 24 in.
Courtesy the artist

Willard E. Worden
(Philadelphia, Pa. 1868-1946 Palo Alto, Calif.)
Photographer. Learned photography in the Philippines during the Spanish-American War. Arrived in California in 1900. In 1902 he opened commercial studio in San Francisco. Official photographer for the Panama Pacific International Exposition, 1915.

173. *Seal Rock*, ca. 1906
Gelatin silver print, 4 x 8 in.
Collection of The Oakland Museum of California, gift of Dr. Robert Shimshak

174. *Presidio and Angel Island, San Francisco Bay*, ca. 1910
Gelatin silver print, 4 x 8 in.
Collection of The Oakland Museum of California, gift of Dr. Robert Shimshak

Raymond Dabb Yelland
(London, England, 1848-1900 Oakland, Calif.)
Painter. Emigrated to New York in 1851. Attended National Academy of Design, New York, studying with William Page, L.E. Wilmarth, and James Brevoort (1869-71). Also studied privately with Luc Olivier Merson in Paris (1886). Taught at National Academy of Design (1872), Mills College (1874-77), CSD/MHIA (1877-94), and UC Berkeley. Traveled to Europe in 1877 and 1886. Maintained a studio in San Francisco. Lived in San Francisco and Oakland, spending summers in Monterey.

175. *Cities of the Golden Gate*, 1893
Oil on canvas, 55 x 96½ in.
University Art Museum, University of California, Berkeley, gift of the artist

Video Program

The two-hour video program was produced by Constance Lewallen exclusively for The Fine Arts Museums of San Francisco. Post-production by Video Free America, San Francisco. The producer extends special thanks to the artists, Skip Sweeney and Sue Marcoux of Video Free America, and Leslie Asako Gladsjo.

This video program aired continuously during the exhibition. The first part of the program presented important Bay Area performances, events, and installations as preserved and documented in videotapes. The second part of the program featured hallmark videos, created in and of themselves as works of art, that explore the landscape of the Bay Area.

The following lists the contents of the video programs according to their order of presentation.

Program A – *Documentation: Urban Performance and Installation*, 1968-1994

Mel Henderson (with Joe Hawley, Alf Young, and Bob Campbell)
Documentation of 1969 Performances: Yellow Cabs, Searchlights, and Oil, 1994
Black and white, color, sound
8 minutes, 30 seconds

Bonnie Sherk
Excerpts of Work from 1970-1994, 1995
Black and white, color, sound
12 minutes

Darryl Sapien (with Michael Hinton)
Excerpts from Performances, 1974-1979, 1994
Black and white, sound
9 minutes, 4 seconds

Mark Pauline
Survival Research Laboratories: Excerpts from San Francisco Performances, 1979-1992
Black and white, color, sound
9 minutes, 21 seconds

Tony Labat
David Ireland's House, 1976-77
Black and white, sound
10 minutes

Mark Thompson
Immersion, 1976
Color, sound
6 minutes, 59 seconds

Ned Kahn
Digital Wind, 1987
Color
2 minutes

Timothy Collins
Offshore Residence (Everyone's Home by the Bay), 1988-89
Color, sound
1 minute, 30 seconds

John Roloff
Gradient, 1994
Color, sound
6 minutes, 10 seconds

Program B – *Video Works*, 1979-1994

Tom Marioni
Studio 1979, 1979
Color, sound
14 minutes, 30 seconds

Tom Marioni
San Francisco, 1984
Color, sound
10 minutes

Doug Hall
Prelude to the Tempest, 1985
Color, sound
15 minutes

Mary Lucier
Asylum (A Romance), 1986
Color, sound
11 minutes, 48 seconds

Joanne Kelly
Hear Us Speak, 1987
Color, sound
3 minutes, 55 seconds

Paula Levine
Coyote Cow, 1994
Color, sound
4 minutes, 20 seconds

Chip Lord
Bi-Coastal, 1981
Color, sound
40 seconds

Index of Artists and Designers

Illustrations
Works in exhibition are starred.

Photography Credits
Other than those accompanying illustrations

Introduction
page xii Cecile Keefe
fig.3 Joseph McDonald
fig.4 Courtesy Anne Kohs & Associates,
　Inc., San Francisco
fig.5 © Christo, 1976
fig.7 Robert Campbell

Rearranging the Environment
figs.15-16 Ben Blackwell
fig.18 Courtesy the National Archives,
　Pacific Sierra Region, San Bruno, Calif.
fig.19 Courtesy Cameron & Co., Inc., San
　Francisco
fig.21 Rondal Partridge, courtesy Grace Hall
fig.26 William J. Schwarz
fig.30 Catherine Harris

Pastoral Visions at Continent's End
page 30, figs.2, 7 M. Lee Fatherree
figs.1, 13-14 Ben Blackwell
figs.3-4, 9-12, 15,17, 21, 23 Joseph McDonald
figs.5, 24, 26-28 Cecile Keefe
fig.6 John H. Garzoli
fig.8 Helga Photo Studio, N.J.
fig.19 Courtesy James Graham & Sons,
　New York
fig.22 Lyn McCracken
fig.25 Wayne McCall
fig.29 Lee Stalsworth
fig.30 D. James Dee

**Celebrating Possibilities and
Confronting Limits**
page 60, figs.10-14 Joseph McDonald
fig.2 ©Bliss Photography, 1994
fig.3 Ilmari Kalkkinen
figs.4-6, 20-21 Don Beatty
fig.7 Ben Blackwell
fig.8 Christina Lillian
fig.15 Courtesy Hirschl & Adler Galleries,
　Inc., New York
fig.16 Copyright © 1994 by The Metropoli-
　tan Museum of Art, New York
fig.17 David W. Hawkinson, copyright
　courtesy Museum of Art, Brigham
　Young University. All rights reserved.
fig.18 Tibor Franyo, 1990
fig.22 Luc de Champris
fig.23 Courtesy Denenberg Fine Arts, Inc.,
　San Francisco
fig.24 Courtesy Jan Holloway Fine Art, San
　Francisco

Nature and Self in Landscape Art
page 88, figs.1-2, 6-7, 10, 15 Joseph McDonald
fig.3 Ben Blackwell
fig.5 Courtesy Carlson Gallery, Carmel,
　Calif.
fig.8 Ira Schrank, Sixth Street Studio, San
　Francisco
fig.9 Geoffrey Clements, New York
fig.11 Michael Agee
fig.12 ©1995, The Museum of Modern Art,
　New York

fig.13 George Holmes
fig.14 Gene Ogami
fig.16 M. Lee Fatherree
fig.19 Courtesy Koplin Gallery,
　Santa Monica
fig.21 D. James Dee
fig.22 Ken Showell
fig.23 Schopplein Studio, San Francisco
fig.24 Elizabeth Davis, Buffalo, N.Y.
fig.25 Scott McCue Photography, Orinda,
　Calif.

Metaphor, Matter, Canvas, Stage
fig.2 Jeanne-Claude
fig.3 Courtesy L.A. Louver, Inc., Venice,
　Calif.
fig.4 John Roloff
figs.5-6 George Bolling
fig.9 Vicente Saval
fig.10 Joseph McDonald
fig.12 Robert Campbell
fig.13 Peter Levitan
fig.14 Courtesy Performance Foundation,
　San Francisco
fig.15 Courtesy Newton and Helen Mayer
　Harrison
fig.16 John Wilson White
fig.19 Douglas Hollis
fig.20 Susan Schwartzenberg
fig.21 Richard Barnes Photography

Changes like the Weather
page 138, figs.14-15, 25 Ira Schrank, Sixth
　Street Studio, San Francisco
fig.1 Ben Blackwell
figs.2, 16-20, 23 (panels 1-2), 26 M. Lee
　Fatherree
figs.4, 23 (panels 3-4) Schopplein Studio, San
　Francisco
fig.5 Pam Maddock
fig.6 Eva Heyd
fig.10 Ken Showell
fig.11 Courtesy The Saint Louis Art Museum
fig.12 Courtesy O.K. Harris Works of Art,
　New York
fig.13 Greg Heins, Boston, copyright ©1990
　Richard Estes
fig.22 John Wilson White
fig.23 (panel 5) © Bliss Photography, 1994
fig.24 Doug Hall
fig.27 Sam Woo, Davis, Calif.

Seeking Place
figs.2, 10 Camera Corner, Oakland
figs.5, 15 Ben Blackwell
fig.13 Copyright© 1994 by the Trustees of
　Princeton University. All rights
　reserved.
fig.16 Copyright© 1994 by the Trustees of
　the Ansel Adams Publishing Rights
　Trust. All rights reserved.

Facing Eden
100 Years of Landscape Art in the Bay Area
Produced by the Publications Department of
The Fine Arts Museums of San Francisco.
Ann Heath Karlstrom, Director of Publications;
Karen Kevorkian, Editor. Designed by Jack
Werner Stauffacher, The Greenwood Press,
San Francisco. Set in Cycles Display and Cycles,
designed by Sumner Stone. Typesetting by
Francesca Stauffacher. Printed on 128 gsm
Japanese matte art paper by Regal Printing,
Hong Kong, through Overseas Printing
Corporation, San Francisco.